GRACIOUS ENTERTAINING
Southern Style

GRACIOUS ENTERTAINING
Southern Style

by

DAISY KING

Rutledge Hill Press
Nashville, Tennessee

ACKNOWLEDGEMENTS

To so many people, my family, my sharing friends, my thoughtful, hard-working restaurant staff, I owe a debt of gratitude. Without them this cookbook would not have been possible.

My family is small—my mother and father-in-law, Hazel and Herman King, affectionately known as Nannie and Da Dee Dee, my husband Wayne, and our sons Kevin and Patrick. I dedicate this book to them for without their loyal support I would not have been able to compile this collection of menus and recipes for you, my Gracious Friends.

Happy eating!

Daisy King

The publishers wish to acknowledge and thank the following companies, and organizations for their help in securing photos and recipes: North American Blueberry Council; State of Florida Bureau of Marketing and Extension Services; Kitchens of Sara Lee; United Fresh Fruit and Vegetable Association; North Carolina Yam Commission, Inc.; International Apple Institute; the McIllhenny Co.; Hershey Foods Corporation; Pacific Kitchens Division, Evans Food Group; California Prune Board; California Artichoke Advisory Board; Lenox, Inc.; Oneida, Ltd.; Pfaltzgraff Co.; Association for the Preservation of Tennessee Antiquities.

Published in Nashville, Tennessee, by Rutledge Hill Press, Inc., 513 Third Avenue South 37210

Photographs of Daisy King by Doug Brachey, Brentwood, Tennessee
Art by Tonya M. Pitkin
Typography by Bailey Typography, Nashville, Tennessee
Printed in Singapore through Palace Press.

Library of Congress Cataloging-in-Publication Data

King, Daisy, 1945-
    Gracious entertaining, southern style.

    Includes index.
    1. Cookery, American—Southern style.   2. Entertaining.
3. Menus.   I. Title.
TX715.K5144   1987   641.5975   87-20784
ISBN 0-934395-67-5

        1   2   3   4   5   6   7   8   9—94   93   92   91   90   89   88   87

CONTENTS

Recipes

Index

GRACIOUS ENTERTAINING
Southern Style

A Legacy

*T*here's something about being reared a Southerner that never quite filters out of a person. You may move to Montana and lose your accent along the way, but if you are a true Southerner you will always define yourself by your origins no matter how long you have been gone.

Knowing where you are from helps you know who you are. For a Southerner, this means accepting your roots—your family and friends—and realizing that no matter what happens to you, you will always be a Southerner. It also means treasuring your family and friends and remaining close to them, emotionally as much as geographically. Indeed, over the years good friends gradually become like an extended family.

This sense of place and closeness to one's family and friends reveals itself in the "Southern hospitality" for which the South—from Virginia to Savannah, from Charlotte to Texas—is known. Hospitality is our way of life. It is not a myth. And in spite of the quickening pace below the Mason-Dixon line, we have managed to hold on to our love of hospitality. Southern hospitality means always taking time for others. It means taking time to greet one's neighbors on the street. It means having parties where one brings together a mixture of congenial people to enjoy good food. It also means that hosts and hostesses want to share a part of themselves and their lives with their guests. In short, Southern hospitality comes from the heart and is wrapped in love.

It has been suggested that the roots of our Southern hospitality come from the loneliness of living in a predominantly rural society, which made getting together a special occasion. When the South was a frontier society, newcomers to a settlement were welcomed and invited to stay with an established family until a new cabin could be built. Usually, the established settlers helped the new ones build a cabin, after which they would bring them gifts to help furnish the new home. It may be that the remnants of this simple habit of kindness may underlie much of the Southern habits of hospitality.

Even in a frontier society, the South had plenty of examples of gracious entertaining. In the early nineteenth century, visitors to Andrew Jackson's Hermitage just outside of Nashville described the General's manners as "perfectly easy and polished" and those of his wife Rachel as "replete with kindness and benevolence" in spite of the fact that twenty people were gathering at their dinner table for a "sumptuous meal."

In 1856, U.S. President Andrew Johnson, a Southerner, lovingly penned on three folded blue pages, these words to his "dear daughter":

I hope it will be your constant effort to contribute to the happiness of both [you and your husband] in all the domestic relations of life as I know you can do. . . . I hope you will spend a portion of your time in reading something that is useful and profitable and habit yourself to writing letters to someone of the family. . . . My dear child, cultivate all these enduring relationships and by so doing you enlarge the better feelings and passions of the heart, so essential to a woman who expects to occupy position in society and to command the esteem and admiration of those in her immediate vicinity.

A Southerner cultivates the enduring relationships of life. We have grown up knowing that we can drop in unannounced at friends' homes and not be considered unwelcome, but rather "a sight for sore eyes." We look upon guests as a compliment to our home. Even if it's the next door neighbor, time is taken to share a glass of tea and conversation. Southerners love to visit, to spend time together, and to talk, talk, and talk some more. This "cultivates the enduring relationships of life." This is why it seems we enjoy entertaining more than those in other regions in our country.

We know it takes a lot of time to plan a

Picnic honoring Confederate veterans at Belle Meade Mansion, Nashville, circa 1886.

dinner, a tea, or a luncheon, but we also know that it's always worth the effort. Although we may feel physically exhausted when the event is over, we will be emotionally and mentally refreshed.

Southerners have always linked the gathering of friends with the sharing of good food, whether at a family reunion where people gather from across the country, a dinner on the grounds at the anniversary of the founding of a church, or a formal dinner party for a few select friends. True, some occasions do require entertaining as a "duty," but usually we entertain because we want to spend more time with people we enjoy and value. We may want to know them better. We want to keep up with their lives. After all, they are "family."

Whatever the occasion, when we decide to entertain, we want to honor our friendships with the best of ourselves. We do so with our hospitality, as well as with our best home-grown food, decorated with the best flowers from our garden, and served with our best china, crystal, and silver. But above all, Southern hospitality is sharing ourselves, not just our possessions. Giving of yourself is the hallmark of gracious entertaining, Southern style. It is a willingness to share with others, a desire to care for others, and a sense of pride in oneself and one's relationships.

Gracious entertaining Southern style was best described by a six-year-old neighbor of mine, who said, "I love to visit my friend's house because when I leave I always feel full." Southern hospitality will make you feel comfortably full— full of food and full of well-being, served up by a gracious host or hostess.

Whether you are in Michigan or Massachusetts, Wyoming or West Virginia, the secret's out! Southern hospitality can extend far beyond the geographical borders of the former states of the Confederacy. This book is your map to creating those special times for your guests and yourself.

*W*hatever else they may have to offer, many Southerners can still set a fine table and surround it with conversation and laughter and love. On such occasions special things can happen. . . . It's an old Southern skill, a habit, a custom, a tradition, and it deserves to last as long as the corn grows tall.
—John Egerton, *Southern Food*

Party Planning

*T*he secret of any successful party lies in the planning. To your guests, a good party will appear to be effortless. But in order to have a relaxed party for you—the host or hostess—and in order to appear to be effortless, a party must be carefully planned. This means that from the moment you decide to invite some people over, you must begin a well-structured organizational strategy. With proper planning and strategizing, your party cannot help but be a success. This is true whether you entertain two people or two hundred.

The Party's Purpose

First, establish in your mind why you are having a party. To celebrate a birthday? To complement a bride? Because it's Christmas and the house is decorated? Or just because you want to have a party?

Whatever your reason, state it to yourself and use this as the guide in creating the ambiance you want. The party should reflect you—your personality and taste. Never imitate someone else. If your boss entertained you at a formal seated dinner with maid service and a white-coated bartender, you do not have to repay in kind. Never ruin your budget or try to do what is untrue to your own personality. Be yourself. That is the reason people come to your parties. You can have a simple supper and, if the food, presentation, and a cordial mix of guests are well planned, your party will be a success.

The Party Format

Next, decide what format the party should take—a sit down dinner or a backyard barbecue. The party's purpose, your own schedule and commitments, your space and equipment, available help, budget, the time of year, and the people you want to entertain all are factors in establishing the format. Suit the style to the guest list. An elderly woman might not really enjoy a picnic; a man, a lap-buffet meal; or avid teetotallers, a cocktail party. Consider if people, including you, must get up early for work the next day. If you want to entertain outdoors, is there a suitable alternative in case of rain?

Above all, invite a congenial mix of guests. There must be some glue to hold the party together. If you have church, political, school, and business friends, as well as friendly neighbors, don't lump them all together indiscriminately. Draw from only two—at most three—of these groups. Try to have everyone there know at least one person other than you. Plan back-to-back parties, if necessary, but never overcrowd your space.

When you plan your guest list, consider the personalities of the people you invite. Make sure you have compatible people who will be comfortable with each other. Have life-of-the-party types who will ease your entertainment load, but also have listeners. The people you choose to come to your party will have as much to do with its success as the food you serve. An old proverb says, "The company makes the feast."

An easy to prepare party: Cheese and fruit.

Invitations

The method of issuing invitations depends to a great extent on the type of party you are having. Traditionally, written invitations were expected, but today people find telephoning satisfactory. Telephoning is ideal for a seated dinner where you really need to know at once about acceptances. If you receive negative responses from the first two calls, you can change the date to a better time. When you call, don't trap your potential guest with, "What are you doing Saturday night?" Ask, instead, "Can you come for dinner Saturday?" Never leave a message to be relayed. Call back and talk to the member of the household who makes social plans, giving the invitation and confirming the response.

Be sure your invitations—written or by phone—contain all the necessary information: time, date, type of party, location, and directions, if necessary. It is both courteous and important to indicate the appropriate clothing so that you will avoid embarrassing your guests. Formal invitations, of course, include a notation such as "black tie," but extend this to other affairs. If you want people to dress up, don't hesitate to add "festive attire" to the invitation or over the telephone say, "We'll be eating on the patio, so dress casually."

For a crowd of twenty or more when no immediate answer is needed, it is a good idea to send written invitations. Usually the traditional R.S.V.P. is omitted now and replaced with "Regrets Only" and a phone number or address. Only the most formal invitations are engraved and sent to both husband and wife. Wedding invitations now often include an acceptance card to be returned. Printed invitation cards are usually sent for very large gatherings, and these are really the most impersonal of all. If you send out 2,000 invitations to a political gathering, for instance, you can expect only about 10 to 20 percent to come. For a big cocktail buffet, if you mail 500 cards, you will probably receive 250 replies, but plan on 350 to attend. If the guests are close friends, however, you can expect a greater number to accept the invitation.

Written invitations can be printed, handwritten, filled in on purchased cards, or designed and made by you. I once heard of a clever hostess who saved wine labels, pasted them on cards, and wrote the date on the back for a wine and cheese party.

For a huge party, send invitations four weeks in advance; for up to sixty guests, about three weeks ahead of time. Unless it's a spur-of-the-moment affair, all other invitations should be issued about ten days to two weeks before the event.

The Menu

As soon as you decide on the type of party you will have—even before the invitations are sent or called—plan your menu. Of course, the kind of party dictates what you will serve—a tea party or a buffet, for instance.

It is thoughtful to consider if your guests have special dietary needs, religious taboos, health restrictions, or strong aversions. If you know a guest is diabetic, for instance, serve fresh fruit as an alternative to a chocolate mousse for dessert.

If you are going to do all the cooking and serving yourself, plan things that can be made in advance, then frozen or refrigerated, that require little last-minute attention. You should also plan around the equipment you have on hand. Refrigerators and freezers are not expandable. What can they reasonably hold? (You can use ice chests as extra cooling space for food, beverages, even flowers.) If you have just one oven, will all the dishes fit? Do your dishes require the same oven temperature for the same length of time? How will you keep them warm?

If you are a novice cook or one pressed for time, you can hire a caterer to supply all or part of the meal or you can buy specialty items at a good deli, a French bakery, a seafood place, or a Chinese restaurant. Bring the food home and put it in your own dishes and it will fit right in. Check the Yellow Pages of your telephone book

for gourmet shops, restaurants, food wholesalers, and caterers who help in party planning and execution. But the important point is to plan carefully everything on the menu ahead of time.

Think about color, taste, and texture. Most people know that for food to look appetizing on a plate there must be color contrast. You should also consider varying the ingredients. For example, don't combine vichysoisse (potato soup) and mashed potatoes in a menu. If the main dish is a casserole, serve plain vegetables. Avoid cream sauces in more than one dish. If the salad contains fruit, don't have a fruit dessert. If cheese is an appetizer, forget cheese sauces. Have both hot and cold, and soft and crunchy dishes.

Should you practice a dish ahead of time? Many experienced cooks never do. They like to try out something new for a party, and they don't want to go to the trouble and expense of preparing complicated dishes just for themselves. Most recipes work fine if you follow directions as written and do not attempt creative variations the first time around. However, other experienced cooks always have a trial run. And certainly, if you are a beginner, the nervous type, or don't cope well in emergencies, do practice in advance.

One hostess I know constructs a good menu, serves it first to a small group of close friends, repeats it until everyone she knows has experienced it, and then devises a different menu and starts over. It is helpful to have some tried-and-true menus on file. You can avoid serving a guest the same menu twice by maintaining files of party menus so that you can check what dishes were served to whom.

In some cases there is nothing wrong with serving a dish more than once to the same people. Your Thanksgiving dinner may be a family tradition, or guests may look forward to your Christmas eggnog, or you may have a special dessert they can't get anywhere else.

A working woman I know lives in a tiny efficiency apartment with very limited space, yet she entertains a few friends at a time in a charming manner. I know I will always be served

For an elegant table decoration, use large brandy snifters and float one or two flower blossoms on the surface.

To help guests identify ashtrays from collectibles, drop a few cigarette ashes into each ashtray.

a beautifully seasoned stew from her cherished tureen, a nice green salad, crusty French bread, special cheese, and a fine wine. Her guests sit on folding chairs and eat from a card table. We all look forward to going there, for she provides good food and a friendly atmosphere. What else really matters?

Necessary Lists

The secret of a successful party lies in the planning, and the secret to making your plans work lies in list-making. I make lists for everything. It starts when you plan your menu. If you try to remember every detail, you will either overlook something crucial or you will become a basket case as swarms of items roll around in your brain. Well-organized lists make execution much simpler. A loose-leaf notebook is ideal for keeping party plans together. Use a separate page for each list.

List #1: The Complete Menu: Everything you plan to serve as food or drink. Note the name of the cookbook and the page number for each recipe and/or pull recipe file cards and place them in the notebook.

List #2: Service Needs: Figure out exactly what silverware, dishes, glassware, serving equipment, and pots and pans you will need to prepare the menu. This will prevent the horrible experience a friend of mine had. With great effort and expense she had prepared a seafood gumbo for a supper party. Two hours before the eight guests were to arrive, as she was setting the table, she realized that gumbo could not be eaten off dinner plates with forks, and she had only four soup spoons and no soup bowls unless she counted five everyday cereal bowls, one of which was chipped!

Search your cabinets. Everything does not have to match, but it should blend. Is there crossover, an unusual use for a serving piece, such as using a pedestal cake stand to hold pie or a punch bowl to hold shrimp or a cobbler for dessert? Will your tureen be effective for the centerpiece? There are so many interesting, different uses for familiar pieces: Stick cocktail picks in your

children's baby-gift silver cups, serve trifle in champagne glasses, juice from wine decanters, or bread baked in small clay flower pots.

If you cannot serve the menu you have planned with what you have, change the menu (List #1) or make List #3.

List #3: Rental or Purchase Needs: Call or browse through a rental or retail store and make your reservations or purchases. Sometimes you can save money by using some items twice. For example, you could rent beverage glasses that, with a quick wash, could contain the dessert.

List #4: Diagram: Make a blueprint of your service. What food will go in what containers and where will they be placed? Vary shapes and heights on a table.

List #5: Ingredients: Using List #1 (the menu) and your recipes, make a master shopping list of all ingredients you will need. Don't forget to check the spice shelf (does the oregano need replacing?) and your staples (are you about out of baking powder?). Divide the list according to early and last-minute purchases.

List #6: Reservations: List any special food that must be ordered, such as a Smithfield ham that has to be shipped. Decide if you need to hire extra help: a maid, a bartender, or a valet for parking. Arrange for a member of the family or a friend to help, if need be. If a friend is hosting the party with you, now is the time to decide exactly what each one will do.

List #7: Time Schedule: Make a cooking schedule of what can be prepared days in advance and frozen, made the day before and refrigerated, or made the day of the party. For the day of the party, give exact times, figuring backwards from when the dish should be ready. For example, a partial schedule might be:

4:30 p.m.: Make rolls and set them out to rise.
4:45 p.m.: Remove casserole from refrigerator to warm to room temperature.
Bathe and dress.
5:30 p.m.: Set out cheese.
5:45 p.m.: Place casserole in oven.

Jot down everything you can think of that must be done to construct your timetable.

The lists that you made previously were all for early organization, done anywhere from two to three weeks before the party. This schedule picks up at the last week and carries you to the moment you greet your guests. Details of planning vary, of course, with the size and complexity of your party and your personal schedule. For example, if you work in an office all day, your cooking schedule will differ from that of someone who is home all day.

Here are some things to consider on a time schedule:

About one week ahead: Shop for staples and buy film. Prepare food that can be frozen. Wash seldom-used dishes and glassware. Polish the silver. Purchase wines and liquors. Decide on flowers or whatever else you will use for the centerpiece. Order items from the bakery. Arrange to have the lawn mowed and clipped along driveways and borders during the week. Make place cards and write out a seating chart. Decide on what you will wear and get it ready.

Three days before: Shop for the remaining food. Begin freezing extra ice cubes and placing them in plastic bags in the freezer.

Two days before: Clean the house. Prepare what food you can. Rearrange the furniture if needed. Make sure there are sufficient hangers in the guest closets.

One day before: Do serious cooking. Place ingredients needed for last minute cooking in baskets so that you or your help will have them at hand. Stock and set up the bar. Press table linens and set your table.

Day of the party: Arrange your centerpiece. Clean the bathrooms and put out guest towels. Remove all personal items and store out of sight, e.g., deodorant cans, toothbrushes, glasses, sleepware, etc. Get extra ice if needed. Clear table surfaces to accommodate plates and extra ashtrays. Give yourself time to rest, get dressed, and be ready fifteen minutes before guests are due to arrive.

After the Party

But that's not all! After the party, besides the inevitable cleaning up, do two things as soon as possible.

Count the silver—not because you think a guest made off with a teaspoon, but because it is so easy to accidentally dump a fork in the trash. It will be too late to retrieve it after the garbage truck comes.

Also, make entries for the event in your party journal. Record the guest list; the menu with citations for finding the recipes; your table diagram; what centerpieces, decorations, and linens were used; names and phone numbers of hired help and rental services; how much liquor was consumed; and any comments such as what you ran short of and what you would do differently next time. Later, paste in photos taken at the party and reflect on the good time you and your guests had.

Turn a brunch or luncheon into an outdoor garden party.

Party Presentation

A party is like a stage or musical performance. The real key to success in both is the planning and preparation. When the doorbell rings for your party, rehearsal time is over and the curtain is rising on the actual performance. Think of yourself as the star who must carry the show and consider your home as the set.

Your guests must be able to find your house easily, and the first impression should be a festive, welcome one. Let's assume you have given good directions and your guests have found your street. In the dark, however, house numbers are hard to read and driveways can be confusing. Finding the right apartment in a large building can be even worse. Make it easy for your guests. Illuminate your house number on the door. Or perhaps attach a bow or balloons to your mailbox so that your guests won't have to drive up and down the street or knock on a neighbor's door for guidance. If there are any tricks to finding your apartment, be sure to let the guests know ahead of time.

Have all the outside lights on and brighten walkways with torches, lanterns, or luminaries, which can be made easily by inserting emergency candles in sand-filled paper bags. It should be obvious where cars are to be parked or you should give directions with the invitations. If you expect many cars, you might provide a parking attendant. Engage a teenage boy to shuttle guests in your car up a long, steep driveway. If it's icy, be sure you sprinkle the steps with salt, and if it's raining, have an umbrella holder handy.

Before the guests even enter the house they should be made to feel welcome, taken care of, and put in a party mood. Hang a wreath on the front door; place a vase of flowers in the foyer; set around baskets of apples studded with cloves, or boil cinnamon sticks on the stove.

You should have everything ready ahead of time so that you can be

Welcome to my home!

near the door. Greet each person, giving him or her a feeling of not only being welcome, but honored. You and your spouse can take turns, one staying with guests while the other greets new arrivals. Direct guests to the area that will house their coats or bags. Most people do not have closet space for a lot of garments, and a pile of clothing on the guest room bed is messy. You might want to consider renting a portable hanging rack for coats.

You are the star of the show, but unlike a stage performance where everyone makes the star look good, it is your responsibility to make the guests feel welcome and a part of the party. At a large party, don't try to introduce everyone around the room. When a new guest arrives, introduce him or her to the guest of honor and then integrate the new arrival into a nearby group. Bring up a topic that the new person can discuss with other people in the group. It will take creativity and awareness on your part but it will work wonders in making your guests feel at ease. Mention that the new arrival grows roses to a person who is a gardener or that his father started the company

for which another guest works. A hobby, a career, an interest, all make good potential discussion starters. Because you do not have to carry the conversation, you are able to slip away gracefully to greet other guests. If making introductions is not easy for you, read a good etiquette book detailing prescribed rules and practice ahead of time.

In your leading role of the party drama, you should be prepared with possible topics for conversation to fill in lulls, and you should be alert to steer the conversation away from unpleasant, embarrassing, or controversial subjects.

Be aware of what's going on and make your guests feel comfortable by offering a drink refill, by suggesting a second helping, by emptying ashtrays, removing empty glasses, and being sure no timid soul is called upon to give a toast.

Watch out for loners and try to draw them into a friendly circle; watch out for others who may be entrapped by a too-avid talker and try to extract them by a gentle detachment maneuver. Tact is required and also subtlety. Always remember it is your role to see that everyone has a good time, but don't hover and regiment like a zealous tour guide.

Be determined beforehand to keep your sense of humor at all times, to ride with the unpredictable, to keep disasters private, to accept with serenity broken plates, spilled drinks, hardened fondue, and the fact that the cat ate half the turkey.

Your clothing is important. Wear comfortable shoes and clothes for your duties—no flowing ruffles that will get in the way if you are doing the cooking or serving. Also be aware of how the color of your clothing blends with the decor of your living room. After all, you and the room are both part of the same "set."

Expanding Party Space

Most homes are not normally arranged for extra people and you will probably have to do some creative rearranging. To keep food and bar services well separated for convenient traffic flow, for instance, you could convert a utility room into a bar. Place ice in the sink, lay a cloth-covered board over the washer and dryer, and you have another party room.

Utilize all your rooms and furniture. Stash dirty glasses in a room you are not using for the party to free counter space for dessert preparation. Ice down beer in a bathtub. Place hors d'oeuvres trays on desks, chests, a coffee table, or serving carts. Serve appetizers in the den and desserts in the playroom. Look at your space critically and rearrange the furniture to loosen up congested areas around the entrance, the bar, the buffet table. A small dining table can be enlarged by laying a big piece of plywood over it, and covering it all with a mammoth cloth made especially to size.

Table Linens

Since food is always the focus of a party, its presentation is of paramount importance, and its backdrop, of course, is the tablecloth. Traditional cloths are always in excellent taste and fine linens are a good investment because they last for years and one never tires of looking at them.

In a formal setting, white damask or linen is unsurpassed. Use a custom-made pad underneath or cut a white blanket the size of your table. Only one fold line is permissible, straight down the cloth lengthwise. Even rolling cloths on a dowel or hanging them in a closet produces wrinkles. Therefore, press cloths just before use.

The damask cloth for a formal seated dinner should overhang the table about eighteen inches all around, while a lace or sheer cloth should overhang about fifteen inches. For a semi-formal dinner or for a luncheon, lighter linens are used and the overhang should usually be about twelve to fifteen inches. Buffet tablecloths should extend to the floor.

Napkin sizes vary. Formal dinner napkins of matching damask are about twenty-two inches square; semiformal dinner, breakfast, and luncheon napkins are fifteen to eighteen inches square, and tea napkins are usually twelve to fifteen inches square. Dinner napkins are folded to form triangles with the points sometimes tucked back to make a wedge shape.

While traditionally folded napkins are correct at all times, for less formal occasions you might like to try some fancy folds. There are good books available which contain diagrams and show you various folds. Practice these when you are not pressured so that you can see which fold you like best.

At formal luncheons or informal dinners, organdy, linen, or lace mats with matching napkins may be used.

Except for the most formal seated dinner, for which you can rent damask cloths, today's entertainers strive for beauty through a creative use of color, texture, and design. Whatever suits your house, the type of party, and enhances the food presentation is what you should use. Look for tablecloth material in slipcover and drapery fabric stores, and consider colored sheets or even forms of wall hangings for tablecloths. Embroider or stencil tablecloths, place mats, and napkins to complement your furniture and your lifestyle. On occasion, let the natural beauty of the wood show.

Think of striking color combinations. You might make bright red napkins for use against a white cloth at Christmas or Valentine's Day. At Christmas, the centerpiece could be a styrofoam-based apple tree, while for Valentine's Day you might spray paint a bare branch white and tie foil-covered hearts to it with red ribbons. Use yellow napkins to match a centerpiece of daffodils in the spring or orange napkins in the fall to blend with a copper pot filled with pyracantha berries.

Plan your cloths to enhance what you often use for centerpieces. Choose a color to bring out a shade in the design of an antique tureen or a favorite piece of pottery. Use a brown cloth with orange and beige napkins to go with a dried arrangement, or use a navy cloth with all-white dishes and a milk glass vase for a centerpiece.

Platters and dishes for hot meats and vegetables will hold the heat longer if warmed briefly in the oven before using. Plates and bowls for salads and desserts may be chilled in the refrigerator.

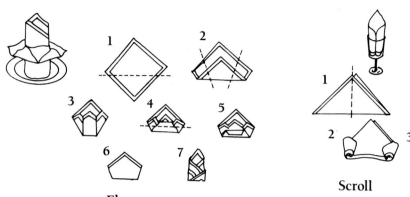

Flame

Scroll

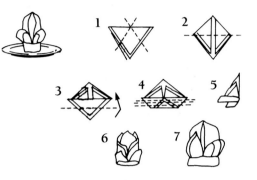

Fleur-de-lis

Napkin Folds

Flame

1) Fold lower ⅓
2) toward center.
3) Fold edges inward. 4) Fold bottom up over edges. 5) Turn lip of edge downward.
6) Front view.
7) Fold edges inward and tuck under; peel outer edges downward.

Scroll

1) Fold into triangle shape.
2) Roll edges inward. 3) Place in glass.

Fleur-de-lis

1) Fold into triangle shape. 2) Fold outer corners toward bottom.
3) Fold points up over themselves.
4) Fold bottom point

Centerpieces

Centerpieces can be conversation pieces and contribute to the atmosphere, but they should never dominate the table nor should they be used at all if they make the table too crowded. Instead, use part of the food as the centerpiece—bread sticks in a ceramic pitcher, a bowl of fruit, or a cheese tray.

Use your imagination. Almost anything can be used effectively as a centerpiece—gaily decorated Easter baskets; wine glasses of various heights filled with colored candy; or huge, vivid paper flowers in a black spray-painted clay pot. (Silk, ceramic, and even paper flowers have their place; just avoid cheap plastic ones.) Pin clusters of sweetheart roses, baby's breath, and ribbons to the corners of a tea table. Wander the fields and roadsides for interesting additions to your center-pieces. Queen Anne's lace found beside the highway is a wonderful addition to an arrangement of garden flowers. In fact, I once picked some Queen Anne's lace seeds and now grow my own.

At a seated dinner or luncheon, everything must be strictly symmetrical, with the centerpece exactly in the center of the table. However, asymmetrical arrangements are nice when placed on a sideboard or buffet table that is pushed against the wall. An attractive—and inexpensive—centerpiece can be made using a simple Japanese flower arrangement of three carefully shaped branches in a flat bowl with one large chrysanthemum at their base.

When using candles, be sure to keep them out of sight line. Don't use them at all if guests must reach across a buffet table. Candles should be used only after sunset. On a dining table, you should always light them. When you want to use them unlit, however, you should always char the wick first.

Dressing the Food

How your home, your table, and your centerpieces look is important. But don't forget the food itself. Even when you throw on some clothes and head out the door, you give thought to how you look, and for a party you would carefully select accessories to enhance your outfit. You should plan the appearance of your food—not just its taste—with the same care that you plan what you will be wearing.

Think of every dish you set on the table as a three-dimensional picture you are creating. Consider food for color, texture, shape, and height. Choose the background (the plate) carefully. For instance, deviled eggs look appetizing on a glass plate, but somehow they aren't quite as appealing on a copper one. Plain white plates are good foils for colorful hors d'oeuvres. Always leave some of the plate showing to frame the food.

The way the food is placed and the garnishes used with it work together to create a design. You could make a leafy oval border of celery leaves or endive to frame the food. You could twine ivy around the handle of a basket of bread. Or you could make an asymmetrical arrangement by placing a ball of cream cheese and caviar at the corner of a tray with crackers leading the eye up to it from the opposite corner.

Use hollowed-out oranges, lemons, or grapefruit as bowls for sauces. A hollowed green pepper makes a fine dip container in the center of raw vegetables. Spiced sweet potato casserole just naturally goes in orange shells.

Mix and match vegetables—their color, texture, shape, and height. Fill a rice ring with lima beans or make a ring of mashed potatoes and heap peas and water chestnuts in the center. Arrange asparagus bunches "tied" with strips of red pepper down one side of a platter with broiled tomatoes on the other.

Dress foods according to the holidays. You might tint coconut green on St. Patrick's Day or arrange blueberries and raspberries around confectioners' sugar or whipped cream on the Fourth of July.

Dressing food is not difficult. It just takes some thought and planning. It will give a professional finishing touch to your meal and make a simple dish more pleasing to the eye and the appetite.

After Dinner

After-dinner entertainment can take different forms, but the important thing is for you to know what you want to happen rather than just hoping something does. Obviously there can be good conversation with friends. Sometimes a game is in order—cards, board games, mental games—although it is best when everyone can participate together. You might ask a guest to bring a guitar or have everybody gather around the piano to sing favorite songs. You might consider having a magician, a handwriting analyst, or a caricaturist. Newspapers, city magazines, or the Yellow Pages can all help you find such entertainment as well as give you ideas.

Finally, there is the old Southern custom of gift-giving in reverse. Instead of guests' bringing a hostess gift, the host or hostess sends departing guests home with a little something to preserve the memory of a happy evening: flowers cut from the yard, ripe tomatoes from the garden, a jar of homemade jelly, a needlepoint Christmas tree ornament.

Even at the largest party, a good host and hostess notice when guests are preparing to leave and wish them a good night. The host walks with unaccompanied women to their car or taxi. Do not shut the front door until guests are well on their way.

After-dinner activities do not have to be unduly long. Luncheons usually last from one and one-half to two hours. Unless special entertainment is provided, dinner guests plan to stay forty-five minutes to an hour after coffee, making the dinner party about three to three and one-half hours long—although no one should leave before the guest of honor. Cocktail party guests stay about forty-five minutes to one hour and should leave no later than twenty minutes past the ending time on the invitation.

However, sometimes it is necessary to gently help those who can't seem to tear themselves away. Don't offer more drinks; casually close the bar; mention early rising; excuse yourself to begin kitchen cleanup duties; and warmly thank each guest for coming.

to reach halfway touching center points. 5) Fold bottom over itself. 6) Fold outer ends behind each other. 7) Pull down loose corners to form fleur-de-lis.

Note: These folds work and look best when napkins are stiffly starched.

Don't wash fruits and vegetables you use in a centerpiece. Instead, spray them with a nonstick vegetable oil spray to make them glisten.

Party Drinks

*D*ispensing Southern hospitality is as easy as serving coffee, tea, or a favorite mixed drink. We don't just drink to quench a thirst, but as a focal point for a social occasion. An afternoon tea, a morning coffee, or an after-dinner liqueur all provide opportunities to be with friends. Your choice of party beverages will depend on your personal preference, your budget, and the type of party.

Coffee

There are a great many types and blends of coffees available and serving an exotic coffee after dinner is one way of making your party memorable. Most coffee is a blend of many coffees. A blend may contain coffee from South America, Mexico, Hawaii, or Africa. Visit a local gourmet shop to gain ideas for the right coffee for your party.

To make coffee, follow directions for your coffee maker exactly. Never mix stale and fresh coffee. You should keep your coffee maker and the pot very clean because an invisible film of coffee oil will gather on the surface of any coffee maker, quickly become rancid, and contaminate the flavor of successive brewings. Measure carefully. (The rule of thumb is one standard coffee measure or two level tablespoons for each three-fourths cup of water. If you prefer strong coffee, use three level tablespoons. If you like it weak, use two scant tablespoons). Always start with fresh cold water. Brew no less than three-fourths of the capacity of your coffee maker. Remove grounds as soon as the coffee is brewed. Keep the coffee hot at all times; never reheat it. Figure on one minute per cup for brewing time and arrange for coffee to be ready close to serving time. Coffee will become bitter after it stands for twenty minutes.

Coffee can be served in many ways, some requiring unique blends. Demitasse is extra-strong coffee, served in small cups, and usually

Serve coffee or tea with a favorite dessert, such as this Triple Chocolate Cake, page 150.

When pouring hot liquids into fine glassware, place a teaspoon in the glass and pour hot liquid over it. This will help prevent breakage.

drunk black. Iced coffee is served like iced tea. Make it double strength and pour it hot into tall ice-filled glasses. Cafe au lait (strong coffee mixed with milk), Irish coffee (strong coffee mixed with whiskey), Viennese coffee (coffee with whipped cream), and espresso (coffee made in a special Italian coffee pot) are some of many coffee specialties you might try.

Tea

Drinking hot tea is a well-established institution in England, and it is only recently that the British would even consider serving iced tea. In the South, however, asking someone if he would like tea is assumed to mean iced tea. And although iced tea is a standard part of any day-time gathering in the South, hot tea is also a favorite.

Flavored and scented teas are refreshing alternatives to coffee, and spiced teas and tea punches are wonderful additions to any party.

To make hot tea, fill a tea kettle with three-fourths cup of cold water per serving. Bring to a full boil. Meanwhile, heat a china, glass, or porcelain (not metal) teapot by pouring in scalding water. Empty the water and measure in one regular teaspoon (not a measuring spoon) of tea or one tea bag for each cup. Pour the boiling water over the tea and steep three to five minutes. Aficionados say that the water should be as close to boiling as possible and you should "take the pot to the kettle, not the kettle to the pot." Serve with lemon, sugar, or warm milk (never cream).

For iced tea, bring one quart of cold water to a boil in a glass or enamel pot, remove from heat, and add one-third cup of loose tea or fifteen tea bags. Steep for four to five minutes. Strain into a pitcher containing one quart of cold water. This makes eight to ten servings. Tea will cloud if you refrigerate it while hot. To clear, stir in a little boiling water.

To make hot tea for a crowd:

20 servings: 7 tablespoons of loose tea or 20 tea bags and 3 cups of water

40 servings: 1 cup + 2 tablespoons of loose tea or 40 tea bags + 1½ quarts of water

60 servings: 1¼ cups + 1 tablespoon of loose tea or 60 tea bags + 2 quarts and 1 cup of water

For a large party, make a tea concentrate. Bring water to a full boil in a non-aluminum saucepan. Remove from heat, add tea, steep five minutes. Strain the tea into a scalded pot. Serve by pouring about 2 tablespoons of tea into each cup and fill the cup with very hot, freshly boiled water. By varying the amount of concentrate, you can vary the strength of the tea.

Punch

Punch is a good addition to most larger parties, especially if you are not going to have a bar staff. Punch provides not only a drink that people can serve themselves, but a festive decoration as well.

One way of decorating with punch is to use your imagination in devising ice rings in punch bowls for special occasions: red and green maraschino cherries at Christmas or sweetheart rose buds for wedding receptions. To make an ice ring, use a ring mold, a metal loaf pan, or a bowl that will fit your punch bowl. A twelve-cup ring will allow a ladle to fit through its center for easy service. Make the mold from chilled distilled or boiled water since tap water produces a cloudy ring. Freeze about one-half inch of water in the bottom of the mold until a thin layer of ice appears. Crack this with a spoon so that water seeps up and quickly arrange your garnishes (candied cherries, pineapple chunks, fruit slices, etc.) partially submerging them in the water. Freeze until solid. Then freeze the rest of the mold in layers, one inch of chilled distilled water at a time. Do not keep the mold longer than twenty-four hours as it will turn cloudy. An ice ring usually lasts about two hours in the punch.

Another way of decorating with punch is with an ice float. Place a one-quart metal bowl into a three-quart metal bowl that has been half-filled with water. Weight down the smaller bowl and let the water freeze. Remove the small bowl by filling it with hot water. Quickly dip the large bowl in hot water and remove the ice from it. Now you have an ice float for your punch bowl. You can fill it with flowers or fruit. It also makes an eyecatching container for ice cream or fruit desserts.

Frozen fresh fruits both look pretty and help keep punch cold. Wash peach slices, melon balls, berries, and slices of orange, lemon, or lime (grapes and cherries won't float as these do); freeze them on a sheet of foil and put in the punch when it is ready to serve. You can also freeze ice cubes with fruit or mint leaves in them.

Wine

Although more and more Americans are discovering the joys of wine, many are still a little insecure about serving it. This brief introduction to wines will help you become more at ease with the appreciation and selection of it.

The four major types of wine are table wines, sparkling wines, dessert wines, and fortified wines. Table wines—red, white, rosé or blush—are poured at the table as part of the meal. Dry white and fruity reds are also often served as appetizer wines. Popular table wines are Beaujolais, Chianti, Cabernet Sauvignon (red) and Chablis, Riesling, and Chardonnay (white). Sparkling wines, of which champagne is one, are often thought of as special occasion wines, but they are also good with meals. Sparkling burgundies, Anjou (rosé), and Vouvray (white) are in this group. Dessert wines, which can also be served at other times, include Sauternes, Madeira, Muscat, port, tokay, and sweet sherry. A fortified wine has brandy added to it. Sherry, marsala, and Madeira are fortified wines. Aromatized or aperitif wines such as dry and sweet vermouth or Dubonnet, are other types of fortified wine.

Wines should be stored in a cool, dry, dark place with a non-fluctuating temperature, away from heat or air-conditioning sources and vibrations of appliances like refrigerators or washing machines. The floor of a closet is fine. Ideally the temperature should be about 60 degrees, but temperatures up to 70 degrees can be tolerated by most wines. Table and sparkling

Wine is a perfect complement to an After Theater Supper.

There are the two basic shapes for bar glassware: stemware (which does not leave rings on furniture) and tumblers. Some people limit themselves to an all-purpose, tulip-shaped, stemmed wine glass (6 to 8 oz. or even up to 13 oz.); tall highball tumblers (8 to 15 oz.) which can double for punches, coolers, and iced teas; and perhaps short old-fashioned or on-the-rocks tumblers (6 to 8 oz.) for such things as Bloody Marys or fruit juices. Other standard shapes and sizes:

A. 8 oz. tulip shape white wine

B. 12 oz. tulip shape red wine

C. 8 oz. old-fashioned

D. 14 oz. cooler/ice tea

E. 12 oz. highball/cooler

F. 5 oz. champagne glass

G. 5 oz. champagne flute

H. 12 oz. pilsner

I. 10 oz. brandy snifter

wines should be stored on their sides so that the cork will remain moist. Wine cartons are good for this purpose. If you have a wine rack on display in a lighted area, stock it with wines you plan to serve soon.

Red wines should be served at 60–65 degrees. (The old saying that they must be at room temperature applied to English homes that did not have central heating.) White wines should be served at about 50 degrees and rosés at about 55. Never put wine in the freezer for quick chilling. You can't cool wine quickly. You should try not to chill wine, allow it to warm up, and then rechill it, as this spoils the taste of fine wine. The flavor can also be altered by refrigerating the wine for too long before serving. The best way to chill wine is in a bucket with half ice and half water. Then, before serving, wrap the wine bottle in a white napkin to absorb the water.

To serve wine, get a *good* corkscrew, preferably one with an open-centered screw, and practice using it. Sparkling wine should not open with a loud pop and a spurt of foam. To avoid this, point the bottle away from yourself and others, holding it by the neck with your thumb on the cork. If the cork is in tight, undo the wire, but if

the cork is beginning to ease out, leave the wire in place. Twist the *bottle* carefully from the cork so that there is only a low pop and hiss.

Red wines should be opened about an hour before serving so that they can "breathe." This breathing is also achieved by the process of putting wine in a decanter. If the wine has heavy sediment, you must decant it carefully. Stop pouring when the sediment reaches the neck.

When serving wine at home, sample it in the kitchen ahead of time to be sure it is good. Fill a wine glass no more than one-third to one-half full so that the liquid can be swirled, the better to savor the bouquet. Twist the bottle slightly as you lift it from the glass to prevent drips.

Wines turn to vinegar once they are opened. Whites keep a few days in the refrigerator, reds a little longer. Use wine that has turned to vinegar in salad dressings and keep a jar of white wine in the refrigerator for use as a quick stain remover when red wine is spilled.

The first consideration in deciding on a wine is the occasion. For a select dinner party, you may prefer a very special wine, but for a large gathering you could feel comfortable with an adequate wine that comes in a large bargain jug. (There are really three genres of wines: vintage, premium, and jug. Jug wine accounts for 80 percent of all wines drunk in the United States. Jugs got their name because they have long been sold in bottles larger than a fifth and formerly were only generic wines. Today, however, many are perfectly acceptable.)

Next, consider your menu, choosing the wines that will complement the food. One of the greatest delights of wine is its use as a flavor enhancer. You don't have to follow the old guide of serving red wine with red meats and white with white meats. Instead, serve whatever you and your guests prefer. Let your palate decide if a strongly flavored dish overpowers a light wine or if an assertive wine fights with a delicate dish. The more you become acquainted with wines, the easier it is to choose what goes best with what food. Until you feel secure, ask someone on whose judgment you can rely. Often liquor store managers can give good advice or call the food and wine editor of your newspaper.

Dry (which means "not sweet") sparkling wines can be served with appetizers and during meals. With cold hors d'oeuvres, try a dry or medium dry white wine or rosé. Brie cheese and dry sherry or Sauvignon Blanc are good together. For hot hors d'oeuvres, serve a medium dry white or a light red blend. Sherry has always

been a pre-dinner favorite and goes well with soup courses. Chardonnays and Sauvignon Blancs go well with creamed soups, while light reds fit tomato-based soups.

Fish and shellfish pair well with dry Sauternes, Rhine wines, and Chablis, but rosé wines also may be served as well as such light reds as Gamay, Pinot Noir, Zinfandel, and Cabernet. With steamed, poached, or broiled fish, try a dry Chenin Blanc or a light Chardonnay. Trout and other freshwater fish team with a dry Riesling. With grilled or baked salmon, consider a

Store infrequently used cocktail glasses in empty liquor cartons. Get these free at your favorite liquor store.

Wine, Cheese, and Fruit

Here are some combinations of fruit, wines, and cheeses that I like. At the end of a meal (not a rich one), I often like to pass the centerpiece—fruits—along with a tray of cheeses and crackers.

Fruit	Cheese	Wine
Apples	Camembert	Red Burgundy
	Gorgonzola	Claret
	Sharp Cheddar	Port
Apricots	Cream cheese	Light Muscat
	Jack	Gamay Beaujolais
		Chemin Blanc
Cherries	Mild Cheddar	Port
Grapes	Baby Gouda	Riesling
	Cream cheese	Red Burgundy
	Gruyère	Light Muscat
	Swiss	
Melon	Jack	Light Muscat
	Mild brick	Sweet Sauternes
	Swiss	
Peaches	Camembert	Champagne
	Cream cheese	Light Muscat
	Mild brick	
	Swiss	
Pears	Camembert	Medium Sherry
	Cheddar	Port
	Gorgonzola	Tokay
	Liederkranz	Sweet Sauternes
	Roquefort	

Basic Bar Equipment

Jigger—1 oz. and 1½ oz.
Corkscrew
Bottle opener
Can opener (punch type)
Long bar spoon/ stirrer
Small knife and cutting board for fruits and peels
Juice squeezer
Ice bucket and tongs
Ice chest
Cocktail shaker
Pitchers with stirrers
Wine coolers
Blender for daiquiris or foamy drinks
Electric ice crusher
Small dishes for lemons, limes, olives, onions
Decanters
Carafes for wine or juices
Coasters
Cocktail napkins
Punch bowl and cups
Absorbent cloths or sponges

California Chardonnay or medium reds like Volvay or Merlot. Fish in cream sauce blends with Chardonnay, while sauces full of spices require a more assertive wine such as a Sauvignon Blanc. Champagne and oysters are traditionally served together.

Chicken goes well with both red and white wines. Try medium reds such as Cabernet Sauvignon or dry whites such as Chablis or Chardonnay with roast or grilled chicken. Beaujolais (red) goes well with barbecued chicken, but so does a good white. Coq au vin is usually made with a red Burgundy and you should use the same wine to accompany it. Chicken salad can be served with dry Chenin Blanc or Riesling. Try California Chardonnay with a chicken in cream sauce.

With roast turkey, try a red, a rosé, or Riesling or white Zinfandel.

Duck requires a medium red Burgundy and game birds are excellent with a light red Burgundy such as Pinot Noir or Chianti.

Most people prefer red wines with beef, lamb, and game, and white wines for pork and veal. Try Pinot Noir, Cabernet, or Zinfandel with beef. However, full-bodied whites and dry rosés are fine with cold roast beef.

Mature Bordeaux or Cabernet Sauvignon is excellent with lamb.

For veal in cream sauce, serve Chardonnay or Cabernet Sauvignon.

Fresh pork takes a dry white or light red. With ham, you could choose Pinot Noir Blanc, Tavel Rose, or Beaujolais, or perhaps Gamay.

With roast lamb, select a light or medium red.

These are guidelines. Use them until you feel confident enough to experiment with what you feel goes best with your meal.

Alcoholic Beverages

If you are going to serve alcoholic drinks, consider what drinks you plan to serve and check the recipes. For instance, will you make whiskey sours with a 1½-ounce or a 2-ounce base? Will you need cherries, olives, cocktail onions, or lemons? What mixers will you need? In stocking mixers such as club soda, tonic water, ginger ale, or cola drinks, plan on a 28-ounce bottle for every two people. A person drinking three gin and tonics, for instance, would use twelve to fourteen ounces of mixer. For ease in handling, buy the small ten-ounce sizes if guests are pouring their own.

When stocking your bar remember that one 750 ml bottle of liquor will make sixteen 1½-ounce drinks or twelve 2-ounce drinks. For wines, one 750 ml bottle will serve 2 to 3 people. For brandies and liqueurs, one 750 ml bottle will serve 6 to 8 people.

When beer is served at an informal picnic or barbecue, plan on three bottles or cans per person.

When stocking the bar, it is better to err on oversupply than to run short. Liquor stores will

Wine Guide

Wine Class	Types
Appetizer Wines	Sherry
	Vermouth
	Flavored Wines
White Wines	Sauternes
	Chablis
	Rhine Wine
	Riesling
Red Wines	Burgundy
	Chianti
	Claret
	Rosé
Dessert Wines	Muscatel
	Angelica
	Cream Sherry
	Port
	Tokay
Sparkling Wines	Champagne
	Sparkling Burgundy
	Cold Duck

often allow you to return unopened bottles if arrangements have been made in advance.

Always have a good choice of non-alcoholic drinks for those who cannot drink or who choose not to. Provide a good choice of sparkling water, diet and regular colas, ginger ale, tonic, and fruit juices.

After-Dinner Drinks

For many people, a good cup of coffee is all that is needed to end the perfect meal. However, dessert wines, brandy, and liqueurs add an especially nice finishing touch to a dinner. Sauternes, Madeira, sparkling wines, sweet sherry, and port are all excellent to serve with dessert. Do not pair wines with ice cream or chocolate. It is best to serve only simple cakes and cookies or fresh fruit, nuts, and cheeses with dessert wines.

Brandies and liqueurs or cordials can be served as dessert or served with coffee or ice cream.

Stocking the Home Bar

For a basic home bar, you might like to stock the following, making variations according to what's popular with your friends and your drink specialties,

2 liters of bourbon	Cognac
1 liter of gin	6 bottles of white wine
2 liters of vodka	
2 liters of Scotch	3 bottles of red wine
1 liter of blended whiskey	1 six-pack of light beer
1 liter of light rum	1 six-pack of dark beer
1 liter of dark rum	1 six-pack of imported beer
Dark sherry	Mixers (sparkling water, club soda, tonic,
Dry vermouth	
Cointreau	ginger ale, colas;
Grand Marnier	juices, such as tomato,
Amaretto	orange, grapefruit)
Kahlua	

A Parade of Parties

For generations, seated dinner parties have been synonymous with gracious entertaining, and they certainly continue to be so, even though most people do not have household help. The general rules for all successful parties apply here: congenial guests, a well-planned menu of well-prepared food served competently in an attractive setting, and a gracious, cordial host and/or hostess.

For a relaxing evening, the perfect number for a seated dinner party is six to eight, and a person can manage that number nicely without help. If twelve to sixteen are invited, you really must have assistance for smooth service. A spouse or friend can take over bartending duties, but someone else is required to superintend cooking, serving food, and attending to the pile of dirty dishes. For a larger number, of course, you will need more professional help.

More than for any other type of party, the selection of the guest list is crucial for a dinner party because of the length of time conversation continues with a dinner partner and because of the relatively small number of people involved. Use as a criteria those who are congenial with each other, not just those whom you like personally or to whom you owe an invitation.

The time for the party depends on the prevailing dinner hour where you live and among your circle of friends. Young marrieds often like a later hour, like 8 p.m., so they can feed and bed their children first. Older couples may prefer an earlier evening, beginning at 6:30 or 7 p.m. Take into account the next day's activities such as early rising for work or a special event.

If there is both a host and hostess giving the dinner, one should greet guests at the door and introduce those who do not know each other while the other helps with the drinks.

If pre-dinner drinks are served, plan for dinner to be served about an hour after the invitation time. If you serve no drinks, allow twenty minutes for all the guests to arrive. Dinner should never be delayed longer than fifteen minutes waiting for a late guest, as it is rude to those who have come on time.

While guests are enjoying the pre-dinner time, slip away to do last minute chores or to consult with the help in the kitchen. Check the table, light the candles, and return to the living room to invite guests into the dining room. Ladies lead the way and as the guests near the table, the host or hostess tells each one where to sit or indicates place cards.

If you have an odd number of couples—three or five, for instance—the hostess may sit at the end of the table nearest the kitchen with the host at the opposite end. However, with an even number of couples at the table, that won't work if you wish to alternate men and women. Solve the problem by having the hostess move one place to the left of the traditional hostess spot opposite the host.

The woman guest of honor always sits at the host's right and the man guest of honor is at the hostess' right. With eight at the table, the man guest of honor would be opposite the host. Separate married couples, but seat engaged couples side-by-side. If there is no guest of honor, give the honored seats to a first-time guest or to an older or distinguished person. The hostess sits first and then guests sit, from the left of their chairs.

The table should be beautiful, but this does not necessarily mean costly. If you have a white damask tablecloth or placemats, sterling silver, and gold-rimmed china, use them. You can also have a stunning table, however, by combining colors and textures effectively using pottery or even odd soup, salad, and dessert plates. Be ingenious with inexpensive decorations. It isn't necessary to call a florist for a centerpiece. In the summer, make a centerpiece of cut garden flowers, in the early spring make a group of blooming potted plants. Nothing is prettier for Christmas than an arrangement of holly in a silver bowl, perhaps with fruit or Christmas ornaments. Keep the centerpiece low so as not to obstruct the view across the table, and avoid burning candles at eye level. Place them in tall candlesticks or use low, squat votive candles set in old-fashioned glasses on a mirror.

A damask cloth with an eighteen-inch overhang should be placed on top of a pad or a thin flannel blanket. Sheer cloths, laid directly on the table, need a fifteen to eighteen-inch overhang and may have a colored undercloth the same size. A sheet will do. Use large dinner napkins, folded in thirds into an oblong shape with the open corner at the lower right. Lay them on the service plates in the center of the place settings, or in the center where the service plate would be, or to the left of the forks if food is in place when the guests are seated. Smaller luncheon napkins are folded in triangles or shields (triangles with points turned under).

Silverware is placed one inch from the edge of the service plates in the order of use, beginning at the outside. Have no more than three pieces of silver on each side of the plate. Forks go on the left and knives and spoons on the right, but cocktail forks go on the right of the spoons. If the salad accompanies the main course or is served after the entree, place its fork to the right of the dinner fork. Dessert spoons and forks are brought with the dessert plates, and coffee spoons on the saucer with the coffee. Butter plates are placed above and to the left of the place setting. Place the butter knife across the plate parallel to the edge of the table, the blade facing the diner. Plates for salad served with the main course go to the left or the right of each place setting.

At a luncheon when no knife is needed, place the luncheon fork in the knife position. Service plates are not used for an informal dinner and the dessert fork and spoon can be placed parallel to the edge of the table, pointing to the left, above the place setting.

Left: *Standard table setting.*

Right: *Table set to indi-cate salad will be served after the entree. Note placement of salad fork.*

Glasses are arranged in descending order of size beginning with a water goblet above the dinner knife to the right of the plate.

The lady guest of honor is served first with service continuing around the table counterclockwise; the host is served last. Dishes are served from the left, but beverages are poured from the right, never lifting the beverage glasses. To exchange plates, remove the used plate with the left hand and place the new one with the right. Leave each course of plates on the table until all guests are finished.

When a maid is serving, she brings heated dinner plates from the kitchen one at a time, exchanging the previous course's plate. Then she serves vegetables, bread, and salad, if it accompanies the main course. Everything is removed from the table except water and dessert wine glasses before dessert is served.

While coffee may be served with dessert, it is pleasant to serve it, and possibly liqueurs, from a tray in the living room after dinner. A thoughtful host or hostess provides decaffeinated as well as "real" coffee.

If you engage temporary help, you must prepare adequately. Have help arrive early so that you can stage a dress rehearsal. Write out your menu and even a checklist of serving tips. Cover even elementary concepts: Do not touch guests when serving. Refill water goblets when empty,

but do not lift them from the table. Hold a napkin in your left hand to catch stray drops. Do not extend your thumb over the rim of a plate. Sit down and visualize every conceivable serving situation and write it down. Use the same list over and over again.

If you have no maid, simplify your service. Choose a simple menu, two courses for an informal dinner, never more than three. Consider arranging the main course on plates in the kitchen. Serve the salad yourself from a big bowl at the table or place individual salads on the table before the guests are seated.

Dishes may be placed on the table family-style with hot pads underneath. Stack the plates (always hot for hot dishes, chilled plates for cold ones) before the host. Let him serve the main dish and one vegetable with the person on his left serving another vegetable. He passes the plate to her and then the filled plate is passed to the one being served. Other dishes are handed around.

If the host is proficient at carving and likes to be a bit of a star, by all means give him the opportunity to do so. Many people, however, prefer to carve ahead of time in the kitchen.

After the table is cleared, the dessert is brought in and the hostess serves it onto the dessert plates placed to her left.

In clearing the table, it is helpful to use a

A beautiful setting for a dinner party.

room is connected to the living room and the dirty dishes will show for the rest of the evening, whisk off the dessert plates and turn out the light while the guests are drinking coffee in the living room.

Buffets

A meal served buffet style is a delightful alternative to a seated one. Because guests serve themselves, most buffets have a more informal atmosphere. But for special occasions, a wedding breakfast, an anniversary celebration, or entertainment in honor of an important guest, a semiformal or formal buffet can be very elegant. Buffet service lends itself to breakfasts and brunches, to luncheons, and to dinners. A buffet can approach a seated dinner in formality or can be as casual as the most informal cocktail party.

More people can be entertained at a buffet than the average dining room table will seat. In fact, you don't even need to own a dining room table for a buffet—a sideboard, a living room table, a low bookcase, or even a chest of drawers will suffice. However, you do need to have a place for each guest to sit down.

Moreover, at a buffet, a host or hostess can single-handedly serve the meal graciously and enjoy the guests at the same time. For a large group, a buffet is ideal for the budget-conscious because costs per serving can be minimal. Requirements for china, glassware, silver, and linens are not large. With proper planning, you can get by with one dinner plate, perhaps a dessert plate, a cup and saucer, a fork and spoon and a glass per person. And these do not have to match.

For guests, a buffet is enjoyable because they can choose what they wish to eat and move about visiting with different people in an informal way.

A buffet dinner should start with a light first course served in the living room while you are attending to last-minute details. Serve cocktails with finger food, for instance.

Throughout the meal, what you choose to

tiered tea cart. First remove the serving dishes, then the plates and silver. Use a tray to take out salt and pepper and unused silver. If you are removing plates without a cart, it is permissible to place a bread and butter plate on a dinner plate, but don't stack anything else. Take them to the kitchen, stack them in the sink, in a nearby utility room, or place them in the dishwasher if you can do it quickly. The main consideration is smooth, rapid efficiency in changing courses so that your guests will not be uneasy with the work you are doing.

Never accept offers for help unless you have prearranged for help from a relative or very close friend. The same is true at the end of the meal. Inevitably, someone will say, "Let's all pitch in and wash up." Be firm and do not relent. Simply close the door to the dining room or put up a screen and leave everything as is. If your dining serve will be influenced by the unique problems of eating on one's lap. The main dishes should be ones that can be eaten with a fork alone—forget knives. Be sure what you have will fit on one plate, but have plenty from which to choose. Your preparation will be simplified if you select food that can be prepared ahead of time. Casseroles that go straight from oven to table and keep hot a long time are ideal. All hot dishes should be able to withstand being kept hot at least thirty minutes. Butter your breads ahead of time. Do not plan desserts requiring parfait or sherbet glasses. Instead, have something that sits easily on a plate like a piece of pie or cake. You can simplify service by having finger desserts such as cookies and fruit. Do not serve beverages in stemmed glasses since they are awkward to hold while eating.

To make dining more pleasant, invest in lap trays, scatter small stackable tables around the room, and reserve places at desks and at side tables for elderly and "anti-buffet" people. The agile can sit on the floor around a coffee table or on stairs.

At a seated buffet, guests serve themselves and then eat at the dining room table or card tables. Cover the tables with napkins, silverware, and glasses. For this kind of buffet, you can serve food requiring a knife. Water is poured just before the guests come to the tables and wine is poured by the host after they are seated.

When the main course is over, ask a friend to help you remove the plates (unless you have a maid). Clear the buffet table and reset it with dessert plates and coffee service for guests to help themselves. Alternatives are to serve dessert and coffee from the kitchen, set up dessert and coffee on a sidetable, pass finger foods for dessert, pass a dessert that goes directly on the dinner plate—crackers, cheese, and fruit, for instance—or use as your table centerpiece—a basket of fruit or a decorated cake—as dessert.

If you use card tables in the living room, they should be taken down when the meal is over, although not if games are scheduled.

The placement of the buffet table and the arrangement of food on it are important. You can set up the buffet anywhere—in the dining room, kitchen, den—as long as guests can move easily with no backtracking or crisscrossing through those in line. Be sure electrical outlets are available for food warmers. Setting the buffet table close to the kitchen helps the hostess.

Put things on the table in logical order: (1) napkins, (2) forks, (3) plates, (4) entrees, (5) salads, (6) relishes, (7) vegetables, (8) bread. Desserts and drinks may be on a separate table or set out later.

If an entrée is to be served over noodles or rice, be sure the noodles or rice are placed just before the entrée. Sauces and gravies should be adjacent to what they are used on. Have the proper serving piece beside each dish. Leave space to set down a plate if the service requires two hands, such as to get a tossed salad or to grind a pepper mill.

For a large buffet meal, set up two lines to speed service. Have duplicate dishes so guests do not have to reach across the table and so everyone has a choice of everything. Alternatively, you might use one set of dishes on a narrow table with a line on either side.

Make your buffet table stunning. You don't need the most expensive serving pieces, but you do need to achieve something special. Be willing to give it thought and a degree of inventiveness. Formal or informal, your table's appearance complements the desired mood.

Use color creatively, tying in holiday or seasonal schemes. Add interest to your buffet table by original use of an everyday object: a large punch bowl for salads, a soup tureen for the centerpiece, or a pitcher for serving soup.

If you have a great many serving dishes, avoid an overcrowded look by dispensing with a centerpiece and using a dramatic dish instead. For a sideboard against a wall, create an asymmetrical effect by placing the centerpiece at one end.

Invest in an electric hot plate or tray to keep

your dishes warm and by all means start off with heated plates. You can heat them by putting them in the oven for an hour on warm or by running them through the dry cycle of the dishwasher and leaving them there until needed.

Styrofoam ice chests can do double duty as warmers for plates or as extra coolers. Place a warming pad set on medium in the bottom of the chest or wrap an oven-heated brick in a towel, and place the plates on top. To keep extra food cold, line the bottom with ice cubes or chemical ice packages, cover with heavy foil, and then set the food on a towel.

Cocktail Parties

There is no such thing as a standard cocktail party. A cocktail party can be small and informal or large and elaborate. It can be as simple as drinks and a few hors d'oeuvres or as elaborate as a cocktail buffet.

A cocktail party involves less expenditure of time, trouble, and money than a seated dinner, and more people can be entertained in small quarters in a relatively short period of time. Cocktail parties provide an excellent opportunity to share your home with new or casual acquaintances you wish to know better.

You should also consider a cocktail party's negatives by remembering ones you did not enjoy because there was no place to sit down, a high noise level, an elbow-to-elbow crowd, a guest list composed of everyone that had to be "paid back" but whose only common denominator seemed to be they knew the host or hostess from somewhere.

Avoid these pitfalls by planning a series of smaller parties or staggering the hours, inviting different people at different times: 5:00-7:00, 5:30-7:30, and 6:00-8:00 p.m.

Try to invite approximately an equal number of men and women who are congenial. Don't mix too many different personalities and try to make sure that each guest knows at least one other person on the invitation list.

If the party is to be small, telephone the

invitations. Otherwise send written ones with a "Regrets Only" line and your telephone number added. In every case, be specific. State the time limits: "Cocktails from 5:00 to 7:00 p.m." The early hour and the ending time alert guests to the fact that the party does not include a buffet supper and they should plan to stay only forty-five minutes to one hour. Considerate guests always telephone if they must decline the invitation, and always appear if they have indicated acceptance.

You can serve all sorts of hors d'oeuvres. Just don't place them all on the same table. Space them around the entertaining area to lure people into moving around. Stand long cheese breadsticks in a flower vase on a side table. Place salted nuts on an end table and tiny meat balls on a desk. Don't put everything out at once; replenish hot appetizers throughout the evening and have fresh trays prepared for later arrivals.

You do not need plates and eating utensils, but you should have plenty of available receptacles for throw-away items like olive pits and toothpick skewers. Be lavish with supplies of paper cocktail napkins and coasters.

Decide on the kind of drinks to serve, keeping them simple if there are no hired bartenders. Assemble all necessary ingredients and provide plenty of extra glasses as guests often forget where they have put down a drink. Plastic glasses are acceptable to use. Figure on three drinks per person and be sure to include nonalcoholic beverages.

Be aware of your guests' consumption of alcohol and never ever urge drinks on anyone. If a guest has too much to drink and is not with someone who can drive safely, it is your responsibility to arrange transportation home with a mutual friend or by taxi.

If more than twenty people are coming, consider hiring a bartender and having a maid in the kitchen. For more than thirty people, you may need two bartenders. For huge affairs, get plenty of professional help, including waiters to pass hors d'oeuvres trays and drinks. Give your help exact serving preferences, especially in measuring drinks. If you calculate drinks at 1½ oz. per drink and the bartender puts 2 oz. in each drink, you may run short.

Without hired help, the host usually acts as bartender and the hostess passes trays. A single woman can delegate bar service in advance to her date or any close male friend or relative. The hostess passes hors d'oeuvres and then leaves the trays for guests to help themselves. She removes or replenishes platters as necessary. The host-bartender asks each guest what he or she would like to drink, and then suggests that guests refill their own glasses.

You may decide to have a cocktail buffet, which combines elements of a simple cocktail party and a more elaborate buffet dinner. Call it a "cocktail buffet" when you issue the invitations so that guests do not make other dinner plans. The arrival time may be slightly later than for cocktails only, say at 6:00 or 7:00 p.m., and the invitations do not necessarily give an ending time as cocktail party invitations should do, but may state that the party is from 6:00 to 9:00 or 7:00 to 9:00 p.m. The fact that your party extends over the dinner hour reveals that a dinner substitute will be offered.

For a cocktail buffet, prepare a cloth-covered serving table well separated from the bar area to avoid congestion. Offer more than just appetizers: platters of meats, breads, raw vegetables and dips, hot foods in chafing dishes, cheeses, even candies and cakes. Generally, it is best to have stacks of small plates available. For a more elaborate buffet dinner you may need forks.

If the serving table does not have room for an elaborate centerpiece, use one of the dishes as a conversation piece instead. You might place a can of Sterno in a hollowed-out cabbage for guests to cook little bits of meat on picks over the flame, or fill a hollowed-out rind of pumpernickel bread with dip.

Because food at a cocktail party is not being served according to a schedule, it is important that the host and hostess be aware of their guests'

needs at all times and keep food and drink available.

Wine and Cheese Parties

Increasingly popular is the wine and cheese party, perhaps because wine is becoming a favorite beverage, but also because such a party is so simple to put together, yet so festive to attend. While it requires the basic logistical planning common to all parties, a wine and cheese party does not necessitate long hours of fancy food preparation.

A wine and cheese party is one that does not call for silver accessories. Cheese lends itself to wooden boards. You can even press your chopping and bread boards into service or use marble or tile slabs.

Have a different knife or slicer for each cheese and do not pair strong and mild flavors on the same board. Plenty of slicing room is needed for each cheese.

Garnishes should be minimal. Just set out the cheese at least an hour before starting time so that it can warm up to room temperature.

Natural fiber baskets or wooden trays holding bread and crackers can be placed nearby. Provide crusty French bread, rye bread, lightly salted or bland crackers—all with fairly unobtrusive flavors that don't compete with those of the wine and cheese.

If you like, add bowls or trays of red and green grapes and sliced apples or pears that have been treated with something like Fruit Fresh to keep them from darkening. Platters of fresh raw vegetables with a mild dip also go well. I like to add a plate of plain cookies for those who prefer drinking fruit juices.

A simple white cloth—perhaps a sheet or even good quality paper—allows the table focus to be on the reason for the party, and the centerpiece can emphasize it. Try placing three long-stemmed lilies in a wine carafe. Elongate the arrangement by adding a smaller carafe on either side with a single blossom, tying them all

Cocktail glasses should be chilled before using. Either put them in the refrigerator or stir cracked ice in them.

To frost glasses, immerse in very hot water until thoroughly heated and, while still dripping, place in the refrigerator for several hours.

A delightful way to serve cocktails or coolers is in sugar-frosted glasses. Dip the rims in about one-fourth inch of water. Then rub the rims with orange, lime, or lemon wedges and dip in sugar or dip the rims into a syrup or liqueur and then into sugar. Make these ahead and store them in the refrigerator or freezer.

Pasta Salad Bar

For an easy meal, prepare any combination of the following items and place in serving dishes for a tempting and cool meal.

Cooked pasta: *rotini, spirals, macaroni twirls, ditalini, salad macaroni, curly-roni, shel-roni, rotelle, shell macaroni, rigatoni, small shells, cut fusilli, elbow marcaroni, cut ziti.*

Chopped or sliced raw vegetables: *carrots, celery, broccoli, tomatoes, onion, green pepper, cauliflower, zucchini, avocado, radishes, asparagus, mushrooms, cucumber, bean sprouts.*

Cubed or sliced cooked meat: *chicken, turkey, beef, ham, pork, veal, tuna, salami, bologna, pepperoni, crab, shrimp, corned beef.*

Salad Dressings: *creamy cucumber, bleu cheese, mayonnaise, Italian, creamy buttermilk, thousand island, French, creamy Italian, vinegar and oil, Russian, tomato and bacon, sweet and sour, avocado, hot bacon.*

together with strands of intertwined ivy. A huge bowl of fruit to be eaten serves well as a centerpiece, or a jug of extra-long loaves of bread or a tray of interesting twists of bread.

Place glasses and decanters and carafes of wine and juice on another table or opposite the food end of the main serving table. Always provide an alternative to alcoholic beverages. Stock catawba juice, white grape juice, grapefruit juice, and any other fruit juices you want.

Plan to have at least three kinds of cheese and a minimum of two wines, one red and one white. Expand on this as much as you like. Figure about one-fourth pound of cheese and one half liter of wine per person.

Have plenty of all-purpose wine glasses. Ideally, have two glasses for each guest so that they may sample more than one type of wine.

Aim for variety and balance in selecting cheeses from the following sample categories:

Soft: Camembert, Brie, Liederkrantz, cream cheese

Semi-soft: Bel Paese, Port du Salut, Muenster, Monterey Jack

Firm: Cheddar, Swiss, Jarlsberg

Hard: Gouda, Gruyère, Provolone

Spicy: Harvarti with dill, Esrom with herbs or peppers, Tilsit with caraway

Blue-veined: Danish blue, Bleu, Gorgonzola

With the same criteria in mind, choose a slightly sweet white Chenin Blanc or a rich Riesling wine. Contrast this with a fruity red Beaujolais. If you wish, add a dry Chablis (white) and a tart Cabernet Sauvignon (red).

Wine and cheese tasting parties lend themselves nicely to a variation of the familiar BYOB party. Ask each guest or couple to bring a favorite vintage for others to sample. Provide three glasses per person and bowls of fresh water nearby for rinsing glasses.

Teas

Generations of Southern ladies have learned their social amenities by attending a progression of teas, from small, intimate gatherings of close friends, to large affairs such as those traditionally honoring high school graduates and Cotillion Club holiday tea dances. They then turned to giving teas as the way to repay social obligations.

Teas are always elegant. With flowers and candlelight, the dainty food and refreshing hot tea make a party so enchanting that to most women, teas have a glamor that cannot be equaled.

For a while it seemed that other, more informal affairs were in greater vogue, and, certainly, career women cannot take time off in mid-afternoon to sip and chat. However, a renaissance seems to be occurring. Fine hotels and restaurants have started advertising late afternoon tea times as an alternative to the cocktail hour, and many people are rediscovering this extremely pleasant social occasion for a late afternoon or weekend diversion.

Types of teas range from the small and intimate to the large and formal which can merge into a reception where a punch bowl may be added. Actually, teas and coffees are interchangeable, but we often associate coffees with morning affairs when muffins and pastries are served and teas with afternoon parties featuring little sandwiches and cakes.

The traditional tea hour is four o'clock, but the time can vary from two to six o'clock. One hotel in Nashville, Tennessee, serves tea from 3:30 until 5:30 in the afternoon and then the room becomes the usual cocktail lounge.

Your seating capacity determines how many guests you invite to a tea. Unlike cocktail parties, teas are sit-down affairs.

Make the tea in the kitchen and bring it in with the tea things on a bare tray. Arrange the tray for your convenience, usually with a teapot on the right and a jug of hot water for diluting the tea just behind the teapot. The tray should also contain a small plate of lemon slices with a fork, a pitcher of warm milk (not cream), and a bowl of lump sugar with tongs.

Tea cups and saucers may be stacked in twos with teaspoons. Small plates are stacked with a napkin between each plate and butter knives or forks arranged on top with handles facing the guests. Sometimes saucers are eliminated and only dessert plates are used.

Use a small cloth-covered table in the living room to serve the tea. After it is poured, bring in and pass other food—tiny sandwiches such as cucumber and watercress, smoked salmon, cream cheese on date-nut bread; tea cakes and cookies; fruitcake; toasted muffins spread with jam or honey. The light food at a tea differs from that of cocktail parties, for the emphasis is on sweets; sandwiches are made on very thin, crustless bread and are usually cold.

For a larger, more formal tea, service is most often from the dining room table, although the tea table may be any that has space around it for movement of guests. Always use a pretty organdy, lace, or linen cloth with cutwork, embroidery or applique. It may barely cover the table or have an eighteen-inch overhang.

Your best china, crystal, and silver are appropriate, although all plates and cups need not match. Centerpieces should not be "cute" or "creative." Strive for traditional beauty. Fresh flowers are lovely, as is fruit or a decorative object. You can light the candles, even in the daytime, to heighten the sense of elegance.

Set a large tray at each end of the table, one for tea service, the other for coffee. Have all equipment necessary for proper tea making: a pot with boiling water over a flame, if possible; a teapot and strainer; tea bags or loose tea in a caddy; milk pitcher; sugar bowl; lemon slices. Coffee should be in an urn or pot with a flame beneath it. The coffee tray should also contain a cream pitcher and sugar bowl.

If you do not have elaborate equipment, make the beverages in the kitchen and keep bringing pots to the serving table.

CHEESE SAMPLER

Cheese	Texture & Taste	Uses
Blue	Semisoft; crumbly; tangy	Appetizers, salads, dips, dressings, with fruit for desserts
Brie	Soft; mild to pungent	Appetizers, with fruit for desserts
Camembert	Soft; mild to pungent	Appetizers, with fruit for desserts
Cheddar	Firm, grates easily; mild to strong	Appetizers, snacks, sandwiches, sauces, casserole toppings
Cottage cheese	Soft curds; mild	Appetizers, dips, snacks, casserole fillings
Cream cheese	Soft; mild	Dips, spreads, appetizers, cake fillings, frostings
Edam	Firm; mild, mellow, nut-like flavor	Snacks, salads, sandwiches, desserts
Emmentaler	Firm; sweet, slightly salty nut-like flavor	Snacks, salads, sandwiches, with fruit for desserts
Gorgonzola	Semisoft; tangy, pungent	Salads, with pears for dessert
Gouda	Semisoft to firm; mild to mellow	Salads, snacks, appetizers, with fruit for desserts
Gruyère	Firm; buttery, nut-like flavor	Sauces, salads, fondues, soups, omelets, snacks
Jack	Semisoft; mild	Snacks, sandwiches, casseroles
Jarlsberg	Firm; mild, nut-like flavor	Snacks, salads, sandwiches
Muenster	Semisoft; mild to pungent	Snacks, sandwiches, salads, desserts

Cups and saucers are arranged around the tea and coffee trays. Stack tea plates with small napkins folded between each one along the sides of the table. Arrange the food being served behind the cups. If a large, square cake is offered, slice about a quarter and leave the knife for guests to cut the rest. Have forks if iced cakes are served. If the table cannot accommodate everything, place some of the plates on a sideboard or small table nearby.

A host or hostess can easily manage a tea without a maid because nothing needs to be cooked or passed. Set out the tea things, greet guests, show them where to leave their coats, and all that has to be done is to bring in boiling water from the kitchen stove.

Pouring is done by close friends of the hostess who are asked in advance. It is considered an honor to be asked. If the party is long, the hostess should plan for relief pourers. The hostess and possibly a friend take the empty cups and plates to the kitchen as guests finish.

Between these two kinds of teas described, there can be variations. Plan your tea party the way that is most comfortable for you. But do strive for as much elegance as possible, for that is what makes tea time so special.

Brunch

A delightful start to any day is the informal, relaxed entertainment of brunch, combining menu elements of both breakfast and lunch. Usually served between 10:30 a.m. and 1:00 p.m. (as opposed to a luncheon's beginning time of 12:30 or 1:00 p.m.), brunch is a perfect way for busy career people to entertain on weekends. Brunch can be combined with watching sports events on television or it can be a way to get together casually after church. Big brunches are often planned for out-of-town guests who have come for a special occasion like a horse race or a charity ball.

Bloody Marys or Mimosas are usually served as are martinis and other cocktails, but pitchers of plain fruit juice and lots of coffee are also required. While some serve sit-down style, as at a luncheon but with less formal linens, more people plan a brunch just as they do a buffet supper. The big difference is that food is arranged much less elaborately and breakfast-type dishes such as eggs, sausages, and bacon are included. Creamed chicken or turkey hash is a Southern brunch tradition as are cheese grits.

The later in the day the brunch starts, the more the menu lends itself toward luncheon fare. It is, however, a hearty meal because it really combines two meals. Actually the term "brunch" is flexible enough to mean whatever the host or hostess wishes, even an elegant luncheon.

Interesting, unusual containers used as centerpieces fit the mood perfectly: a colander of fresh fruit, an egg basket filled with eggs (dyed for Easter), a coffee pot filled with garden flowers, or a cannister filled with interesting utensils such as wire whisks, beaters, graters, and wooden spoons.

At a seated brunch I once attended for out-of-town guests before a wedding, each table was centered with a different ceramic teapot filled with field daisies and black-eyed Susans picked from the roadside. It was lovely. Once again, attention was turned toward the flowers nature provides. Daisies and Queen Anne's Lace often grace Southern tables for this reason.

Overnight Guests

Preparing for house guests requires more preplanning than for any other type of entertaining because the "party" extends over a longer period of time, involving more meals and diversions. Here are some ideas that may help both you and your company to have a satisfying visit.

For the peace of mind of all, settle gracefully exactly when arrival and departure times will be. This applies to relatives as well as friends. A friend once shared a family joke with me that when she was a new mother and went home to visit her parents, it was so pleasant that she stayed first one week, then two, then three (while

CHEESE SAMPLER

Cheese	Texture & Taste	Uses
Mozzarella	Semisoft; mild	Appetizers, sandwiches, salads, Italian cooking
Parmesan	Hard; sharp, pungent	Casseroles, Italian cooking, sauces, with fruit for dessert
Provolone	Firm; mild to sharp smoky flavor	Sandwiches, snacks, appetizers, salads, pasta dishes, with fruit for dessert
Roquefort	Semisoft; sharp and pungent	Appetizers, salads and dressings, desserts
Swiss	Firm; mild, nut-like flavor	Sandwiches, snacks, salads, sauces, soups

her newspaperman husband covered a political campaign). The next time she visited her parents, her father met her at the door with, "How long do you propose to stay?"

When the invitation is extended, give some indication of the plans, perhaps inviting input from the guests: "Would you like to spend a day at an amusement park or would you prefer to sit by the pool? Would you enjoy seeing an exhibit at the museum Saturday afternoon and then going to the symphony?" Knowing these arrangements will make a difference in the wardrobe your guests will pack as well as in your menu planning.

If it's not possible to discuss plans at the time of the invitation, consider your options and get back in touch as soon as possible. Don't overschedule; you are not a tour director, and it is tiring for all if every minute is filled. Set aside time for rest and solitude.

Map out your strategy. Plan your own wardrobe and write out all your menus—and don't forget breakfast! Shop early, cook, and freeze dishes so that you will have time to be with and enjoy your guests.

Prepare the guest room thoughtfully. All hosts

and hostesses should spend a night in their guest room, just to see what it is really like. Is the lighting adequate for reading in bed and to apply makeup? Are the pillows comfortable? Where would your guests put a suitcase? Does the closet contain enough clothes hangers, including some for skirts and pants? You should have plastic or padded hangers for your guests instead of wire ones from the cleaners. Remove all the junk you have been stashing in the closet.

Consider the room's amenities—a box of tissues, pins and a threaded needle, magazines, a radio, a clock. Lay out an extra blanket or an afghan for naps. Leave a labeled house key on the dresser. Make up the bed with freshly washed sheets and clear some drawer space. Set out a jar of dried rose potpourri or place a single rose in a bud vase as a silent extra welcome.

Bathrooms need critical examination and not just for scrupulous cleanliness. In the guest bath is there plenty of tissue, soap, bath salts, an extra tube of toothpaste, and even a new toothbrush?

If the bath is shared by the family, lay out guest towels of a different color and tell your family members and your guests which towels belong to whom.

Upon arrival, the guests may want refreshments or a nap after a long drive. Then explain the family schedule and make them feel as though they are part of the routine.

A host or hostess usually remembers to send instructions on how to get to the house, but it is equally important to write out directions for going away, especially if the guests will not be reversing their route, but will be going elsewhere. Draw a diagram to get to the interstate and have a road map handy to give away, marked with the way to any interesting nearby sites.

If the guests are leaving by plane, plan plenty of time to get to the airport. Then you and your guests can be relaxed when you say goodbye and begin to plan ahead for another visit.

Menus

Derby Day Breakfast

Compote of Melon Balls
Eggs Derby
Herbed Tomatoes   Cheese Strata
Sour Cream Coffee Cake
Maple Bran Muffins   Oatmeal Cake

Eggs Derby

6   hard-boiled eggs
³/₄ cup cooked, minced country ham
2 to 3 tablespoons heavy cream
     Salt and pepper to taste
2   tablespoons butter
2   tablespoons all-purpose flour
1¹/₂ cups milk, scalded
1¹/₂ cups heavy cream, scalded
6   large mushrooms, sliced
¹/₄ cup butter
¹/₄ cup grated Parmesan cheese
2   tablespoons butter
¹/₂ teaspoon paprika

Halve eggs. Mix yolks with ham, cream, salt and pepper. Return yolks to whites and place in buttered casserole. Melt 2 tablespoons butter, stir in flour until smooth. Remove from heat. Add scalded milk and cream, heat and stir until smooth. Add salt and pepper to taste. Simmer 10 minutes. Sauté mushrooms in ¹/₄ cup butter. Season with salt and pepper and add to the cream sauce. Pour over eggs. Top with Parmesan, butter and paprika. Bake in a 450 degree oven for 8 to 10 minutes until golden. Yield: 6 servings

Herbed Tomatoes

6   large ripe tomatoes
1   teaspoon salt
¹/₄ teaspoon black pepper
¹/₄ cup finely snipped parsley
¹/₄ cup fresh or frozen chives
²/₃ cup vegetable oil
¹/₄ cup tarragon vinegar

Peel tomatoes; cut crosswise in half. Place in deep bowl, sprinkling each layer with seasonings and herbs. Combine oil and vinegar and pour over tomatoes. Cover; chill an hour or more, basting often. Drain off dressing and arrange tomatoes on platter. Yield: 12 servings

The Derby Day Breakfast is pictured on pages 32-33.

Cheese Strata

4   tablespoons butter
8   slices day-old white bread
1   pound sharp cheese, grated
2¹/₂ cups milk
6   eggs, lightly beaten
1   medium onion, minced
1   teaspoon seasoned salt
     Dash of pepper
1   tablespoon brown sugar
1   tablespoon Worcestershire sauce
¹/₂ teaspoon dry mustard
     Dash of hot sauce

*S*pread butter on bread and cube 6 slices. Remove crusts on remaining slices and cut into 4 triangles. Layer bread cubes and cheese into a 2-quart buttered casserole. Combine remaining ingredients and pour over cheese. Arrange triangles around edge of casserole. Chill overnight. Set out at room temperature for 1¹/₂ hours before baking. Bake in a 325 degree oven for 1¹/₂ hours or until brown. Yield: 6 to 8 servings

Sour Cream Coffee Cake

1   cup butter, softened
1¹/₄ cups sugar
2   eggs
1   cup sour cream
1   teaspoon vanilla
2   cups all-purpose flour
1   teaspoon baking powder
1   teaspoon salt
4   tablespoons sugar
1   teaspoon cinnamon
1   cup chopped nuts

*C*ream butter and sugar; add eggs, sour cream, and vanilla. Sift flour, baking powder and salt together; stir into first mixture. Pour half the batter into a greased bundt or tube pan. Combine remaining ingredients; sprinkle half over batter. Pour on remaining batter and top with remaining sugar mixture. Bake in a 350 degree oven for 1 hour. Yield: 10 to 15 servings

Maple Bran Muffins

1   cup sour cream
1   cup maple syrup
2   eggs
1   cup all-purpose flour
1   teaspoon baking soda
1   cup bran flakes
¹/₃ cup raisins
¹/₃ cup chopped pecans

*C*ombine sour cream, maple syrup and eggs. Sift flour and soda: add bran flakes, raisins and nuts. Stir in sour cream mixture. Spoon into greased muffin tins. Bake in a 400 degree oven for 20 minutes. Yield: 18 muffins

Oatmeal Cake

2   cups oats
3   cups boiling water
4   eggs
2   cups sugar
2   cups brown sugar
1   cup shortening
3   cups flour
2   teaspoons cinnamon
2   teaspoons baking soda
1   teaspoon salt
     Topping

*C*ook oats in water; set aside. Cream eggs, sugars and shortening, add remaining ingredients and beat well; stir in oatmeal. Bake in two 13x9-inch cake pans in a 350 degree oven for 30 to 35 minutes or until a skewer inserted in center comes out clean. Prepare Topping and pour over cake. Yield: 10 to 12 servings

Topping

1 cup chopped pecans	1 cup milk
1 pound brown sugar	2 cups coconut
1 cup butter	1 teaspoon vanilla

*M*ix together and bring to a rapid boil. Pour over hot cakes.

Morning Coffee

Mimosas
Creamy Milk Punch* and Tomato Juice
Assorted Breads
Strawberry Butter   Cream Cheese
Honey   Fresh Fruit
Sausage Balls in Apple Butter
Coffee with Whipped Cream and Cinnamon

• ———————— •

Mimosas

Champagne, chilled
Orange juice, chilled

Combine equal parts of champagne and orange juice. Serve in large wine glasses.

Honey Banana Bread

1 **cup butter**
3/4 **cup honey**
2 **eggs**
1 **cup mashed, overripe bananas**
2 **cups all-purpose flour**
1 **teaspoon baking soda**
1/4 **teaspoon salt**
1 **cup chopped pecans**
1 **8-ounce package chopped dates**

Cream butter and honey. Add eggs, then mashed bananas. Blend well. Add flour, soda, salt and mix well. Add pecans and dates; stir. Pour mixture into greased and floured 9x5x3-inch loaf pan. Bake in a 350 degree oven for 30 minutes or until a skewer inserted in center comes out clean. Yield: 14 to 16 slices per loaf

Harvest Yam Bread

4 1/2 **cups all-purpose flour**
1 1/2 **teaspoons salt**
3 **cups sugar**
1 **tablespoon baking soda**
3 **cups cooked pureed yams**
1 1/2 **cups vegetable oil**
6 **eggs, beaten**
3/4 **teaspoon nutmeg**
3/4 **teaspoon cinnamon**
3/4 **teaspoon allspice**
3 **cups peeled, chopped apples**
2 **cups chopped pecans**

Sift together flour, salt, sugar and baking soda. Mix pureed yams, oil, eggs and spices together, then combine just until mixed with dry ingredients. Do not overmix. Stir in apples and pecans. Pour into well-greased 9x5x3-inch loaf pans or muffin cups, filling muffin cups about two-thirds full. Bake in a 350 degree oven for 60 to 70 minutes and muffins 20 to 25 minutes or until skewer inserted in center comes out clean. Remove from pan and cool on rack for several hours before slicing. Can be rewarmed just prior to serving. Yield: 3 loaves or 36 muffins

*Recipe for Creamy Milk Punch is on page 50.

Harvest Yam Bread, page. 47.

Strawberry Bread

    3   cups all-purpose flour
    1   teaspoon baking soda
    1   teaspoon salt
    1   tablespoon cinnamon
    2   cups sugar
    4   eggs, beaten
    2   cups sliced frozen strawberries, thawed
    1½ cups vegetable oil
    1¼ cups broken pecans

*S*ift dry ingredients together. Combine eggs, strawberries, and oil and add to sifted ingredients. Add pecans. Pour into 2 well-greased 9x5x3-inch loaf pans. Bake in a 325 degree oven for about 1 hour or until a skewer inserted in center comes out clean. Cool in pan for 5 minutes, then cool on wire rack. Yield: 14 to 16 slices per loaf

Strawberry Butter

    ½   cup butter, softened
    ⅓   cup strawberry jam
    ½   teaspoon lemon juice
    ½   teaspoon confectioners' sugar

*C*ombine all ingredients until thoroughly blended. Chill until serving time. This may be placed in decorative molds. Yield: Approximately ¾ cup

Sausage Balls in Apple Butter

    1 pound mild sausage
    1 large jar apple butter

*M*ake marble-sized sausage balls. Sauté in skillet until done. Drain on paper towels. When ready to serve, heat apple butter in saucepan or chafing dish and add sausage balls. Keep warm while serving. Yield: 5 dozen

St. Patrick's Day Brunch

Spicy Breakfast Casserole
Apples in Sauterne
Yeast Rolls*
Crème de Menthe Cake
Irish Coffee*

•⸺•

Spicy Breakfast Casserole

1 dozen eggs, beaten
³/₄ cup milk
Salt and pepper to taste
1 pound bulk pork sausage, cooked, crumbled and drained
1 4-ounce can green chiles chopped and drained
4 ounces Cheddar cheese, grated

Combine eggs, milk and seasonings. Place sausage in a 1¹/₂-quart baking dish. Pour egg mixture over sausage. Sprinkle with chiles and cheese. Bake, uncovered, in a 325 degree oven for 20 minutes. Yield: 6 servings

Apples in Sauterne

7 medium apples, peeled and cored
¹/₂ cup sauterne
1 tablespoon candied orange peel
¹/₂ teaspoon nutmeg
2 tablespoons orange juice
1 tablespoon lemon juice
Whipped cream, optional

Combine apples, wine, orange peel, nutmeg and juices; poach until apples are soft. Take half of one apple and combine with pan juices in blender. Use as a sauce for remaining whole apples. Serve with whipped cream, if desired. Yield: 6 servings

Crème de Menthe Cake

1 package white pudding cake mix
3 tablespoons crème de menthe
1 16-ounce jar hot fudge topping
3 tablespoons crème de menthe
¹/₂ pint heavy cream, whipped

Prepare cake according to directions, substituting 3 tablespoons crème de menthe for the water. Bake in a 13x9x2-inch pan according to package directions. Cool. Heat the fudge topping and smooth over top of the cake. Cool. Fold remaining crème de menthe into whipped cream and spread on cake. Yield: 24 servings

To help prevent tears when chopping onions, refrigerate them first, then breathe through your mouth while chopping.

*Recipe for Yeast Rolls is on page 58.
*Recipe for Irish Coffee is on page 100.

Father's Day Brunch

Creamy Milk Punch
Grillades*
Hot Fruit Compote   Garlic Cheese Grits
Cheese Biscuits*
Bourbon Chocolate Pecan Pie*
Iced Tea or Coffee

·————·

Freeze stock, gravies, soups, and liquid from cooked vegetables in ice cube trays, and then store the cubes in bags.

Creamy Milk Punch

2   quarts vanilla ice cream
1½ cups brandy
4   tablespoons sugar
2   teaspoons vanilla
2   cups cold milk
    Nutmeg

Place ice cream in blender. Add brandy, sugar and vanilla. Blend 5 seconds or until well mixed. Add milk and blend 5 seconds longer. Serve in champagne glasses. Sprinkle with nutmeg. This recipe should be halved if prepared in a home blender. Yield: 16 to 24 glasses or 1 gallon

Hot Fruit Compote

1   16-ounce can pear halves
1   16-ounce can sliced peaches
1   16-ounce can pineapple chunks
1   16-ounce can apricot halves
12 maraschino cherries
¾ cup light brown sugar
3   teaspoons curry powder
⅓ cup melted butter
⅔ cup slivered almonds

*Recipe for Grillades is on page 142.
*Recipe for Cheese Biscuits on page 51.
*Recipe for Bourbon Chocolate Pecan Pie is on page 155.

Drain all fruit. Add sugar and curry powder to melted butter. Arrange fruit and nuts in layers in casserole. Pour butter mixture over all and bake for 1 hour in a 325 degree oven. Refrigerate overnight. Reheat at 350 degrees before serving. Yield: 10 to 12 servings

Note: Be sure to prepare this a day ahead of serving time.

Garlic Cheese Grits

1¼ cups grits, uncooked
3½ cups boiling water
1   roll garlic cheese
½ cup butter
2   eggs
1   cup milk
½ cup Cheddar cheese, grated

Cook grits in boiling water about 30 minutes or until done. Crumble garlic cheese and butter into grits. Blend eggs and milk together. Combine with grits. Pour into 2-quart greased casserole and bake for 45 minutes, uncovered, in a 350 degree oven. Sprinkle with grated cheese and bake 15 minutes longer or until cheese is melted. Yield: 8 to 10 servings

Ladies' Luncheon

Chicken Divan
Fresh Fruit Salad with Poppy Seed Dressing*
Cheese Biscuits or Bran Muffins
Bread Pudding with Brandy Sauce
Iced Tea with Fresh Mint

· ———— ·

Chicken Divan

2 10-ounce packages frozen broccoli spears
6 cooked boned chicken breasts, cut
   into chunks
   Garlic salt
   Butter
1 10³/₄-ounce can cream of chicken soup
1 cup sour cream
3 tablespoons milk
1 cup grated Cheddar cheese
3 tablespoons sherry
   Paprika
   Toasted almonds

Cook broccoli according to package directions. Place a layer of broccoli and a layer of chicken pieces in casserole. Sprinkle with salt and dot with butter. Combine soup, sour cream, milk, Cheddar cheese, and sherry. Pour half over chicken. Repeat layers; sprinkle with paprika and toasted almonds. Bake in a 375 degree oven for 45 minutes. Yield: 6 servings

Cheese Biscuits

3   cups sifted all-purpose flour
5   teaspoons baking powder
1¹/₂ teaspoons salt
¹/₂ teaspoon cayenne pepper
¹/₂ cup shortening
1   cup grated sharp cheese
¹/₄ cup chopped pimiento
1 to 1¹/₂ cups cold milk
     Melted butter, optional

Sift dry ingredients together. Cut in shortening, cheese and pimiento. Add enough milk to make a soft dough. Roll out onto a floured board to a ¹/₂-inch thickness. Fold over and roll again. Cut with a 2-inch biscuit cutter and place on a greased cookie sheet, leaving space between each so all sides can brown. Brush with butter, if desired before baking. Bake in a 450 degree oven for about 15 minutes. Yield: 36 biscuits

Bran Muffins

1 cup shortening
3 cups sugar
4 eggs, beaten
2 cups 100% Bran cereal soaked in 1 quart
   buttermilk until moist
5 cups all-purpose flour
5 teaspoons baking soda
1 teaspoon salt
4 cups All Bran cereal soaked in 2 cups
   boiling water until moist
2 cups raisins

Note: These muffins are served in Miss Daisy's Restaurant in Nashville, Tennessee.

Cream shortening with sugar. Add eggs. Add bran cereal soaked in buttermilk. Sift flour, soda and salt. Add to above mixture. Add bran cereal soaked in boiling water. Pour in raisins. Mixture will last for 6 weeks in refrigerator. When ready to serve pour into greased muffin tins. Bake in a 400 degree oven for 15 to 20 minutes. Yield: 5 dozen

*Recipe for Poppy Seed Dressing on page 108.

52 ·

For a ladies' luncheon, use a small nosegay of flowers at each place instead of a centerpiece.

Bread Pudding with Brandy Sauce

10 slices day-old bread
4 cups scalded milk
1 cup heavy cream
4 eggs
1 cup sugar
1 teaspoon vanilla
1 teaspoon cinnamon
$^1/_2$ teaspoon nutmeg
$^1/_4$ cup melted butter
$^1/_2$ cup seedless raisins
   Brandy Sauce
   Whipped cream

Break bread into pieces and combine with milk and cream. Beat eggs and add sugar; add next 5 ingredients. Pour over bread mixture. Pour into 3-quart baking dish; place dish into pan of warm water. Bake in a 350 degree oven for $1^1/_2$ hours. Serve Brandy Sauce over pudding and top with whipped cream. Yield: 8 servings

Brandy Sauce

3 egg yolks
1 cup sugar
1 teaspoon vanilla
$1^1/_2$ cups milk
1 tablespoon cornstarch
$^1/_4$ cup water
$1^1/_2$ ounces brandy or bourbon

In saucepan slightly beat yolks; add sugar, vanilla and milk; heat. Blend cornstarch into water; stir into hot mixture. Continue cooking until thickened. Remove from heat and stir in brandy or bourbon. Cool and serve over pudding.

Bridge Luncheon

Chicken Crêpes with Velouté Sauce
Fresh Steamed Broccoli Spears
Fruit Salad with Poppy Seed Dressing*
Sherried Angel Cake
Coffee or Tea

· ———— ·

Chicken Crêpes

- 6 tablespoons butter, divided
- 1 cup sliced fresh mushrooms
- 1 cup diced chicken
- 3 hard-boiled egg yolks, mashed
- 1/2 cup sour cream
- 1 tablespoon minced fresh parsley
- 1 teaspoon salt
- 1/4 teaspoon pepper
- 1/2 10-ounce package frozen spinach, cooked and well drained
- 12 to 18 crêpes
- 3 tablespoons grated Parmesan cheese
  Velouté Sauce

Melt 3 tablespoons butter and sauté mushrooms. Remove from heat. Mix in chicken, egg yolks, sour cream, parsley, salt, pepper and spinach. Fill crêpes and roll tightly. Arrange in ovenproof dish. Sprinkle with cheese. Dot with remaining butter. Bake in a 425 degree oven for 15 minutes. Serve with Velouté Sauce. Yield: 12 to 18 crêpes

Velouté Sauce

- 2 tablespoons butter
- 2 tablespoons all-purpose flour
- 2 cups chicken stock
- 1/4 cup chopped mushrooms
  Pinch of nutmeg
  Salt and white pepper to taste

Melt butter in top of double boiler and stir in flour. When blended, add stock and cook, stirring until thickened. Add mushrooms and simmer about 1 hour. Add nutmeg and seasonings to taste. Yield: 1 1/2 cups

Sherried Angel Cake

- 1 envelope unflavored gelatin
- 1/4 cup cold water
- 4 eggs, separated
- 1 cup sugar, divided
- 1/2 cup sherry
- 1/2 pint heavy cream
- 1 large angel food cake

Line bottom of tube pan with foil. Soak gelatin in cold water. Mix egg yolks, 1/2 cup sugar and sherry; cook in double boiler over hot water, stirring constantly, until thickened. Add gelatin to egg yolk mixture and blend thoroughly. Remove from heat. Whip egg whites, adding 1/2 cup sugar, until stiff. Whip cream. Fold together egg whites, whipped cream, and sherry mixture to form custard. Break cake into small chunks and layer cake pieces in bottom of prepared pan. Pour some of custard mixture over top. Repeat layers, ending with custard layer. Chill 3 to 4 hours and serve cold. Garnish with dollop of whipped cream and strawberries if desired. Yield: 10 to 12 servings

*Recipe for Poppy Seed Dressing is on page 108.

Valentine Luncheon

Chicken Saltimbocca
Strawberry Nut Mold
Wild Rice with Mushrooms
Refrigerator Rolls
Chocolate Valentine Torte or Red Velvet Cake
Kir

· ———— ·

Chicken Saltimbocca

3 large chicken breasts, skinned, boned, and halved lengthwise
6 thin slices baked ham
3 slices Mozzarella cheese, halved
1 medium tomato, chopped
1/2 teaspoon sage
1/3 cup fine dry bread crumbs
2 tablespoons grated Parmesan cheese
4 tablespoons crushed parsley
4 tablespoons melted butter

Flatten chicken breasts. Place one ham slice and 1/2 slice of cheese on each breast; trim to fit. Top with some tomato and a dash of sage. Tuck in sides and roll up jelly-roll style. Secure with toothpicks, pressing to seal well. Combine bread crumbs, Parmesan cheese, and parsley. Dip chicken in butter and roll in crumbs. Place in shallow 2-quart ovenproof dish and bake in a 350 degree oven for 40 to 50 minutes. Yield: 6 servings

Strawberry Nut Mold

1 cup boiling water
1 6-ounce package strawberry gelatin
1 envelope unflavored gelatin
1 20-ounce can crushed pineapple, drained
1 cup broken pecan pieces
2 10-ounce packages frozen strawberries with syrup, defrosted

3 mashed bananas
Sour cream
Fresh strawberries

Pour boiling water over strawberry gelatin and unflavored gelatin in a large bowl. Stir until dissolved. Add remaining ingredients except sour cream and strawberries; mix well. Pour into 8-cup mold. Refrigerate. Serve with sour cream and fresh strawberries. Yield: 8 servings

Wild Rice with Mushrooms

1/2 pound wild rice
3/4 pound fresh mushrooms, sliced
1/2 cup butter
2 tablespoons all-purpose flour
1 cup heavy cream
1/2 cup sherry
Salt to taste
1 cup buttered bread crumbs

Cook and steam rice; set aside. Sauté mushrooms in butter. Add flour, then cream, stirring constantly, until thickened. Remove from heat and stir in rice, sherry and salt. Place mixture into a greased 2-quart ovenproof dish and top with bread crumbs. Bake in a 350 degree oven for 20 to 30 minutes. Yield: 6 to 8 servings

Refrigerator Rolls

2 packages dry yeast
1 cup warm water
1 cup boiling water
1 cup vegetable shortening
3/4 cup sugar
2 teaspoons salt
2 eggs
6 cups all-purpose flour
  Melted butter

Dissolve yeast in warm water and set aside for 5 minutes. Pour boiling water over shortening, sugar and salt in large bowl. Blend well; set aside to cool. Beat eggs into yeast water and add to cooled shortening mixture. Gradually add flour and mix well. Place in large oiled bowl; cover and refrigerate. Three hours before serving, roll out dough and cut with biscuit cutter. Dip into melted butter; fold over and place in greased pans. Set aside to rise until doubled in size. Bake in a 400 degree oven for 10 to 15 minutes. Yield: 5 to 6 dozen rolls

Chocolate Valentine Torte

1 1/2 cups sour cream
1 3/4 cups unsifted all-purpose flour
1 3/4 cups sugar
3/4 cup unsweetened Hershey's cocoa
1 1/2 teaspoons baking soda
1 teaspoon salt
2/3 cup butter or margarine, softened
2 eggs
1 teaspoon vanilla
  Vanilla Cream Filling
  Chocolate Glaze (recipe on page 56)
  Decorator's Frosting (recipe on page 56)
  Sliced almonds, optional

Heat sour cream in saucepan or microwave to lukewarm; set aside. Combine flour, sugar, cocoa, baking soda and salt in large mixer bowl. Blend in butter, sour cream, eggs, and vanilla on low speed. Beat 3 minutes on medium speed. Grease and flour two heart-shaped pans or two 9-inch round layer cake pans. Pour batter into pans. Bake in a 350 degree oven for 30 to 35 minutes or until skewer inserted in center comes out clean. Cool 10 minutes; invert onto wire racks. Cool completely. Prepare Vanilla Cream Filling or flavor variation. With sharp serrated knife, cut layers in half horizontally. Place cut-side down; spread with 1/3 of filling. Top with cut layer, repeat procedure ending with plain layer on top. Prepare Chocolate Glaze; pour onto top of torte. Spread evenly allowing some to run down sides. Prepare Decorator's Frosting. Pipe onto top of cake. Garnish with sliced almonds, if desired. Yield: 8 to 10 servings

Vanilla Cream Filling

1/4 cup unsifted all-purpose flour
1/2 cup milk
1/4 cup butter or margarine, softened
1/4 cup shortening
2 teaspoons vanilla
1/4 teapoon salt
4 cups confectioners' sugar

Combine flour and milk in a small saucepan. Cook, stirring constantly with wire whisk, until mixture thickens and just begins to boil; (mixture is very thick) cool to room temperature. Cream butter and shortening until light and fluffy; add vanilla, salt and flour mixture. Gradually add confectioners' sugar beating until spreading consistency. Yield: About 3 cups filling

Variations:
Strawberry: Decrease vanilla to 1 teaspoon; add 3/4 teaspoon strawberry extract and 1 or 2 drops red food color.
Almond: Decrease vanilla to 1 teaspoon; add 1 teaspoon almond extract.
Cherry: Stir in 1/4 cup chopped maraschino cherries, well-drained. Add 1 or 2 drops red food coloring.

The colors, shapes, and sizes of baskets today are endless. Use one as a starting point for a centerpiece. Fill with flowers, fruits, shells, vegetables, colorful autumn leaves and more.

Say "love" deliciously with this Chocolate Valentine Torte, pages 55-56.

Chocolate Glaze

1 tablespoon butter
2 tablespoons unsweetened Hershey's cocoa
2 tablespoons water
1 cup confectioners' sugar
¼ teaspoon vanilla

*M*elt butter in small saucepan over low heat; add cocoa and water, stirring constantly until mixture thickens. Remove from heat; beat in confectioners' sugar and vanilla until smooth and of spreading consistency. Add additional water, ½ teaspoon at a time, if needed.

Decorator's Frosting

2 tablespoons butter
2 tablespoons unsweetened Hershey's cocoa
1 cup confectioners' sugar
½ teaspoon vanilla
1 tablespoon milk

*C*ombine all ingredients until smooth.

Red Velvet Cake

½   cup butter
½   cup shortening
2   cups sugar
4   eggs
2½ cups all-purpose flour
1   teaspoon baking soda
¼   teaspoon salt
4   tablespoons cocoa
1   cup buttermilk
1   teaspoon vanilla
4   tablespoons red food coloring
    Frosting for Red Velvet Cake

*C*ream butter, shortening, and sugar. Add eggs one at a time. Combine flour, soda, salt, and cocoa, and gradually add to butter mixture alternating with buttermilk. Add vanilla and food coloring. Blend well. Pour into 3 greased and floured 9-inch cake pans or 1 tube pan. Bake in a 350 degree oven for 25 to 30 minutes or until a skewer inserted in center comes out clean. Cool cake. Prepare Frosting and ice cake. Yield: 8 to 10 servings

Frosting

1   16-ounce box confectioners' sugar
1   cup butter, softened
1   teaspoon vanilla
4   tablespoons heavy cream
½   cup shredded coconut
    Red food coloring

*B*lend confectioners' sugar, butter, vanilla and cream with mixer until smooth and fluffy. Additional cream may be needed to achieve fluffy consistency. Frost layers and assemble. Tint coconut with red food coloring and sprinkle over top.

Easter Sunday Lunch

Salad of Mixed Greens with Caesar Dressing
Leg of Lamb
Herbed Green Beans   New Potatoes
Yeast Rolls   Onion-Cheese Sauce
Kahlua Mousse
Coffee or Tea

· ———— ·

Caesar Dressing

1   teaspoon salt
1/2 teaspoon pepper
1/4 teaspoon garlic powder
1   teaspoon Worcestershire sauce
1/4 cup vegetable oil
1   egg, coddled
1/2 cup vegetable oil
1/4 cup lemon juice
1/4 cup grated Parmesan cheese

Combine first five ingredients in blender. Coddle egg for 1 minute. Add egg to blender. Add remaining ingredients and blend well. Chill until ready to serve. Yield: Approximately 1 1/4 cups dressing

Leg of Lamb

1   clove garlic, cut into thin slivers
1   6-pound leg of lamb, boned and rolled
2   tablespoons vegetable oil
2   tablespoons all-purpose flour
1   teaspoon chopped fresh rosemary
1   teaspoon thyme
1/4 teaspoon mace
1   teaspoon marjoram
    Salt and freshly ground pepper to taste
1   cup dry white wine
1   cup chicken broth

Insert slivers of garlic into meat. Combine oil, flour, and herbs; rub over meat. Sprinkle with salt and pepper. Pour wine and broth over lamb in roasting pan. On top of the stove, bring liquid in pan to a boil. Place roasting pan in oven. Bake in a 325 degree oven for 30 minutes, basting occasionally. Cover and continue cooking 1 1/2 hours longer or until meat thermometer registers desired degree of doneness. Remove lamb; skim fat from pan juices, bring remaining liquid to a boil; serve with sliced meat. Yield: 8 servings

Herbed Green Beans

2   pounds young, tender green beans, snapped
6   tablespoons olive oil
2   cloves garlic, minced
2 1/2 tablespoons chopped fresh basil
1 1/4 teaspoons chopped mint
2 1/2 tablespoons minced parsley
2 1/2 cups tomatoes, peeled and chopped
    Salt to taste

Soak beans for 15 minutes in water to cover; drain. Combine remaining ingredients; sauté for 5 minutes. Blanch beans in boiling salted water for 1 minute; drain and plunge into cold water. Drain. Add to sautéed herbs and cook for 15 minutes. Yield: 8 servings

Hardened brown sugar can be made useable by sprinkling it with a few drops of water and heating it in a slow oven for a minute or two. Two other techniques are to pulverize it in a blender or to cover it in a glass bowl with an apple slice and microwave it on a very low setting for a minute or two.

58 ·

*The following foods
should not be frozen:
Gelatins
Refrigerator doughs
Potatoes and other
water foods
Creamed cottage cheese
Sandwich spreads
made with mayonnaise
or boiled salad dressing
and hard cooked egg
whites
Crisp salad-type
materials such as
tomatoes, greens, and
cucumbers
Bananas and pears
Cakes with egg-based
filling and/or icings
containing egg whites
or syrups
Cream or custard pies*

New Potatoes

4 pounds tiny new potatoes, unpeeled
4 tablespoons butter
2 tablespoons cream
2 tablespoons minced parsley
    Salt and pepper to taste

Cover potatoes with boiling water to cover. Cook until tender when pricked with a fork, about 20 minutes, drain and stir in remaining ingredients. Yield: 8 to 10 servings

Yeast Rolls

2   cakes yeast
1½   cups lukewarm water
2   tablespoons sugar
1½   teaspoons salt
⅔   cup shortening
2   eggs, beaten
7½   cups all-purpose flour
     Butter

Dissolve yeast cakes in ½ cup of lukewarm water. In a large mixing bowl, cream together sugar, salt, and shortening. Add beaten eggs and the yeast and mix well. Stir in half the flour and the remaining cup of water. Knead in remaining flour by hand until smooth. Place dough in warm, buttered bowl. Set aside to rise until doubled in size. Roll out on floured board to ½-inch thickness. Shape rolls as desired. Butter baking sheets. Arrange rolls on baking sheets. Set aside to rise in warm place for 25 minutes or until doubled in size. Bake in a 425 degree oven for 10 to 15 minutes until golden brown. Yield: 4 dozen rolls

Onion-Cheese Sauce

3   tablespoons butter
¼   cup chopped onion
2   tablespoons all-purpose flour
1¼   cups milk
1   cup shredded Cheddar cheese

Melt butter in a 1-quart saucepan. Add onion and sauté for 5 minutes. Blend in flour. Remove from heat; gradually blend in milk. Return to heat and cook, stirring constantly, until mixture thickens. Cook 2 minutes longer. Remove from heat and stir in cheese until melted. Serve with green beans as an alternate sauce. Yield: 1¾ cups

Kahlua Mousse

½   cup sugar
½   cup water
2   eggs
     Dash salt
1   6-ounce package semi-sweet chocolate chips
2   tablespoons cognac
3   tablespoons Kahlua
½   pint heavy cream, whipped
     Toasted slivered almonds

Heat sugar and water until dissolved. Set aside. Mix eggs, salt, and chocolate in blender. Slowly blend in sugar mixture until thick. Set aside until cool. Add cognac and Kahlua. Fold in ½ the whipped cream. Chill for several hours before serving. Serve topped with remaining whipped cream and toasted almonds. Yield: 6 servings

Afternoon Tea

Southern Tea Cakes
Sherry Frosted Pound Cake
Shortbread Wedges   Lemon Tea Cookies*
Chocolate Petit Fours
Lemon Curd*
Assorted Teas

· ———— ·

Southern Tea Cakes

2¼ cups all-purpose flour, sifted
¼ teaspoon salt
2 teaspoons baking powder
½ cup butter
1 cup sugar
2 eggs, beaten
½ teaspoon vanilla
1 tablespoon milk

Sift first 3 ingredients together. Cream butter, sugar and eggs. Add remaining ingredients and flour mixture. Blend well. Roll dough out on floured board to a ½-inch thickness. Use cookie cutter to cut out shapes. Place on ungreased cookie sheet. Bake in a 350 degree oven for 12 to 15 minutes or until lightly browned. Yield: 24 tea cakes

Sherry Frosted Pound Cake

1 cup butter or margarine, softened
4 eggs
2 cups all-purpose flour
1 teaspoon baking powder
¼ teaspoon salt
1 cup sugar
1 teaspoon vanilla
1 teaspoon grated orange rind
1 cup sifted confectioners' sugar
3 tablespoons cream sherry

Have butter and eggs at room temperature. Combine flour, baking powder and salt. Cream butter with mixer set on medium speed for 30 seconds. Slowly add sugar, beating for 6 minutes. Add vanilla, then eggs, one at a time, beating for 1 minute after each addition. Scrape down sides of bowl frequently. Slowly add flour mixture, blending on low speed until mixed. Add orange rind. Pour into greased and floured loaf pan. Bake in a 325 degree oven for 55 to 65 minutes. Cool for 10 minutes on wire rack. Remove from pan to cool. Combine remaining ingredients. Drizzle onto top of cake. Yield: 12 servings

Shortbread Wedges

1 cup butter or margarine
¼ cup sugar
½ teaspoon vanilla
2½ cups all-purpose flour

Cream butter, sugar and vanilla until light and fluffy. Stir in flour. Divide dough in half. Pat each half into a 7-inch diameter circle. Place on ungreased cookie sheet. Prick dough with fork to make pie-shaped wedges. Bake in a 325 degree oven for 20 to 25 minutes or until lightly golden. Cool 1 minute; place on wire rack to cool. Break into wedges. Yield: 16 servings

*Recipe for Lemon Tea Cookies is on page 159.
*Recipe for Lemon Curd is on page 168.

Everything is ready for a lovely tea.

and almond extract. Beat egg whites in large mixer bowl until foamy; gradually add ¼ cup sugar and continue beating until stiff peaks form. Carefully fold chocolate mixture into beaten egg whites. Spread batter evenly into prepared pan. Bake in a 375 degree oven for 16 to 18 minutes or until top springs back when lightly touched. Invert onto cooling rack; peel off foil. Turn right side up; cool. To prepare Petit Fours: Cut cake into hearts, diamonds, circles or squares with small 1½-inch cookie cutters. Sandwich similar shapes together with a thin layer of raspberry or apricot preserves. Place petit fours on wire rack with wax paper covered cookie sheet below to catch drips. Cover until ready to glaze. Prepare either Milk Chocolate or Semi-Sweet Chocolate Glaze. Frost by spooning glaze over the cake pieces until entire piece is covered. (Glaze that drips off can be reheated and used again.) Allow glaze to set. Chill, if needed. Pipe decorations with tubes of glossy decorating gels or tinted frostings. Cover; store in cool place (will keep several days). Yield: 2 dozen petit fours

Chocolate Petit Fours

4 eggs, separated
½ cup sugar
¾ cup ground blanched almonds
⅓ cup unsifted all-purpose flour
⅓ cup unsweetened Hershey's cocoa
½ teaspoon baking soda
¼ teaspoon salt
¼ cup water
1 teaspoon vanilla
¼ teaspoon almond extract
¼ cup sugar
Raspberry or apricot preserves
Milk Chocolate or Semi-Sweet Chocolate Glaze

Line 15½x10½x1-inch jelly roll pan with aluminum foil; generously grease foil. Set aside. Beat egg yolks in small mixer bowl for 3 minutes on medium speed of mixer. Gradually add ½ cup sugar and continue beating 2 minutes longer. Combine almonds, flour, cocoa, soda and salt; add alternately with water to egg yolk mixture on low speed of mixer, just until blended. Stir in vanilla

Milk Chocolate Glaze

½ pound Hershey's milk chocolate bar
2 tablespoons vegetable shortening

Break chocolate bar into pieces; melt slowly with shortening in top of double boiler over hot water. Cool slightly, stirring occasionally.

Semi-Sweet Chocolate Glaze

1 cup Hershey's semi-sweet chocolate Mini Chips
¼ cup unsalted butter
2 teaspoons vegetable oil

Melt Mini Chips with butter and oil in top of double boiler over hot water; stir until smooth. Cool slightly, stirring occasionally.

Tailgate Picnic

Gazpacho   Spicy Cheese Straws*
Cold Tenderloin   Dijon Mustard
Rice Salad*   Yeast Rolls*
Tennessee Brownies
Lemonade or Iced Tea

• ———— •

Gazpacho

1	cup chopped peeled tomatoes
1	cup finely chopped green pepper
1	cup diced celery
1	cup diced cucumber
1/4	cup minced green onion
2	tablespoons parsley flakes
1	teaspoon chives
1	teaspoon fresh chopped basil
1	small clove garlic, minced
1/4	cup red wine vinegar
1/4	cup olive oil
1	teaspoon salt
1	teaspoon Worcestershire sauce
2	cups tomato juice
	Sour cream

*C*ombine all ingredients except sour cream. Chill. Top each serving with a teaspoon of sour cream. Yield: 6 servings

Cold Tenderloin

3	to 4 pounds beef tenderloin
	Freshly ground pepper

*R*ub meat with pepper and place on rack in pan. Roast in a 425 degree oven for 15 to 20 minutes or until meat thermometer registers desired degree of doneness. Cool. Slice thinly and refrigerate. Yield: 8 servings

Tennessee Brownies

1	cup butter or margarine
2	cups sugar
3	eggs
1	cup all-purpose flour
1	teaspoon baking powder
1/4	cup cocoa
1	teaspoon vanilla
1 1/2	cups nuts, optional
	Icing

*M*elt butter; add sugar and mix well. Add eggs, flour, baking powder, cocoa, vanilla and nuts, if not used in icing. Pour into 13x9x2-inch pan. Bake in a 350 degree oven for 30 minutes or 25 minutes if using glass baking dish. Cool and frost with Icing. Yield: 12 to 16 servings

Note: These brownies are good without the icing, in which case add the nuts to the batter.

Icing

1/2	cup butter or margarine
3	tablespoons cocoa
1 1/2	tablespoons Karo syrup
18	large marshmallows
1	box confectioners' sugar
1	teaspoon vanilla
1 1/2	cups nuts

*C*ombine butter, cocoa, Karo syrup, and marshmallows over low heat, stirring until melted. Add confectioners' sugar, vanilla, and nuts. Pour over warm brownies.

*Recipe for Spicy Cheese Straws is on page 91.
*Recipe for Rice Salad is on page 103.
*Recipe for Yeast Rolls is on page 58.

Backyard Barbecue

Spinach Dip with Raw Vegetables
Barbecued Chicken
Parmesan Cheese Ball   Crackers
Best Baked Beans   Corn on the Cob
Creamy Slaw   Garlic Bread with Butter
Homemade Peach Ice Cream
Oatmeal Cookies
Fudge Nut Bars
Iced Tea

· ———————— ·

Using proper pan sizes is important. If yours aren't marked, measure across the top from inside edge to inside edge for linear measurements or pour water by cups or quarts until the pan is full for volume measure. Mark the measurements on the pan.

Spinach Dip

2   cups mayonnaise
1   10-ounce package frozen chopped spinach, cooked and well drained
$^1/_2$ cup chopped green onion
$^1/_2$ cup chopped fresh parsley
1   teaspoon salt
1   teaspoon pepper

*C*ombine all ingredients, stirring well. Serve with raw vegetables. Yield: 4 cups

Barbecued Chicken

$^1/_3$ cup melted butter
$^1/_3$ cup vegetable oil
2   tablespoons lemon juice
2   teaspoons prepared mustard
$^1/_3$ teaspoon prepared horseradish
1   clove garlic, finely chopped
2   teaspoons barbecue sauce
6 to 8 chicken breasts
    Ac'cent

*C*ombine all ingredients except chicken and Ac-cent; bring sauce to a boil and simmer 5 minutes. Sprinkle chicken breasts with Accent. Brush both sides of chicken with sauce and place on grill. Cook slowly for 1 to 1$^1/_4$ hours, turning and basting often with sauce. Yield: 6 to 8 servings

Parmesan Cheese Ball

1   8-ounce package cream cheese
$^1/_2$ cup grated Parmesan cheese
$^1/_4$ teaspoon garlic salt
2   tablespoons finely chopped green pepper
2   tablespoons finely chopped pimiento
    Chopped parsley or nuts

*C*ombine cheeses and garlic salt until well blended. Add green pepper and pimiento. Mix well and chill. Form into desired shape. Roll in chopped parsley or nuts. Serve with crackers. Yield: 1 cheese ball, enough for 8 to 10 servings

Best Baked Beans

2   green peppers, finely chopped
1   small onion, finely chopped
$^1/_2$ cup brown sugar
$^1/_2$ cup catsup
1   teaspoon prepared mustard
1   teaspoon Worcestershire sauce
1   large can pork and beans
6   slices bacon

*C*ombine all ingredients, except bacon. Place bacon across top of mixture. Bake, uncovered, 1$^1/_2$ to 2 hours in a 325 degree oven. Yield: 6 servings

Creamy Slaw

10 cups shredded cabbage
1 cup shredded carrot
$^2/_3$ cup chopped green pepper
$^1/_2$ cup evaporated milk
$^1/_2$ cup mayonnaise
$^1/_4$ teaspoon hot sauce
$^1/_3$ cup vinegar

$\mathcal{C}$ombine cabbage, carrot and green pepper; set aside. Combine milk and mayonnaise, blending until smooth. Add remaining ingredients to mayonnaise mixture and blend well. Pour dressing over cabbage mixture; toss lightly to mix. Refrigerate overnight. Yield: 8 servings

Homemade Peach Ice Cream

5 eggs
2 cups sugar
1 14-ounce can sweetened condensed milk
$1^1/_2$ pints heavy cream
2 pints light cream
1 tablespoon vanilla
10 medium-sized, soft peaches
$^2/_3$ cup sugar

$\mathcal{B}$eat eggs well, then combine with 2 cups sugar, sweetened condensed milk, heavy and light cream, and vanilla. Peel peaches, chop and purée in blender, adding $^2/_3$ cup of sugar. Stir peaches and cream mixture together, then freeze according to manufacturer's directions. Yield: 1 gallon

Fudge Nut Bars

1 cup butter
2 cups light brown sugar, packed
2 eggs
2 teaspoons vanilla, divided
$2^1/_2$ cups all-purpose flour, sifted
1 teaspoon baking soda
1 teaspoon salt, divided
3 cups quick-cooking rolled oats

1 12-ounce package semi-sweet chocolate bits
1 cup sweetened condensed milk
2 tablespoons butter
$^1/_2$ teaspoon salt
1 cup nuts, chopped
2 teaspoons vanilla

$\mathcal{C}$ream butter; gradually add sugar. Add eggs, one at a time, beating well after each addition. Add vanilla. Combine flour, soda and 1 teaspoon salt; stir into creamed mixture. Stir in oats. Spread about $^2/_3$ of oat mixture in bottom of 9x12-inch pan. Set aside. Combine chocolate, milk, butter and salt in saucepan. Cook over low heat, stirring until mixture is smooth. Remove from heat; add nuts and vanilla. Spread over layer in pan. Dot with remaining oat mixture, spreading as evenly as possible. Bake in a 350 degree oven for 25 to 30 minutes, or until lightly browned. Cool and cut into bars. Yield: 2 dozen bars

Oatmeal Cookies

$1^1/_2$ cups all-purpose flour
1 teaspoon baking powder
1 teaspoon baking soda
$^1/_2$ teaspoon salt
1 cup shortening
$1^1/_2$ cups light brown sugar
$^1/_2$ cup sugar
2 eggs
1 teaspoon vanilla
3 cups quick-cooking oats
1 cup nuts
Confectioners' sugar

$\mathcal{S}$ift flour, baking powder, soda and salt together. Cream shortening, sugars, eggs and vanilla. Add to flour mixture. Stir in oats and nuts. Form balls and shake in a bag of confectioners' sugar to coat. Place on greased cookie sheet. Press with fork. Bake in a 350 degree oven for 12 to 15 minutes or until light brown. Yield: 2 dozen cookies

Never soak knives or wash them in a dishwasher. Rinse knives gently, dry, and store them in a knife rack or block. Your cutting surface should always be softer than the blade of the knife.

Christmas Open House

Holiday Eggnog and Wassail
Artichoke Spread with Sesame Crackers
Miniature Quiche Lorraine
Hot Cheese Dip with Apple Slices
Country Ham* with Beaten Biscuits*
Spiced Pecans
Assorted Cookies* and Tarts

·————·

Holiday Eggnog

24 egg yolks
2 cups sugar
1 quart bourbon
1 pint brandy
1 quart heavy cream
2 quarts milk
1 quart vanilla ice cream
24 egg whites, stiffly beaten

Beat egg yolks and sugar until thick and lemon-colored. Add bourbon and brandy and stir thoroughly. Blend in cream and milk and continue stirring. Add ice cream and mix well. Fold in stiffly beaten egg whites last. Chill for at least 1 hour before serving. Can be prepared ahead with the exception of adding egg whites. Add egg whites 1 hour before serving. Yield: 30 to 40 servings

Holiday Wassail

1 pint cranberry juice cocktail
1 6-ounce can frozen orange juice, thawed
2 cups warm water
1 tablespoon sugar
1/4 teaspoon allspice
3 1/4 cups dry sauterne
   Red food coloring
1 orange
   Cloves

In large kettle or Dutch oven, combine juices, water, sugar and allspice. Bring to a simmer. Add sauterne and heat through; do not boil. If desired, stir in a few drops of red food coloring. Stud thick orange slices with whole cloves. Pour punch into preheated punch bowl; float orange slices on top. Yield: 32 six-ounce servings

Artichoke Spread

1 cup mayonnaise
1 14-ounce can artichokes, drained and finely chopped
1 cup Parmesan cheese

Combine ingredients in order given. Bake in a 350 degree oven for 20 to 30 minutes. Use as dip or spread on sesame crackers or toast rounds.

*Recipe for Country Ham is on page 139.
*Recipe for Beaten Biscuits is on page 127.
*Recipes for additional cookies are on pages 160-162.

Miniature Quiche Lorraine

- 1   3-ounce package cream cheese, softened
- 1/2 cup margarine, softened
- 1   cup sifted all-purpose flour
- 1/4 pound bacon, fried and crumbled
- 1   cup grated Swiss cheese
- 2   eggs
- 1   cup light cream
- 1/4 teaspoon salt
      Dash of cayenne pepper

*B*lend cream cheese, margarine, and flour; chill 1 hour. Press into 24 tart-size pastry or 16 muffin-size tins. Sprinkle bacon over bottom of unbaked pastry cups. Sprinkle grated cheese over bacon. Blend eggs and cream, but do not beat. Add seasonings and pour over cheese. Bake in a 375 degree oven for 30 minutes on until filling is firm. Serve warm. Yield: 16 to 24 servings

Hot Cheese Dip with Apple Slices

- 6   slices of bacon
- 1   8-ounce package cream cheese
- 2   cups shredded Cheddar cheese
- 6   tablespoons light cream
- 1   teaspoon Worcestershire sauce
- 1/4 teaspoon dry mustard
- 1/4 teaspoon onion salt
- 3   drops hot sauce
      Unpared apples, cut in wedges
      Lemon juice

*C*ut bacon into 1/4-inch slices; sauté until crisp; drain on paper towels. Meanwhile, in top of double boiler or in heavy saucepan, combine the next 7 ingredients. Heat over simmering water on low heat, stirring occasionally, until cheese melts and mixture is hot. Add bacon pieces. Use this as a dip

Egg Nog Cake, page 151; Sugarplums, page 66.

for apple wedges which have been dipped in lemon juice. Yield: approximately 3 cups of dip

Note: The dip may be served in a chafing dish and will keep well for several hours if stirred occasionally. If mixture becomes too thick, more cream can be added. Red Delicious apples are good with this dip.

Spiced Pecans

- 1   egg white, slightly beaten
- 2   tablespoons cold water
- 1/2 cup sugar
- 1/4 teaspoon ground cloves
- 1/4 teaspoon allspice
- 1/4 teaspoon cinnamon
- 1/2 teaspoon salt
- 4   cups pecan halves

*C*ombine all ingredients except pecans, mixing well. Set aside for 15 minutes. Add pecans and mix. Spread evenly on two greased cookie sheets. Bake in a 250 degree oven for 1 hour. Immediately loosen pecans from sheets. Store in an airtight container.

Burnt or stuck-on food easily comes off pots if you boil baking soda and water in the pot for a few minutes. Use about 1 heaping teaspoon to a cup of water.

Petite Tarts

16 pitted prunes
   Sherry
¹/₂ cup sour cream
   Brown sugar
16 prepared 2-inch tart shells
16 candied violets, optional

*P*lump prunes by soaking in sherry. Sweeten sour cream to taste with brown sugar; spoon ¹/₂ tablespoon into each tart shell; top with drained, plumped prunes. Garnish with candied violets. Yield: 16 tarts

Lemon Cornmeal Cookies

1   cup butter or margarine, room
    temperature
1   cup sugar
2   egg yolks
1   teaspoon grated lemon rind
1¹/₂ cups all-purpose flour
1   cup yellow cornmeal

*B*eat butter and sugar with mixer until well-blended. Add egg yolks; mix well. Stir in lemon rind, flour, and meal; mix well. Wrap dough in plastic bag and chill 3 to 4 hours. Roll out dough on lightly floured surface or between sheets of waxed paper. Cut into heart shapes. Place on an ungreased baking sheet and sprinkle with additional sugar. Bake in center of a 350 degree oven for 8 to 10 minutes or until edges are browned. Yield: 3 dozen

Sugarplums

24 pitted prunes
2   tablespoons orange juice
¹/₃ cup butter or margarine, softened
¹/₄ cup sugar
¹/₄ cup packed brown sugar
¹/₄ cup milk
1   egg
¹/₂ teaspoon baking powder
2   cups all-purpose flour
24 whole walnuts
   Glaze
   Colored sugar and candied cherries

*I*n small bowl toss prunes with orange juice; set aside. In large bowl combine butter, sugars, milk, egg, baking powder and flour. Beat until smooth and thoroughly blended. Chill 1 hour. Meanwhile, insert a walnut into center of each prune. Divide dough into 24 equal balls. Flatten each ball into a circle about ¹/₈-inch thick and wrap around a prune to enclose completely, pinching edges to seal. Place 1¹/₂-inches apart on greased baking sheets. Bake in a 325 degree oven for 25 to 30 minutes until firm and lightly browned. Remove to racks to cool completely. Ice tops of cookies with glaze, allowing it to drip down sides. While still wet, sprinkle with colored sugar; top with cherries. Yield: 24 sugarplums

Glaze

*I*n small bowl beat ²/₃ cup sifted confectioners' sugar, ¹/₂ teaspoon vanilla and 1 to 2 teaspoons milk to form an icing of spreading consistency.

Fourth of July Picnic

Fresh Raw Vegetables with Dip
Miss Daisy's Fried Chicken*
Deviled Eggs
Potato Salad in Cooked Dressing
Easy Baked Beans   Roasted Corn on Cob
Homemade Vanilla Ice Cream
Chocolate Pound Cake
Star Spangled Punch

• ———— •

Vegetable or Chip Dip

1   cup sour cream
³/₄ cup mayonnaise
1   tablespoon onion
1   tablespoon parsley
1   teaspoon dill weed
1   teaspoon seasoned salt

*M*ix all ingredients together. Chill. Delicious with vegetables or chips. Yield: Approximately 2 cups

Deviled Eggs

12 hard-boiled eggs, peeled and chilled
¹/₂ cup mayonnaise
1¹/₂ teaspoons Worcestershire sauce
1   teaspoon prepared mustard
¹/₂ teaspoon salt
¹/₂ teaspoon pepper
2   green onions, finely chopped
2   tablespoons well-drained pickle relish
    Paprika

*C*ut eggs in half lengthwise, remove yolks, and reserve whites. Mash yolks until smooth. Combine yolks, mayonnaise, Worcestershire sauce, mustard, salt, pepper, and mix until smooth. Stir in onion and pickle relish. Spoon mixture into center of egg whites. Sprinkle tops with paprika. Yield: 24 egg halves

Potato Salad in Cooked Dressing

2¹/₂ pounds red potatoes, washed
2   eggs, slightly beaten
¹/₃ cup apple cider vinegar
¹/₃ cup sugar
1   teaspoon prepared mustard
1   teaspoon salt
¹/₄ teaspoon pepper
¹/₂ cup mayonnaise
1   teaspoon chopped chives
1   cup diced celery
1   cup chopped onion
    Salt and pepper to taste

*C*ook unpeeled potatoes in water, covered, for 30 to 40 minutes or until tender. Combine next 6 ingredients in saucepan and cook over low heat stirring constantly until mixture thickens. Cool; blend into mayonnaise, stirring until smooth. Add chopped chives. Drain potatoes and place in cold water to cool. Refrigerate until cold. Peel potatoes and slice or cube. Add celery, onion, salt, pepper, and cooked dressing; blend thoroughly. Yield: 12 servings

Perfect hard boiled eggs are hard to come by. Here's a good way to do it, but boil a few more than you need to allow for ones that don't boil perfectly. Use three-day-old eggs. Carefully puncture the small end of each egg with a pin. Let the eggs warm to room temperature (about an hour). Bring water to boil and gently lower each egg into the water. Boil slowly for 14 minutes. Rinse thoroughly under cold running water. Hit the punctured end of the egg on the sink and peel under cool water.

*Recipe for Miss Daisy's Fried Chicken is on page 74.

To peel and pit peaches, immerse peaches in boiling water for 10 to 20 seconds, then run a knife along the indentation of the peach. Twist halves to free the stone. Freestone peaches are easiest to pit.

Easy Baked Beans

1   1-pound 14-ounce can pork and beans
½   cup chopped onion
1   cup dark brown sugar
1   18-ounce can tomato sauce
½   teaspoon salt
½   pound bacon slices

*C*ombine all ingredients placing bacon slices on top. Bake, covered, in a 300 degree oven for 2 hours. Remove cover during last 30 minutes. Yield: 8 servings

Homemade Vanilla Ice Cream

2   cups sugar
3   tablespoons cornstarch
¼   teaspoon salt
3   cups light cream
4   eggs, slightly beaten
4   cups chilled heavy cream
2   tablespoons vanilla

*C*ombine first 3 ingredients in top of double boiler and stir in light cream. Cook, stirring constantly, until mixture thickens. Add a small amount of hot mixture to eggs, stirring constantly. Stir in remaining hot mixture and continue cooking for 5 to 6 minutes, stirring constantly. Remove from heat and cool slightly. Stir in heavy cream and vanilla. Refrigerate until freezing time. Freeze in an electric or hand crank freezer. Yield: 3 quarts

Chocolate Pound Cake

1   cup butter or margarine
½   cup vegetable shortening
3   cups sugar
5   eggs
3   cups all-purpose flour
2   teaspoons baking powder
½   cup cocoa
½   teaspoon salt
1¼   cups milk
1   tablespoon vanilla

*C*ream butter and shortening; add sugar gradually. Add eggs, one at a time, beating well after each addition. Sift together three times, flour, baking powder, cocoa and salt. Add to butter mixture alternating with the milk. Add vanilla. Pour batter into a well greased and floured pan. Bake in a 325 degree oven for 1½ hours or until a skewer inserted in center comes out clean. Yield: 16 slices

Star Spangled Punch

1 6-ounce package cherry-flavored gelatin
2 cups boiling water
6 cups cold water
1 small can orange juice concentrate
1 small can lemonade concentrate
1 large can pineapple juice
1 quart chilled ginger ale

*C*ombine all ingredients except ginger ale and chill until very cold. Add 1 quart chilled ginger ale when ready to serve. Yield: 16 one-cup servings

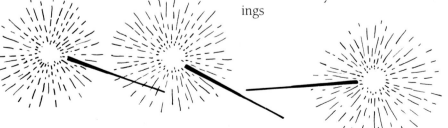

Family Supper

Congealed Carrot Salad
Party Meat Loaf
Corn Pudding*   Fresh Broccoli
Yeast Rolls*
Ice Box Angel Pie
Fruited Tea*

Congealed Carrot Salad

1   8¼-ounce can crushed pineapple
24 marshmallows
1   5-ounce jar cream cheese with pineapple
1   3-ounce package lemon-flavored gelatin
1½ cups boiling water
¾   cup grated carrots

*D*rain pineapple, reserving juice. Heat pineapple juice over low heat; add marshmallows, stirring until melted. Add cream cheese and blend until smooth. Dissolve gelatin in boiling water; cool. Combine marshmallow mixture and gelatin. Chill until consistency of unbeaten egg white. Stir in pineapple and carrots; pour into a 2-quart casserole dish. Chill until firm. Yield: 8 to 10 servings

Party Meat Loaf

1½ pounds ground round or chuck
1   cup bread crumbs
1   medium onion, finely chopped
1½ teaspoons salt
¼   teaspoon pepper
1½ cups tomato sauce, divided
1   cup water
1   tablespoon prepared mustard
2   tablespoons vinegar
2   tablespoons brown sugar
    Hot cooked noodles

*C*ombine beef, bread crumbs, onion, salt and pepper and ½ cup tomato sauce. Shape into one large loaf or 2 small loaves. Combine 1 cup tomato sauce, water, mustard, vinegar and brown sugar; blend well. Pour half of sauce over loaf; bake in a 350 degree oven for 1 hour. Place noodles on a serving platter. Unmold loaf and place on noodles. Heat remaining sauce and pour over meat loaf. Yield: 6 to 8 servings

Ice Box Angel Pie

1 can sweetened condensed milk
  Juice of 1 lemon
1 large carton whipped topping
1 large can crushed pineapple
1 cup finely chopped pecans
1 9-inch graham cracker pie crust

*C*ombine first 5 ingredients. Pour into crust. Chill for several hours before serving. Yield: 6 to 8 servings

*Recipe for Corn Pudding is on page 117.
*Recipe for Yeast Rolls is on page 58.
*Recipe for Fruited Tea is on page 98.

Engagement Dinner

Chilled Consommé with Caviar
Veal Cordon Bleu
Swedish Mushrooms   Crunchy Cheese Noodles
Zucchini Bake
Fresh Rolls
Strawberry Crêpes
Coffee

· ———— ·

Chilled Consommé with Caviar

3 10½-ounce cans consommé
½ pint sour cream
1 3-ounce jar red caviar
   Chopped parsley
6 lemon slices

*P*our consommé into soup bowls. Chill until firm. Before serving, top with a spoonful of sour cream and sprinkle with caviar. Garnish with parsley and lemon. Yield: 6 servings

Veal Cordon Bleu

1½ pounds veal, cut into 12 slices
1 tablespoon anchovy paste
3 tablespoons butter, softened
6 thin slices boiled ham
6 thin slices Gruyère or baby Swiss cheese
1 egg, beaten with 1 tablespoon water
½ cup all-purpose flour
½ cup dry bread crumbs
4 tablespoons butter
   Paprika
6 lemon wedges
6 parsley sprigs

*P*ound veal as thin as possible. Blend anchovy paste with 3 tablespoons softened butter. Spread on 6 veal slices. Cover with 1 slice each of ham and cheese. Top with remaining veal. Fasten edges with skewers. Dip each into egg, then flour, then bread crumbs. In large skillet, melt 4 tablespoons butter; sauté the veal pieces 3 to 4 minutes per side until golden brown. Sprinkle with paprika and garnish with lemon and parsley. Yield: 6 servings

Swedish Mushrooms

3 tablespoons butter or margarine
2 small onions, chopped
2 eggs
⅔ cup dry bread crumbs
¾ cup milk
¾ cup light cream
2 teaspoons salt
¼ teaspoon pepper
1 pound fresh mushrooms, coarsely chopped

*M*elt butter; sauté onion until golden. Beat eggs in 1½-quart casserole. Add bread crumbs, milk, cream, salt, and pepper. Mix well. Gently fold in mushrooms and onion. Bake in a 350 degree oven for 60 to 70 minutes until golden. Yield: 6 servings

Crunchy Cheese Noodles

8 ounces medium egg noodles
   Salt
4 tablespoons butter
4 ounces fine egg noodles
1/2 cup minced onion
1 clove garlic, minced
1 cup grated Cheddar cheese

*B*oil medium egg noodles in salted water until tender. Drain, toss with 2 tablespoons butter. Place in shallow casserole dish. Melt remaining butter in a large skillet and sauté egg noodles, onion and garlic until golden brown, stirring occasionally. Pour over top of casserole and sprinkle with cheese. Heat in a 300 degree oven for 10 minutes. Yield: 6 servings

Zucchini Bake

6 zucchini
1 clove garlic, halved
   Salt, pepper and cayenne pepper to taste
4 tablespoons butter

*S*lice zucchini in half lengthwise. Rub with garlic and seasonings; dot with butter. Bake in a 325 degree oven for 40 minutes. Yield: 6 servings

Strawberry Crêpes

3/4 cup plus 3 tablespoons all-purpose flour
1 tablespoon sugar
1/8 teaspoon salt
3 eggs
2 tablespoons cognac
1 teaspoon grated lemon peel
3 tablespoons melted butter
1 1/2 cups milk
4 ounces cream cheese
3/4 cup sour cream
3 to 4 tablespoons sugar
1/8 teaspoon vanilla
1/8 teaspoon almond extract
2 tablespoons butter
2 cups strawberries
6 tablespoons Kirsch
3 tablespoons strawberry liqueur

*S*ift flour, 1 tablespoon sugar, and salt into mixing bowl. Add eggs one at a time, beating well after each addition. Stir until smooth. Add cognac, lemon peel, 2 tablespoons melted butter and milk. The batter will be thin. Chill for 1 hour or more. Heat a crêpe pan and brush with melted butter. Add 2 tablespoons of batter and swirl around to cover bottom of pan. Pour excess back into bowl. Cook until golden on one side, just a few seconds. Turn and cook other side. These may be made ahead and reheated in oven, covered with a damp cloth to prevent drying. Combine cream cheese and sour cream. Add 1 tablespoon sugar, vanilla and almond extract. Spread cream cheese mixture on warm crêpes and roll up. Combine remaining ingredients in a chafing dish. Heat and stir until strawberries are thick as preserves, then flame. Pour sauce over crêpes and serve immediately. Yield: 6 to 8 servings

Zest is the outer skin of citrus fruit. When using fruit rind, always be careful not to include the bitter white part underneath. Use a fine grater, a vegetable peeler, or a special zester purchased at a cookware store.

Elegant Dinner Party

Country Paté
Cold Strawberry Soup
Butter Lettuce with Vinaigrette Dressing
Veal Scallopine Alla Marsala
Fettuccine Alfredo
Asparagus with Hollandaise Sauce*
Lemon Mousse with Raspberry Sauce*
Wine   After Dinner Coffees

· ———— ·

Country Paté

- 2 cups butter
- 2 pounds chicken livers
- 2 medium onions, quartered
- 1 teaspoon curry powder
- 1 teaspoon paprika
- 1/4 teaspoon salt
- 1/4 teaspoon freshly ground black pepper
- 2 tablespoons cognac

Melt 1/2 cup butter in a saucepan. Add the chicken livers, onion, curry powder, paprika, salt, and pepper. Cover and cook over low heat for 8 minutes. Process the mixture in an electric blender until smooth. Add cognac and remaining butter and blend. Chill until firm. Yield: 5 cups

Cold Strawberry Soup

- 1 cup fresh strawberries
- 1/4 cup honey
- 1/4 cup sour cream
- 3/4 cup cold water
- 1/2 cup dry red wine

*Recipe for Hollandaise Sauce is on page 123.
*Recipe for Raspberry Sauce is on page 156.

Blend all ingredients. It is not necessary to strain. Chill. Stir well before serving. Serve in wine glasses or glass soup bowls. Garnish each serving with a dollop of sour cream and fresh strawberry, if desired. Yield: 3 to 4 servings

Butter Lettuce with Vinaigrette Dressing

- 1/4 cup balsamic vinegar
- 1 teaspoon fresh lemon juice
- 3/4 cup vegetable oil
- 1/2 teaspoon Dijon mustard
- Salt and pepper to taste
- Butter lettuce

Combine first 5 ingredients and chill. Bring to room temperature before tossing with butter lettuce. Fresh chives, parsley or garlic may be added if desired. Yield: 1 cup.

Note: Dressing may be made several days in advance and refrigerated.

Veal Scallopine Alla Marsala

- 2 1/2 lbs. veal scallops
- Flour
- 1 cup unsalted butter
- 8 tablespoons olive oil
- Juice of two lemons
- 1 1/2 cups Marsala wine
- Salt and freshly ground pepper
- Sprigs of fresh thyme

Very lightly coat each scallop with flour. In a large skillet heat butter with oil until very hot, but not smoking. Quickly brown veal on both sides.

Lower heat to medium and add lemon juice and Marsala. Simmer veal about 4 to 5 minutes. Sprinkle with salt and pepper. Serve immediately, garnished with fresh thyme sprigs. Yield: 8 servings

Fettuccine Alfredo

16 ounces fresh fettuccine
1/2 cup butter
2/3 cup grated Gruyère cheese
2/3 cup grated Parmesan cheese
1 cup heavy cream
1 teaspoon salt
Freshly ground black pepper

*C*ook fettuccine until tender and drain. Return pasta to pan over medium heat. Add remaining ingredients. Toss lightly with 2 forks to blend. Serve immediately in a warm serving bowl. Yield: 8 servings

Lemon Mousse

4 eggs, separated
1 1/2 cups sugar
1 tablespoon unflavored gelatin, softened in 1/4 cup cold water
1 teaspoon cornstarch
Juice of 3 lemons, divided
Grated rind of 3 lemons
1/4 cup Grand Marnier, divided
1 1/2 cups heavy cream
3 tablespoons confectioners' sugar

*B*eat egg yolks; add sugar and beat well. Set aside. Place gelatin mixture in double boiler over hot water and stir until dissolved. Combine cornstarch and 1/3 of the lemon juice. Stir until smooth. Add to gelatin; stir in remaining juice and rind. Add beaten egg yolks. Cook until thickened, stirring constantly. Add 1/2 the Grand Marnier; cook 1 minute. Do not boil. Chill until set. Whip cream, remaining Grand Marnier and sugar until stiff peaks form. Fold cream mixture and egg whites into lemon mixture. Spoon into soufflé dish; chill. Yield: 8 to 10 servings

If your sauce is lumpy, whip briskly with a whisk, press through a strainer, or process briefly in a blender.

Southern Sunday Dinner

Miss Daisy's Fried Chicken
Country Gravy
Whipped Potatoes
Garden Green Beans
Squash Casserole
Angel Biscuits
Fresh Blueberry Cheesecake or Chocolate Meringue Pie
Coffee or Fruited Tea*

· ————————— ·

Miss Daisy's Fried Chicken

　　Salt and pepper
4 to 6 chicken breasts
2　cups all-purpose flour
1/2 teaspoon paprika
1　teaspoon red pepper
1　egg, slightly beaten
1/2 cup milk
　　Vegetable oil

Salt and pepper chicken breasts. Combine flour, paprika, and red pepper; set aside. Combine egg and milk; dip chicken in egg mixture; then dredge in flour mixture. Heat oil in skillet. Place chicken in skillet; cover. Cook over medium heat about 30 minutes until golden brown, turning occasionally. Yield: 4 to 6 servings

Country Gravy

4 to 5 tablespoons chicken drippings
4 to 5 tablespoons all-purpose flour
3 cups hot milk
　　Salt and pepper

Add chicken drippings to skillet and place over medium heat. Add flour and stir until browned. Gradually add hot milk. Cook, stirring constantly, until thickened. Salt and pepper to taste. Delicious served over biscuits. Yield: 2 1/2 to 3 cups

Whipped Potatoes

2　pounds Idaho potatoes
3 to 4 cups water
　　Salt (about 1 teaspoon)
1/2 cup light cream
1/3 cup butter, softened
　　Dash of black pepper
　　Fresh parsley flakes

Peel potatoes and slice into medium slices. Cook in boiling, salted water until tender, about 20 minutes. Drain. While hot, mash potatoes with potato masher or whip with an electric hand mixer. Gradually add cream and butter. When mixture is smooth, add pepper and sprinkle with fresh parsley flakes. Yield: 6 servings

Garden Green Beans

1 1/2 pounds fresh green beans
4　cups water
1/4 pound diced salt pork or ham hock
　　Salt to taste
1/2 teaspoon sugar

Prepare beans by stringing them and breaking into 1-inch pieces. Add water to a 2-quart saucepan; add beans, and salt pork or ham hock. Add salt and sugar. Cover and cook over medium heat for 30 to 35 minutes or until tender. Yield: 6 servings

*Recipe for Fruited Tea is on page 98.

Squash Casserole

  3 pounds yellow squash, thinly sliced
  1 medium onion, chopped
  1/4 cup butter
  3 eggs, beaten
  1 10³/₄-ounce can cream of mushroom soup
  1 teaspoon salt
  ³/₄ teaspoon pepper
      Cracker crumbs

Cook squash and onion in water until tender. Drain well. Add butter and mix. Fold in next 4 ingredients. Place in a 2-quart buttered casserole and top with a thin layer of cracker crumbs. Bake in a 350 degree oven for 30 minutes. Yield: 6 servings

Angel Biscuits

  3 cups self-rising flour
  1 tablespoon sugar
  1/2 teaspoon baking soda
  1 cup buttermilk
  1 cup shortening
  1 cake yeast, dissolved in ¹/₄ cup warm water

Sift dry ingredients; cut in shortening. Add milk and yeast mixture to make a soft dough. Turn out and knead about 20 strokes. Roll to ³/₄-inch thickness. Cut out biscuits and place on greased pan in a 425 degree oven for 15 to 20 minutes. Yield: 2 dozen

Fresh Blueberry Cheesecake

      Pastry for single-crust pie
  2 envelopes unflavored gelatin
  1 cup cold light cream
  1 cup light cream, heated to boiling
  2 3-ounce packages cream cheese, softened
  1/2 cup sugar
  2 tablespoons orange liqueur
  1 teaspoon vanilla
  1 cup ice cubes, about 6 to 8
  2 to 2¹/₂ cups fresh blueberries
      Whipped cream

Press pastry into 10x2-inch fluted quiche/flan pan or 9-inch deep-dish pie pan; prick bottom and sides with fork. Bake in a 450 degree oven for 10 minutes or until golden; cool. In 5-cup blender, sprinkle unflavored gelatin over cold cream; set aside 3 to 4 minutes. Add hot cream and process at low speed until gelatin is completely dissolved, about 2 minutes. Add cream cheese, sugar, liqueur, and vanilla; process at high speed until blended. Add ice cubes, one at a time; process at high speed until ice is melted. Set aside until mixture is slightly thickened, about 5 minutes. Arrange 1 cup blueberries in prepared crust; add gelatin mixture. Chill until firm. Garnish with remaining blueberries and whipped cream. Yield: About 8 servings

Chocolate Meringue Pie

  3 egg yolks
  1 cup sugar
  1 1-ounce square semi-sweet chocolate
  1 tablespoon butter
  2 tablespoons all-purpose flour
  1 cup milk, lukewarm
  1 teaspoon vanilla
  1 9-inch pie crust, baked
  3 egg whites
  3 tablespoons sugar

Beat egg yolks and sugar together until creamy. In top of double boiler, melt chocolate and butter. Add chocolate and flour to egg yolk mixture. Add milk and blend well. Blend in vanilla. Cook mixture in top of double boiler until quite thick, stirring often. Pour thickened chocolate into pie crust. Cover with meringue made of 3 egg whites stiffly beaten with 3 tablespoons of sugar. Spoon meringue over chocolate, spreading well to all edges of pie shell. Bake in a 350 degree oven for 10 to 15 minutes. Yield: One 9-inch pie

Dinner from the Grill

Crab-Stuffed Mushrooms
Grilled Steak
Crusty Broiled Tomatoes
Spinach Salad with Sweet and Sour Dressing*
Praline Cheesecake
Iced Tea

· ⸺⸺⸺⸺ ·

For a cookout, plan on ³/₄ to 1 pound of meat per person for bone-in cuts of meat, and ¹/₂ to ²/₃ pound per serving for boneless cuts of meat.

Crab-Stuffed Mushrooms

20 medium mushroom caps
3   tablespoons melted butter
1   6-ounce package frozen crabmeat, thawed and drained
¹/₂ cup breadcrumbs
1   heaping teaspoon salad dressing
1   heaping teaspoon mayonnaise
1   teaspoon lemon juice
¹/₂ teaspoon curry powder
    Pimiento strips

Coat mushrooms with butter, place, upside down, in a shallow pan. Spoon ¹/₄ teaspoon butter into each cap. Combine crabmeat, breadcrumbs, salad dressing, mayonnaise, lemon juice, and curry powder; spoon into mushroom caps, and drizzle with remaining butter. Place a pimiento strip on each, and broil 5 minutes. Yield: about 8 servings

Crusty Broiled Tomatoes

4   medium tomatoes
    Dijon-style mustard
    Salt
    Freshly ground pepper
    Cayenne pepper
6   tablespoons melted butter or margarine
¹/₂ cup seasoned breadcrumbs
¹/₂ cup grated Parmesan cheese

Recipe for Spinach Salad with Sweet and Sour Dressing is on page 104.

Cut tomatoes in half. Spread cut side with mustard; sprinkle with salt, pepper, and cayenne pepper to taste. Combine butter, bread crumbs, and cheese. Spoon crumb mixture on top of each tomato half. Broil until crumbs are brown and tomatoes are tender. Yield: 8 servings

Praline Cheesecake

1   cup graham cracker crumbs
3   tablespoons sugar
3   tablespoons melted butter
3   8-ounce packages cream cheese, room temperature
1¹/₄ cups dark brown sugar
2   tablespoons all-purpose flour
3   eggs
1¹/₂ teaspoons vanilla
1   cup finely chopped pecans, divided
    Maple syrup

Combine graham cracker crumbs, sugar and butter. Press into bottom of 9-inch springform pan. Bake at 350 degrees for 10 minutes. Blend cream cheese, brown sugar and flour. Add eggs, one at a time, beating well after each addition. Add vanilla and ¹/₂ cup pecans; mix well. Pour into crumb crust. Bake in a 350 degree oven for 50 to 55 minutes. Loosen from rim and cool. Remove sides of pan. Chill. Brush with maple syrup. Sprinkle with remaining pecans. Yield: 8 to 10 servings

Mexican Buffet

Zesty Nachos
Tacos with Tomato-Pepper Relish*
Taco Twist Casserole
Enchiladas con Pollo
Pizza Style Tostada Bake
Guacamole Salad
Margaritas
Flan

. ———— .

Zesty Nachos

2 12-ounce bags tortilla chips
1 dozen jalapeño peppers, sliced into rings
1 pound sharp cheese, grated

*P*lace chips on baking sheets; place ½ to 1 pepper ring on each and sprinkle with cheese. Broil 2 to 3 minutes or until cheese melts. Serve immediately. Yield: 8 to 10 servings

Tacos

2   pounds ground beef
2¼ cups minced onion
2   cloves garlic, pressed
5   cups chopped tomatoes
4   teaspoons salt
**   Black pepper and cayenne pepper to taste**
2   tablespoons chili powder
1½ teaspoons cumin
2   jalapeño or chile peppers, minced
24 taco shells
3   cups shredded cheese
3   cups shredded lettuce
**   2 to 3 avocados, sliced**
**   Tomato-pepper relish**
**   Taco sauce**

*S*auté ground beef with 1½ cups of onion and the garlic until browned. Add 1½ cups tomatoes, salt, pepper, chili powder, cumin and jalapeños. Cover and simmer 10 minutes, adding a little water if mixture dries out. Combine remaining tomatoes and onion and chill for 30 minutes. Crisp the taco shells in a 350 degee oven for 5 minutes. Serve accompanied by bowls of meat mixture, tomato-onion mixture, cheese, lettuce, avocados, relish and taco sauce. Yield: 2 dozen

*Recipe for Tomato-Pepper Relish is on page 165.

South of the Border Pasta: Taco Twist Casserole and Pizza Style Tostada Bake, pages 78-79.

Accurate measuring is vital for good cooking. When measuring liquids, be sure your eye is level with the measuring mark on the cup.

Measure shortening in a dry measure cup, packing it down, and scraping it even with the top with a straight knife or spatula.

Sift flour and confectioners' sugar before measuring.

Taco Twist Casserole

1   8-ounce package rotini, twirls or curly-roni, uncooked
1   pound fresh pork sausage links
³/₄ cup chopped onion
³/₄ cup chopped green pepper
1   clove garlic, finely chopped
1   16-ounce can tomatoes, undrained and quartered
1   12-ounce can whole kernel corn, drained
1   8-ounce can tomato sauce
¹/₄ cup pitted ripe olives, sliced
2   teaspoons chili powder
1   teaspoon oregano
1   teaspoon salt
1   6-ounce can tomato paste
1¹/₂ cups hot water
1   cup shredded Cheddar cheese
   Corn Chips

*C*ook rotini according to package directions; drain. Meanwhile, simmer sausage in a small amount of water in a large covered skillet for 20 minutes or until done; pour off water. Brown sausage; remove from pan to cool. Slice into ¹/₈-inch slices. Add onion, green pepper, sliced sausage and garlic to skillet; sauté until tender. (Add 1 tablespoon vegetable oil, if needed). Stir in tomatoes, corn, tomato sauce, olives, chili powder, oregano and salt; bring to boil. Combine sauce with pasta in 3-quart casserole or 13x9-inch oblong pan. Stir together tomato paste and 1¹/₂ cups hot water; add to casserole mixing well. Bake in a 350 degree oven for 25 to 30 minutes or until bubbly; top with cheese and corn chips. Yield: 8 to 10 servings

Enchiladas con Pollo

8   large chicken breasts, halved
   Salt
4   cups chopped onion
4   cloves garlic, minced
¹/₂ cup butter or margarine
4   1-pound cans tomatoes, chopped

1   quart tomato sauce
1   cup chopped green chile peppers
4   teaspoons sugar
4   teaspoons cumin
2   teaspoons salt
2   teaspoons oregano
2   teaspoons basil
48 tortillas
   Vegetable oil
10 cups shredded Monterey Jack cheese
3   cups sour cream

*S*immer chicken breasts in water until fork tender. Drain; remove skin and bones. Sprinkle with salt. Cut each piece into 6 strips and set aside. In a large saucepan, sauté onion and garlic in butter until tender. Add tomatoes, tomato sauce, chiles, sugar, cumin, salt, oregano and basil. Bring to a boil; reduce heat and simmer, covered, for 20 minutes. Meanwhile fry the tortillas in hot oil just until softened; drain and set aside. Place one strip of chicken and about 2 tablespoons of cheese in each tortilla, roll up and place seam-side down in four 9x13-inch casseroles. Blend sour cream into sauce and pour over tortillas. Sprinkle with remaining cheese and bake uncovered in a 375 degree oven for 20 minutes. Yield: 4 dozen

Pizza Style Tostada Bake

8   ounces spaghetti, uncooked
2   eggs
1   cup shredded Mozzarella cheese
¹/₄ teaspoon garlic salt
³/₄ pound lean ground beef
¹/₂ cup chopped onion
1   clove garlic, finely chopped
1   8-ounce can tomato sauce
1   teaspoon chili powder
1   8-ounce can refried beans
1   8-ounce jar taco sauce
¹/₄ cup chopped green chiles, drained
1   cup shredded Monterey Jack or Cheddar cheese
   Diced tomato, shredded lettuce, sliced pitted ripe olives

*B*reak spaghetti strands into 3-inch pieces. Cook according to package directions; drain. (Cooked spaghetti should equal about 4 cups.) Cool. Beat eggs in mixing bowl; add Mozzarella cheese and garlic salt. Stir in cooled spaghetti, mix well. Spread evenly on bottom and up sides of a greased 12-inch pizza pan. Bake in a 375 degree oven for 15 minutes or until set and lightly brown. Meanwhile sauté beef, onion and garlic until beef is brown; drain. Add tomato sauce and chili powder. Spread refried beans evenly over spaghetti crust leaving ¹/₂-inch edge; layer beef mixture, taco sauce, chiles, and cheese. Return to oven and bake at 375 degrees for 15 to 20 minutes, or until bubbly. Serve wedges with diced tomato, lettuce and olives. Yield: 6 to 8 servings

Guacamole Salad

5   avocados, peeled and mashed
2   tomatoes, peeled and coarsely chopped
¹/₂ medium onion, finely chopped
3   green chiles, seeded and chopped
1¹/₂ tablespoons lemon juice
    Salt and pepper to taste
6   cups shredded lettuce

*G*ently combine all ingredients except lettuce. Chill; serve atop lettuce. Yield: 10 to 12 servings

Margaritas

1   fifth tequila
¹/₂ pint Triple Sec
1³/₄ quarts water
4   6-ounce cans frozen limeade
4   ounces lime juice, optional
¹/₄ cup lemon juice
    Salt

*T*he day before serving, combine first 5 ingredients and refrigerate until chilled. Stir well and freeze until 6 hours before serving. Return to refrigerator. To serve, dip rims of champagne glasses in lemon juice, then in a plate of salt; fill. Yield: 28 4-ounce drinks

Flan

2¹/₂ cups sugar
1   tablespoon water
8   eggs, lightly beaten
1   teaspoon vanilla
¹/₂ teaspoon salt
1   quart milk, scalded

*O*ver low heat, caramelize 1 cup sugar by stirring in a heavy saucepan until sugar begins to melt. Add water and stir continuously for 1 minute. Pour caramel into 12 custard cups. Tilt each cup to coat sides. Combine eggs, vanilla, remaining sugar and salt. Blend in milk. Divide mixture among cups. Place cups in a pan. Pour water in pan to a depth of 1 inch. Bake in a 350 degree oven for 30 minutes or until a knife inserted near the edge comes out clean. Before serving invert cups. Leave in place for 1 or 2 minutes so caramel will drip down sides. Yield: 12 servings

To peel tomatoes easily, fill a bowl with boiling water and immerse tomatoes for 10 to 15 seconds or hold a tomato speared on a fork over the flame of a gas range.

Mint Julep Dinner

Mint Juleps
Elegant Mushrooms
Grilled Lamb
Cheesy Squash   Asparagus Vinaigrette
French Bread
Charlotte Russe
Coffee

· ———— ·

Mint Juleps

2   cups sugar
1   cup water
16 sprigs mint
4   pounds finely crushed ice
8   1½-ounce jiggers bourbon
    Mint and confectioners' sugar for garnish

Combine sugar and water; bring to a boil. Stir and remove from heat; cool. Place 2 sprigs of mint in each glass; crush to release flavor. Add 2 ounces sugar syrup; stir gently. Fill glass with ice. Add 1 measure of bourbon. Stir, top with sprig of mint and sprinkle with confectioners' sugar. Yield: 6 to 8 servings

Elegant Mushrooms

1   pound lump crabmeat
1   cup mayonnaise
1½   teaspoons salt
⅛   teaspoon pepper
⅛   teaspoon paprika
1   teaspoon sugar
2   tablespoons lemon juice
2   tablespoons milk
1   teaspoon celery seed
1   tablespoon grated onion
2   pounds large mushrooms, stems removed
¼   pound butter
1   tablespoon all-purpose flour
     Salt, pepper and garlic powder to taste

Combine first 10 ingredients together; chill. Sauté mushrooms in butter. Sprinkle with flour and season to taste. Cover and cook over low heat for 10 minutes or until tender stirring occasionally. Cool. To serve, stuff mushrooms with crabmeat mixture. Yield: 6 servings

Grilled Lamb

2   4-pound racks of lamb
1   cup olive oil
⅔   cup lemon juice
3   cloves garlic, pressed
2   bay leaves
6   sprigs parsley
     Salt to taste
½   teaspoon pepper
1½   teaspoons sage
1½   teaspoons rosemary
1½   teaspoons thyme
½   cup beef stock
¼   cup red wine
2   tablespoons chopped green onions
1½   teaspoons sage
1½   teaspoons rosemary
1½   teaspoons thyme
3   tablespoons butter, at room temperature
3   tablespoons minced parsley

*R*emove all fat and skin from lamb. Combine next 10 ingredients; pour over lamb. Cover and refrigerate for 24 hours, turning occasionally. Drain and reserve marinade. Place lamb flat on hot grill; sear each side. Cover and cook 45 minutes to 1 hour over moderate fire. Brush with marinade. Check temperature with meat thermometer for desired degree of doneness. Set aside at room temperature for 20 minutes. Bring next 6 ingredients to a boil; reduce to ¹/₂ cup. Remove from heat. Whisk butter into sauce a little at a time; stir in parsley. Pour over lamb. Yield: 8 servings

Cheesy Squash

2   pounds yellow squash, sliced
1   onion, sliced
¹/₂ teaspoon thyme
¹/₂ bay leaf
3   sprigs parsley
2   tablespoons butter
2   tablespoons all-purpose flour
1   cup milk
2   egg yolks, beaten
³/₄ cup grated Swiss or Gruyère cheese
¹/₄ teaspoon nutmeg
    Salt, white pepper, and cayenne to taste
¹/₄ cup bread crumbs

*B*oil squash in water to cover with onion, thyme, bay leaf and parsley until just tender; drain. Remove bay leaf and parsley. Place squash and onion in large greased casserole. Melt butter; blend in flour and add milk. Stir and cook until thickened. Add ¹/₄ cup sauce to eggs; blend well. Stir egg mixture back into sauce. Add ¹/₂ cup cheese; stir in remaining seasonings. Pour sauce over squash; cover with remaining cheese and bread crumbs. Bake, uncovered, in a 350 degree oven for 25 minutes. Yield: 6 servings

Asparagus Vinaigrette

¹/₂ cup vegetable oil
1¹/₂ tablespoons white wine vinegar
1   tablespoon finely chopped sweet pickle
¹/₂ teaspoon dry mustard
¹/₂ teaspoon salt
¹/₈ teaspoon pepper
1   teaspoon minced parsley
1   teaspoon minced chives
2   pounds asparagus, cooked and drained
2   teaspoons capers

*B*ring first 6 ingredients to a boil. Stir in parsley and chives. Pour over hot asparagus. Top with capers. Yield: 6 servings

Charlotte Russe

2   tablespoons gelatin
¹/₄ cup cold water
8   egg yolks
1   cup sugar
2   cups milk
1   teaspoon vanilla
¹/₂ cup strawberry liqueur
2   cups heavy cream, whipped
12 ladyfingers, split
1   pint strawberries, sugared

*S*often gelatin in cold water. In a double boiler beat egg yolks and sugar with wooden spoon until smooth. Bring milk and vanilla to a boil; slowly add to egg mixture, stirring rapidly with whisk. Cook over boiling water until mixture thickens, stirring constantly. Add gelatin and cook 1 minute longer. Set aside to cool. Add liqueur; fold in whipped cream. Line a springform pan with ladyfingers, placing them upright around sides. Pour in custard; chill 24 hours. Garnish with strawberries before serving. Yield: 6 servings

When cooking rice, add lemon juice to the water to keep it white. When sautéing mushrooms, add lemon juice to give the mushrooms a desirable high gloss.

French Dinner

Spinach Soup
Fillets Parisienne
Berry Sorbet
Beef Tenderloin with Marchand de Vin Sauce
Peaches with Sherry Sauce   Wild Rice
French Bread
Watercress Salad
Crème Brûlée
Coffee

·———·

Roll olives in a few drops of salad oil to keep their shine.

Spinach Soup

1 onion, finely chopped
2 tablespoons butter
3 tablespoons all-purpose flour
2 cups milk
2 cups cooked spinach, well-drained
1 cup consommé
   Salt and pepper to taste
2 cups light cream
1/2 cup sherry
1 cup chopped toasted almonds

*S*auté onion in butter until tender; remove from skillet with slotted spoon. Stir in flour, then milk. Purée spinach with consommé; add mixture to sauce. Add seasonings. Stir in cream; mix well. Heat just until simmering; stir in sherry. Sprinkle with almonds before serving. Yield: 10 servings

Fillets Parisienne

10 fillets of trout
   Salt, pepper and cayenne
2 cups grated sharp Cheddar cheese
1/2 cup bread crumbs
1/2 cup chopped parsley
4 tablespoons butter

*P*lace fillets in shallow, buttered casserole. Season with salt, pepper, and cayenne. Sprinkle with mixture of cheese, bread crumbs and parsley. Dot with butter. Place about 5 inches below broiler and cook for 10 to 15 minutes or until fish flakes easily with a fork and top is browned. Yield: 10 servings

Berry Sorbet

1   pound cranberries
3   cups boiling water
1   tablespoon gelatin
1/2 cup cold water
2   cups sugar
1/8 teaspoon salt
1 1/4 cups orange juice
1   tablespoon lemon juice

*B*ring berries to a boil; cook until soft. Drain and purée. Soften gelatin in cold water for 5 minutes. Combine purée, sugar, salt, and juices in a large saucepan; bring to a boil. Stir in gelatin; blend until completely dissolved. Cool. Freeze until almost firm. Beat until light and fluffy. Freeze again until firm. Yield: 10 servings

Beef Tenderloin with Marchand de Vin Sauce

1   5 to 6 pound filet of beef at room
    temperature
    Olive oil
    Salt, pepper, and garlic powder to taste
1/2 cup chopped green onions
4   ounces sliced mushrooms
4   tablespoons butter
1   cup claret
1   cup consommé
3   teaspoons cornstarch
1   tablespoon lemon juice

*R*ub meat with oil and seasonings. Bake in shallow pan in a 350 degree oven for 45 minutes or until meat thermometer registers desired degree of doneness. Sauté onion and mushrooms in butter until tender. Add wine; simmer for 1 hour until reduced by half. Mix consommé and cornstarch and stir into mixture; simmer until thickened. Add lemon juice and meat drippings from pan. Yield: 10 servings

Peaches with Sherry Sauce

10 Elberta peach halves
2 to 3 tablespoons butter
2 to 3 tablespoons sugar
10 to 12 macaroons, crumbled
   Sherry Sauce

*P*lace peaches in baking dish, cut sides up. Place a bit of butter into each hollow; sprinkle lightly with sugar. Sprinkle with crumbs, pressing them lightly into the butter. Bake in a 350 degree oven for 30 minutes. Serve bubbling hot with Sherry Sauce. Yield: 10 servings

Sherry Sauce

6   egg yolks
3   tablespoons sugar
2/3 cup dry sherry

*B*eat egg yolks and sugar in top of double boiler over simmering water until light and fluffy. Gradually add sherry. Cook, whisking constantly until smooth and thickened. Chill thoroughly. Yield: 6 servings

Watercress Salad

1   teaspoon salt
1   teaspoon pepper
2   tablespoons prepared mustard
1   tablespoon Worcestershire sauce
4   tablespoons catsup
1/4 cup lemon juice
1   cup vegetable oil
5   bunches watercress, washed, drained, and
    stems removed

*C*ombine first 7 ingredients in blender. Pour over watercress and toss gently so as not to bruise the tender greens. Yield: 6 servings

Crème Brûlée

2   egg yolks, slightly beaten
2   eggs, slightly beaten
1/3 cup sugar
    Dash of salt
2   cups heavy cream, heated until very hot
1 1/2 cups dark brown sugar, sifted

*C*ombine first 4 ingredients in top of a double boiler over simmering water. Add the cream slowly, stirring constantly until slightly thickened. Pour into a 9x6x2-inch dish. Cover and chill. Before serving, preheat broiler. Sprinkle brown sugar evenly over top of cream. Place under broiler and heat just until sugar melts and looks shiny. Serve immediately. Yield: 6 to 8 servings

Parsley keeps a long time if washed and stored in a tightly covered jar in the refrigerator.

New Year's Day Dinner

Bloody Marys*
Pork Roast
Hoppin' John   Southern Turnip Greens
Cole Slaw
Cracklin' Bread*
Sweet Potato Custard
Coffee

· —— ·

*Recipe for Bloody
Marys is on page
100.
*Recipe for Cracklin'
Bread is on page 128.

*To get twice as much
juice from a lemon,
drop the lemon in hot
water and roll between
your hands before
squeezing.*

Pork Roast

1/4 cup vegetable oil
2 tablespoons molasses
1 tablespoon ground ginger
2 teaspoons dry mustard
6 cloves garlic, minced
1/2 cup soy sauce
1 4 to 5 pound pork loin

Combine all ingredients except pork; shake or blend well. Pour marinade over the pork loin; cover and refrigerate overnight. Turn pork loin several times. Place meat, fat-side up on a rack in a greased shallow roasting pan. Baste pork with marinade four to five times while roasting. Roast in a preheated 325 degree oven for about 1 hour or to an internal temperature of 140 degrees. Yield: 6 to 8 servings

Hoppin' John

1 cup dry black-eyed peas
4 1/2 cups water
1/8 pound salt pork, cubed
1 medium onion, chopped
1 clove garlic, minced
1 cup raw rice

1/8 teaspoon cayenne pepper
1 teaspoon salt
1/4 teaspoon pepper
Bay leaf

Boil peas in water for 2 minutes. Set aside to soak for 1 hour. Sauté pork in Dutch oven until browned. Add onion and garlic. Sauté until onion is tender. Add peas, water, and remaining ingredients. Simmer for 1 hour or until peas are tender and water is absorbed. Remove bay leaf before serving. Yield: 6 to 8 servings

Southern Turnip Greens

3 pounds of turnip greens
1/4 pound of "boiling meat" or "hog jowl"
Salt to taste
Pod of red pepper, optional
Hard-boiled eggs

Carefully wash and pick over the greens, removing tough portions. Bring seasoning meat of choice to boil in enough water to cover greens. Add greens. Cook at a low boil until greens are tender, about 45 to 50 minutes. Stir often. Season to taste. Drain and serve hot with slices of hard-boiled egg. Yield: 6 servings

Cole Slaw

1 medium cabbage
1 bunch celery
2 onions
3 green peppers
1 sweet red pepper
1 egg, slightly beaten
3 tablespoons butter
1 tablespoon all-purpose flour
1 tablespoon cornstarch
3/4 cup sugar
1 teaspoon salt
1 teaspoon turmeric
1/2 cup wine vinegar

*S*hred cabbage, chop other vegetables, combine with cabbage and chill. In a small saucepan combine egg, butter, flour, cornstarch, sugar, salt, turmeric and vinegar; boil gently until thick, stirring constantly to prevent lumps. Pour hot dressing over vegetables and chill overnight. Yield: 8 to 10 servings

Sweet Potato Custard

1 1/2 cups cooked, mashed sweet potatoes
1/2 cup dark brown sugar
2 eggs, beaten
1/2 teaspoon salt
1 teaspoon allspice
1 1/2 cups milk
1 9-inch pie crust, unbaked

*C*ombine all ingredients. Pour into pie crust and bake in a 350 degree oven for 20 minutes. Add Topping and continue baking for an additional 25 minutes. Yield: 6 to 8 servings

Topping

4 tablespoons butter, melted
1/4 cup dark brown sugar
3/4 cup chopped pecans

*C*ombine all ingredients. Sprinkle on custard and bake until custard is firm and golden brown, about 25 minutes.

Set a festive buffet table.

Creole Dinner

Potato Soup
Sautéed Frog Legs or Trout Amandine
Herbed Lemon Butter   Seasoned Rice
Tomatoes Florentine
Peach Melba   French Bread
Coffee

· ——————— ·

Potato Soup

    4 potatoes, peeled and thinly sliced
    1 onion, quartered
    2 to 3 cups chicken broth
    4 tablespoons butter
    2 cups milk or light cream
    1 tablespoon chopped parsley
       Salt, pepper and hot sauce to taste

*B*oil potatoes and onion in chicken broth about 30 minutes, or until tender. Add butter. Cool slightly and purée. Stir in remaining ingredients. Serve hot or cold. Yield: 6 servings

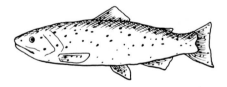

Herbed Lemon Butter

    ¹/₄ cup butter
    1   teaspoon freshly grated lemon rind
    1   tablespoon freshly squeezed lemon juice
    ¹/₂ teaspoon crushed marjoram

*H*eat butter in small saucepan until melted. Stir in remaining ingredients. Serve hot with Trout Amandine, if desired. Yield: 4 servings

Sautéed Frog Legs

    2 eggs
    3 cups milk
    2 dozen frog legs, washed and drained
    2 cups all-purpose flour seasoned with salt
       and pepper to taste
    1 cup butter
    4 tablespoons onion juice
    4 tablespoons garlic juice
    4 tablespoons lemon juice
    4 tablespoons Worcestershire sauce

*B*eat eggs into milk. Dip frog legs in mixture, then dredge in seasoned flour. Melt ¹/₂ cup butter over medium heat in a heavy skillet. Add the remaining ingredients, stirring constantly. Sauté frog legs for 8 minutes or until golden brown. Place on a warm platter. Add remaining butter to the skillet, stir, and pour sauce over the frog legs. Yield: 6 servings

Trout Amandine

    3   pounds trout or bass fillets
    1¹/₂ cups milk
       Salt and pepper to taste
    1   cup all-purpose flour
    ³/₄ cup butter
    ¹/₂ cup slivered almonds
    3 to 4 tablespoons lemon juice
    1 to 2 tablespoons Worcestershire sauce
    1¹/₂ tablespoons chopped parsley

Cover fish with milk; chill for 4 hours. Drain. Season fillets, flour, and sauté in butter until golden brown. Place fish on warm platter. Add almonds to skillet and brown lightly, stirring constantly. Add remaining ingredients. Heat thoroughly and pour over fish. Yield: 6 servings

Seasoned Rice

- 3/4 cup chopped onion
- 6 tablespoons butter or margarine
- 1 10 3/4-ounce can chicken broth
- 1 tablespoon grated orange rind
- 3/4 cup orange juice
- 1 cup water
- 3/4 teaspoon poultry seasoning
- 1/2 teaspoon salt
- 1/2 teaspoon pepper
- 1 1/2 cups rice
- 1/2 cup ripe olives, drained and chopped
- 1 cup sliced celery

Sauté onion lightly in butter; add broth, rind, juice, water and seasonings and bring to a boil. Stir in rice and olives; return to a boil. Cover; reduce heat and cook 10 minutes. Add celery and continue cooking 10 minutes longer or until rice is tender. Yield: 6 servings

Tomatoes Florentine

- 2 10-ounce packages frozen chopped spinach, cooked and well-drained
- 1/2 green pepper, chopped
- 1/4 cup chopped onion
- 2 ribs celery, chopped
- 2 hard-boiled eggs, chopped
  Salt and pepper to taste
- 1/4 cup mayonnaise
- 1 teaspoon lemon juice
- 6 tomatoes, hollowed and drained

Mix spinach with pepper, onion, celery and eggs. Season; stir in mayonnaise and lemon juice. Spoon into tomato shells. Serve warm or cold. Yield: 6 servings

Peach Melba

- 3 peaches
- 3 cups boiling water
- 1/2 cup sugar
- 1 cup water
- 1/2 lemon
  Vanilla ice cream
  Melba Sauce

Immerse each peach in boiling water for 10 seconds. Remove skin; halve and remove seed. Combine sugar with 1 cup water and boil for 2 minutes. Add peaches; cover and poach for 10 to 15 minutes. Drain, sprinkle with lemon juice and chill. To serve, place a scoop of vanilla ice cream in each peach half and top with Melba sauce. Yield: 6 servings

Melba Sauce

- 1 10-ounce package frozen raspberries
- 3/4 cup black currant jelly
- 1/4 cup sugar
- 1/2 teaspoon lemon juice

Cook first 3 ingredients over medium heat stirring until mixture comes to a boil. Simmer, stirring occasionally, for 20 minutes. Strain and cool. Add lemon juice. Chill. Yield: 2 1/2 cups

Never measure liquids, like almond extract, directly over what you are going to put it in as it is too easy to overflow the measuring spoon and get too much in your food.

Thanksgiving Dinner

Steaming Cups of Oyster Stew
Roasted Turkey
Giblet Gravy
Cornbread and Pecan Stuffing
Asparagus with Butter
Sweet Potatoes in Orange Cups
English Trifle*

· ———— ·

A quick test for turkey to see if it is done is to slightly twist the drumstick. If it moves easily, the bird is ready.

Oyster Stew

3   tablespoons butter, melted
1   tablespoon all-purpose flour
    Salt and pepper
1   quart milk, heated
1½ pints stewing oysters
    Chopped chives

Melt butter; add flour and cook until bubbly. Add seasonings to taste. Blend in milk and heat entire mixture thoroughly. Add oysters and cook for about 5 minutes until edges of oysters curl. Serve immediately, topped with chopped chives. Yield: 6 servings

Giblet Gravy

    Turkey giblets
½ teaspoon salt
⅛ teaspoon pepper
4   tablespoons shortening
4   tablespoons all-purpose flour
3   cups giblet or turkey stock
1   hard-boiled egg, chopped

Combine giblets, salt, pepper, and enough water to cover in saucepan. Simmer for 45 to 60 minutes or until tender. Chop giblets and set aside. Melt shortening; stir in flour. Add stock; stir constantly for 5 minutes or until thickened. Add giblets and egg; stir to blend. Yield: 3 cups

Recipe for English Trifle is on page 159.

Cornbread and Pecan Stuffing

8   cups Pepperidge Farm cornbread stuffing
    or 8 cups dry crumbled cornbread
3   cups hot milk
1   cup melted butter
1   cup coarsely broken pecans
2   teaspoons salt
¼ teaspoon cayenne pepper

Combine all ingredients well. Stuff bird loosely. Yield: Stuffing for a 12 to 16 pound bird

Sweet Potatoes in Orange Cups

3   cups cooked mashed sweet potatoes
1   cup sugar
½ teaspoon salt
2   eggs
¼ cup butter
½ cup milk
1   teaspoon vanilla
    Orange half shells
1   cup brown sugar
⅓ cup flour
1   cup chopped nuts
¼ cup butter

Combine first 7 ingredients and pour into orange halves which have the pulp removed. Mix remaining ingredients and sprinkle over potato mixture. Bake for 35 minutes in a 350 degree oven. Yield: 6 to 8 servings

After Theater Supper

Champagne
Seafood Crêpes   Winter Salad
Sunburst Muffins
Amaretto Soufflé

· —————— ·

Seafood Crêpes

24 crêpes
¹/₂ cup chopped green onions
¹/₂ pound mushrooms, sliced
1 3-ounce package slivered almonds
   Butter
1 pound lump crab meat
1¹/₂ pounds shrimp, cooked and chopped
¹/₂ cup cream sherry
   Salt and white pepper to taste
   Garlic salt to taste
   Chopped parsley to taste
¹/₄ cup cornstarch
2 cups light cream, divided
1 cup cream sherry
2 cups heavy cream
3 cups grated Swiss cheese, divided
2 tablespoons butter

Prepare crêpes and set aside. To make seafood filling, briefly sauté onion, mushrooms, almonds, and crab meat in butter. Add next 5 ingredients and heat thoroughly for two minutes. Set aside while preparing sauce. Combine cornstarch and ¹/₄ cup light cream, blending well. Boil sherry until reduced by half. Add cornstarch mixture, remaining cream, and heavy cream; cook, stirring constantly, until thickened. Add 2 cups cheese; stir until melted. Mix half of sauce with seafood filling. Spoon 2 tablespoons mixture onto each crêpe; roll up. Place seam-side down in a buttered baking dish. Cover with remaining sauce, sprinkle with remaining cheese, and dot with butter. Bake in a 400 degree oven for 20 minutes. Yield: 12 servings

Plastic wrap won't stick to itself if you store it in the refrigerator.

Winter Salad

2 cups vegetable oil
²/₃ cup wine vinegar
2¹/₂ teaspoons curry powder
2 teaspoons Worcestershire sauce
6 drops hot sauce
¹/₂ cup catsup
2 teaspoons Italian herb seasoning
1¹/₂ teaspoons salt
¹/₂ teaspoon pepper
2 grapefruit, peeled and separated into sections
2 avocados, peeled and pitted
2 bunches watercress
2 heads Boston or 4 heads Bibb lettuce
¹/₂ cup sunflower seeds, optional

Combine first 9 ingredients, mixing well. Set aside. Cut each grapefruit section into thirds; place in salad bowl. Cut avocado into small pieces; add to grapefruit. Tear greens into bite-sized pieces; add to fruit. Add sunflower seeds, if desired. Serve with dressing. Yield: 12 servings

Sunburst Muffins

1 18¹/₂-ounce box Lemon Supreme Cake Mix
1 3³/₄-ounce package instant lemon pudding mix
¹/₂ cup vegetable oil
1 cup buttermilk
4 eggs
3 tablespoons fresh lemon juice
6 tablespoons fresh orange juice
1¹/₂ teaspoons vanilla
3¹/₂ cups confectioners' sugar, sifted

Combine first 5 ingredients and pour into greased miniature muffin tins filling cups ²/₃ full. Bake in a 350 degree oven for 10 minutes. Combine remaining ingredients. Dip warm muffins into glaze; and place on wire rack to cool. Yield: 3 dozen

Amaretto Soufflé

3 whole eggs
5 egg yolks
¹/₂ cup superfine sugar
¹/₃ cup Amaretto liqueur
1 cup crushed almond macaroons
2 cups heavy cream, whipped

Beat eggs, yolks, and sugar with an electric hand mixer set on high speed for 12 minutes. Reduce speed; add liqueur and crumbs. Blend; fold in whipped cream. Pour into a soufflé dish. Freeze overnight. Yield: 10 to 12 servings

Recipes

Appetizers and Beverages

Party Cheese Ball

- 2 8-ounce packages cream cheese, softened
- 1 8-ounce package sharp Cheddar cheese, grated
- 1 tablespoon chopped pimiento
- 1 tablespoon chopped green pepper
- 1 teaspoon finely chopped onion
- 1 teaspoon lemon juice
- 2 teaspoons Worcestershire sauce
- 1/4 teaspoon cayenne pepper
- 1/4 teaspoon salt
  Finely chopped pecans

*C*ream cream cheese until soft and smooth. Add Cheddar cheese; mix until well blended. Add pimiento, green pepper, onion, lemon juice, Worcestershire sauce and seasonings; blend well. Shape into a ball. Cover and chill at least 24 hours. Roll in chopped pecans. Yield: 24 servings

Ginger Cream Cheese Ball

- 1 8-ounce box pitted dates
- 6 to 8 candied ginger bits
- 1/2 cup pecans or walnuts

- 2 8-ounce packages cream cheese, softened
  Flaked coconut
  Gingersnaps

*C*hop dates, ginger, and nuts in a food processor or mince by hand. Add cheese and blend well. Chill 2 hours and shape into 1 large ball or 2 small ones. Cover with flaked coconut. Serve with gingersnaps. Yield: 20 servings

Spicy Cheese Straws

- 4 cups New York sharp Cheddar cheese
- 1 cup butter, softened
- 4 cups all-purpose flour, sifted
- 4 teaspoons baking powder
- 1/2 teaspoon cayenne pepper
- 1 1/2 teaspoons salt

*S*often Cheddar cheese and blend with butter in mixer. Add remaining ingredients. Chill. Place in cookie press and squeeze onto greased baking sheet. Bake in a 300 degree oven for 15 minutes. Yield: 6 to 7 dozen

Plan to set out cheeses one hour before serving so they will reach room temperature for best flavor and texture.

Baked Gouda Cheese in Pastry with Apples

1 5 x 5-inch puff pastry square
1 egg, well beaten
1 4-ounce wheel Gouda cheese
1 red Delicious apple
  Parsley
  Green grapes, optional

*B*rush puff pastry square with egg and wrap around cheese, covering all of the cheese. Bake in a 375 degree oven for 7 to 10 minutes. Brown pastry under the broiler for 15 to 20 seconds. Remove cheese from baking sheet; place on serving board. Garnish with apple slices, parsley and grapes. Cut into 6 pieces and serve immediately. Yield: 1 to 2 servings

Almond Bacon Cheese Spread

$^1/_2$ cup diced almonds
4 strips of bacon, cooked and crumbled
2 cups grated Cheddar cheese
4 tablespoons chopped green onion
1 cup mayonnaise
$^1/_2$ teaspoon salt

*C*ombine all ingredients thoroughly. Chill to enhance flavors. Serve with your favorite crackers or Melba toast. Yield: approximately $3^1/_2$ cups

Hot Crab and Cheese Toast

1 $6^1/_2$-ounce can crab meat, drained and flaked
1 tablespoon minced onion
1 cup shredded sharp Cheddar cheese
2 tablespoons mayonnaise
  Melba toast rounds
  Paprika

*C*ombine first 4 ingredients thoroughly. Spread on Melba toast rounds and sprinkle with paprika. Broil until bubbly. Yield: 24 toast rounds

Sherry Cheese Pâté

2 3-ounce packages cream cheese, softened
1 cup shredded sharp Cheddar cheese
4 teaspoons dry sherry
$^1/_2$ teaspoon curry powder
$^1/_4$ teaspoon salt
1 8-ounce jar chopped chutney
3 to 4 green onions, including tops, finely chopped
  Sesame or wheat crackers

*C*ombine cream cheese, Cheddar cheese, sherry, curry powder and salt; mix thoroughly. Spread on serving platter, shaping $^1/_2$-inch thick. Chill until firm. Spread chutney over the top, and sprinkle with green onions. Serve with crackers. Yield: 8 servings

Party Cheese Biscuits

$^1/_2$ pound sharp Cheddar cheese, grated
$^1/_2$ pound butter or margarine
$2^1/_2$ cups all-purpose flour
1 teaspoon salt
$^1/_4$ teaspoon cayenne pepper
$^1/_4$ cup ground pecans

*S*often cheese and butter at room temperature. Cream together with flour, salt, pepper and pecans. Divide and shape into long rolls about the diameter of a quarter. Roll in wax paper and store, covered, in refrigerator overnight. Slice thinly and place about $^1/_2$-inch apart on ungreased cookie sheet. Bake in a 400 degree oven for 10 to 12 minutes. Yield: 45 to 60 biscuits

Salmon Ball

- 1 1-pound can red salmon
- 1 8-ounce package cream cheese, softened
- 2 tablespoons fresh lemon juice
- 3 teaspoons onion, grated
- 2 teaspoons horseradish
- 1/2 teaspoon salt
- 1/8 teaspoon Worcestershire sauce
- 1/4 teaspoon cayenne pepper
- 1/4 teaspoon liquid smoke
- 1/2 cup pecans, chopped
- 3 tablespoons fresh parsley, minced

*D*rain, flake and bone salmon. In another bowl mix together cream cheese, lemon juice, onion, horseradish, salt, Worcestershire sauce, cayenne pepper and liquid smoke. Stir in salmon. Combine pecans and parsley and spread onto sheet of wax paper. Spread salmon mixture onto parsley mixture and turn until all sides are covered. Shape into 1 large ball or 2 long rolls. Wrap or cover and chill thoroughly before serving. Yield: 10 to 15 servings

Smoked Oyster Hors D'Oeuvres, page 98; Sherried Pork Roast, page 137; Brandy Spiked Ice Cream, page 157.

When planning appetizers, figure on four to six small appetizers per guest.

Shrimp Mold

1   10³/₄-ounce can tomato soup
1   8-ounce package cream cheese, softened and cut into chunks
3   envelopes plain gelatin, softened for 5 minutes
6   tablespoons water
2   pounds cooked small shrimp
¹/₄ cup diced green onion
¹/₄ cup diced green pepper
¹/₄ teaspoon each: salt, pepper, celery salt, onion salt, and hot sauce
1   cup mayonnaise
2   tablespoons drained horseradish

*H*eat soup and cream cheese. Stir with wire whisk until cheese is melted. Some small lumps will remain. Dissolve gelatin in 6 tablespoons water; add to hot soup mixture. Remove from heat and stir well. Add remaining ingredients. Pour into a well-greased 1-quart ring mold. Refrigerate until firm. Garnish as desired. Yield: 40 to 50 servings as an appetizer spread

Hot Broccoli Dip

1 10-ounce package frozen broccoli
1 medium onion, chopped
1 8-ounce can mushrooms, drained
3 ribs celery, chopped
4 tablespoons butter
1 6-ounce roll garlic cheese
1 10³/₄-ounce can cream of mushroom soup
1 small package chopped or sliced almonds

*C*ook broccoli according to package directions; drain. Sauté onion, mushrooms and celery in 4 tablespoons of butter. Melt cheese in double boiler; add broccoli, onion mixture, and mushroom soup. Pour into chafing dish and sprinkle with almonds. Serve with chips or crackers. Yield: 8 to 10 servings

Hoppin' John Dip

6   slices bacon, cut into ¹/₂-inch pieces
³/₄ cup chopped onion
1   10-ounce package frozen black-eyed peas
2   cups water
1   teaspoon salt
¹/₄ cup raw rice
2   teaspoons vinegar
¹/₄ teaspoon cayenne pepper
    Crackers or chips

*C*ook bacon in large saucepan. Remove with slotted spoon and drain on absorbent paper; reserve. Add onion to bacon fat in saucepan; cook until tender. Add black-eyed peas, water and salt. Cover and cook over medium heat for 15 minutes. Stir in rice; cover and cook over low heat for 25 to 30 minutes, until rice is tender. Purée mixture in food processor or blender. Add vinegar and cayenne pepper. If mixture is too thick for dipping, stir in a little boiling water. Heat. Sprinkle with crumbled bacon. Serve with crackers or chips. Yield: 3 cups

Spinach Crab Meat Dip

3 10-ounce packages frozen chopped spinach
1 large onion, finely chopped
1 green pepper, chopped
2 tablespoons butter or margarine
3 6¹/₂-ounce cans crab meat
2 6-ounce rolls jalapeño cheese
1 6-ounce can chopped mushrooms
3 10³/₄-ounce cans cream of mushroom soup
  Hot sauce
  Worcestershire sauce
  Melba toast

*C*ook spinach according to package directions. Drain well. Sauté onion and green pepper in butter. Add crab meat, jalapeño cheese, mushrooms, and soup. Add hot sauce and Worcestershire to taste. Serve in chafing dish with Melba toast. Yield: 30 to 40 servings

Fire Island Cocktail Spread

1   envelope unflavored gelatin
1/2 cup cold water
1   10³/₄-ounce can condensed tomato soup, undiluted
1   8-ounce package cream cheese, at room temperature
1   cup mayonnaise
1/2 cup finely chopped celery
1/2 cup finely chopped green pepper
1/2 cup finely chopped cucumber
2   teaspoons grated onion
1¹/₂ teaspoons Worcestershire sauce
1/2 teaspoon Tabasco sauce
1/4 teaspoon salt
    Unpeeled thin cucumber slices

*I*n a medium saucepan, mix gelatin with water. Set aside for 1 minute. Stir over medium heat until gelatin is completely dissolved, about 1 minute. In a large bowl, beat together soup and cream cheese until smooth. Fold in mayonnaise, celery, green pepper, cucumber, onion, Worcestershire sauce, Tabasco sauce and salt. Stir in gelatin. Turn into a 4-cup mold; chill until firm. Unmold on serving plate; garnish with cucumber slices. Serve with assorted crackers and breads. Yield: 14 to 16 servings

Mexican Nacho Dip

2   to 3 ripe avocados, peeled and pitted
1/8 teaspoon lemon juice
1   bunch green onions, including tops, chopped
1   16-ounce carton sour cream
1   8-ounce jar picante or taco sauce
2   medium tomatoes, chopped
2   small green peppers, chopped
8   ounces Monterey Jack cheese, grated
    Tortilla chips

*M*ash avocados in a 9-inch pie plate. Sprinkle with lemon juice to prevent discoloring. Layer re-

maining ingredients in order given except chips. Chill 4 to 12 hours. Serve with chips. Yield: 12 to 15 servings

Guacamole

3   large ripe avocados, mashed
1   3-ounce package cream cheese, softened
1   medium onion, chopped
1   medium tomato, peeled and chopped
2   ounces green chiles, chopped
1   tablespoon olive oil
1   teaspoon red wine vinegar
1/2 teaspoon salt
    Freshly ground pepper to taste
    Corn or tortilla chips

*M*ix all ingredients except chips until creamy. If you are making this in advance, place it in a bowl with an avocado pit to prevent discoloring. Remove pit before serving. Serve with chips. Yield: 2 cups

Last of the Red Hot Ham

3   cups finely chopped or ground ham
1   8-ounce package cream cheese, at room temperature
1/3 cup chopped chutney
1¹/₄ teaspoons Tabasco sauce
1   cup chopped pecans, divided
    Pimiento strips
    Parsley

*C*ombine ham, cream cheese, chutney, and Tabasco sauce; mix until smooth. Stir in ²/₃ cup pecans. Line a 4-cup mold or bowl with clear plastic wrap. Pack ham mixture firmly into mold. Refrigerate 1 to 2 hours. Turn mold out onto serving platter; remove plastic wrap. Press remaining 1/3 cup pecans on sides and top of mold. Decorate with strips of pimiento and parsley. Yield: About 4 cups

Freeze juices or tea in ice cube trays. Use in drinks to prevent dilution of juice or tea when cubes melt.

Fire Island Cocktail Spread, page 94; Spinach Pinwheels, this page; Last of the Red Hot Ham, page 95.

Freeze ice cubes or ice rings with fruit in the centers for a festive touch in mixed drinks or punches.

Spinach Pinwheels

2   10-ounce packages frozen, chopped spinach, thawed, drained, and squeezed dry
2   cups cottage cheese, drained
½ cup grated Parmesan cheese
½ cup finely cut scallions
2   tablespoons chopped fresh dill or 2 teaspoons dried dill weed
2   tablespoons processed blue cheese spread
1   teaspoon Tabasco sauce
1   teaspoon salt
1   pre-rolled sheet frozen puff pastry, thawed Dry bread crumbs

$\mathcal{C}$ombine spinach, cottage cheese, Parmesan cheese, scallions, dill, blue cheese, Tabasco sauce and salt; mix well. Cut folded pastry sheet in half. Roll each half to a 8x18-inch rectangle. Sprinkle pastry lightly with bread crumbs to within 1 inch of all edges. Divide spinach mixture in half and spread lengthwise down the center of each rectangle. Fold edges over filling; seal seams and ends with water. Place on ungreased cookie sheet seam-side down. Prick surface with fork. Bake in a 400 degree oven for 25 minutes or until golden brown. Cut spinach rolls 1 inch thick on the diagonal and serve at once. Rolls may be wrapped in foil and refrigerated or frozen for future use. To heat, place uncovered, in a 350 degree oven until warmed through; slice. Yield: About 2½ dozen slices

Ham Biscuits with Mustard Spread

1 cup butter, softened
2 tablespoons poppy seed
2 small onions, chopped
5 heaping teaspoons prepared mustard
  Biscuits
  Swiss cheese
  Ham, thinly sliced

*C*ombine first 4 ingredients in blender until smooth. Refrigerate at least 24 hours. Split biscuits; spread with butter mixture and top with Swiss cheese and ham. Seal in foil and bake in a 350 degree oven until cheese melts, about 5 minutes. Yield: Spread for 20 biscuits

Hot Pecan Spread with Dried Beef

1 cup chopped pecans
1 tablespoon melted butter
1 8-ounce package cream cheese, softened
2 tablespoons milk
1 2¹/₂-ounce package sliced dried beef, cut
  into large pieces
¹/₄ cup finely chopped green pepper
2 tablespoons dehydrated onion flakes
¹/₂ teaspoon garlic salt
¹/₂ cup sour cream
2 tablespoons mayonnaise
¹/₄ teaspoon pepper
¹/₂ teaspoon salt

*H*eat pecans in melted butter; set aside to cool. Combine remaining ingredients and pour into an 8 or 9-inch greased pie pan. Sprinkle pecans on top. Bake in a 350 degree oven for 20 minutes. Serve with crackers or Melba toast. Yield: Approximately 2¹/₂ cups

Stuffed Mushrooms

1 pound large mushrooms
¹/₄ cup butter
¹/₄ cup finely chopped onion
¹/₄ finely chopped celery
1 teaspoon Worcestershire sauce
¹/₂ teaspoon salt
¹/₈ teaspoon pepper
  Parmesan cheese
  Butter, melted

*W*ipe mushrooms with a dampened paper towel; stem. Chop stems; reserve whole mushrooms. In large skillet, heat butter, onion, celery, chopped mushroom stems and seasonings. Brush mushrooms caps with butter. Fill with mixture. Arrange caps, stuffed-side up, in same skillet. Simmer 5 minutes. Yield: 4 to 6 servings

Sausage Balls in Cranberry Sauce

1 pound seasoned bulk pork sausage
2 eggs, beaten
1 cup fresh bread crumbs
1 teaspoon salt
¹/₂ teaspoon poultry seasoning
1 16-ounce can jellied cranberry sauce
1 tablespoon prepared mustard

*C*ombine sausage, eggs, bread crumbs, salt and poultry seasoning. Shape into 1-inch balls. Bake in a 350 degree oven for 30 minutes. Combine cranberry sauce and mustard in medium saucepan: heat until melted. Add sausage balls. Cover and simmer 15 minutes. Yield: 24 to 30 meatballs

A large ice ring melts more slowly in punch than ice cubes, keeping punch from getting watery.

For extra effervescence, always add ginger ale or club soda to punch just before serving.

Cocktail Oysters

$1/2$ cup finely chopped onion
2 tablespoons butter
1 cup catsup
2 tablespoons Worcestershire sauce
1 teaspoon garlic salt
$1/4$ teaspoon hot sauce
1 pint oysters, well drained

*S*auté onion in butter. Add catsup, Worcestershire sauce, garlic salt, and hot sauce; heat to boiling. Add oysters; heat only until edges of oysters curl. Serve hot in chafing dish with Melba toast rounds. Yield: 3 cups

Smoked Oyster Hors D'Oeuvres

20 whole pitted prunes
20 medium-sized smoked oysters
10 lean bacon slices, halved

*S*tuff each prune with an oyster. Wrap each with a half bacon slice; secure with wooden pick. Broil 4 to 5 minutes to cook bacon crisp, turning once. Serve hot. Yield: 20 appetizers

Caviar Potatoes

2 to 3 pounds bite-sized new potatoes
1 pint sour cream
1 2-ounce jar caviar
   Chives, chopped
1 3-ounce package cream cheese
$1/4$ cup mayonnaise
2 teaspoons lemon juice
2 tablespoons grated onion
1 teaspoon Worcestershire sauce

*B*oil potatoes in salted water approximately 20 minutes or until tender. Drain and cool. Using a melon ball scoop, hollow out the top of the potato. Fill cavity with sour cream. Top filling with caviar and sprinkle with chives. As a variation, mix remaining ingredients and fill cavity with mixture. Yield: Filling for 2 to 3 pounds new potatoes

Shrimp Rabbit

2 pounds shrimp, cooked in the shell
3 tablespoons butter
2 cups grated Gruyère or Swiss cheese
2 cups grated Cheddar cheese
$1/2$ cup heavy cream
2 eggs, lightly beaten
1 teaspoon dry mustard
   Worcestershire sauce to taste
   Salt and freshly ground black pepper
   to taste
$1/2$ cup dry white wine
   Toast points

*P*eel and devein the shrimp. If small, leave whole; if large, cut into bite-sized pieces. Melt the butter in a saucepan and stir in the cheeses. Stir until cheese is melted. Add the cream and eggs, then the remaining ingredients except toast. Stir until mixture is slightly thickened and smooth. Stir in the shrimp and heat thoroughly. Serve with toast points. Yield: 6 servings

Fruited Tea

1 quart water
12 small tea bags
10 tablespoons lemon juice
   Juice of 4 oranges
2 cups sugar

*B*oil water; add tea bags and steep 5 minutes. Remove tea bags. Add remaining ingredients and enough water to make $1/2$ gallon.

Tea Punch

6   small tea bags
4   cups boiling water
1½ cups sugar
1   6-ounce can frozen orange juice, thawed
    and undiluted
1   6-ounce can frozen lemonade, thawed and
    undiluted
1   cup pineapple juice
10 cups cold water

Steep tea bags in boiling water about 5 minutes. Discard tea bags. Add remaining ingredients. Serve over ice. Yield: 1 gallon

Summertime Lemonade

1¼ cups sugar
½   cup boiling water
1½ cups fresh lemon juice
4½ cups cold water
    Ice cubes
    Lemon slices

Combine sugar, water, and lemon juice in a 2-quart pitcher and stir vigorously with a spoon until sugar is dissolved. Cover and store in refrigerator until ready to use. To serve, add cold water, ice cubes and lemon slices and stir. Pour over ice cubes into a 10 or 12-ounce glass. Yield: 6 to 8 servings

Sparkling Cranberry Punch

1 6-ounce can frozen lemonade
1 6-ounce can frozen orange juice
1 quart cranberry juice
1 30-ounce can pineapple juice
1 quart ginger ale, chilled

Prepare lemonade and orange juice according to label directions. Pour into large container. Add cranberry juice and pineapple juice. Chill. Add ginger ale just before serving. Yield: 20 to 24 servings

Fruit Punch

1 3-ounce box cherry gelatin
3 cups sugar
1 quart boiling water
3 quarts cool water
1 46-ounce can pineapple juice
1 quart bottle 7-Up

Dissolve gelatin and sugar in boiling water. Add the remaining water and pineapple juice. Store in refrigerator. When ready to serve, pour into punch bowl and add the 7-Up. Stir well. Yield: 50 4-ounce servings

Hot Spiced Apple Cider

9 46-ounce cans apple juice
2 teaspoons cinnamon
2 teaspoons nutmeg
2 teaspoons allspice
2 teaspoons ground cloves

Combine all ingredients in large kettle. Heat until warmed thoroughly. Yield: 50 one-cup servings

A sampling of popular after-dinner drinks:

   Amaretto (an almond flavored cordial)

   B & B (a mixture of half Benedictine and half brandy)

   Cognac (brandy)

   Chambord (fruity black raspberry liqueur)

   Cherry Heering (cherry liqueur)

   Cointreau (an orange flavored liqueur)

   Drambuie (a scotch-based liqueur)

   Grand Marnier (an orange flavored cognac-based liqueur)

   Irish Mist (Irish whiskey-based liqueur)

   Kahlua (a coffee and cocoa bean-based liqueur)

   Southern Comfort (a bourbon-based liqueur)

   Vandermint (chocolate mint liqueur)

Bloody Marys, this page.

Party Punch

15 small cans frozen orange juice
   Water
15 limes
6 lemons
5 46-ounce cans pineapple juice
3 quarts ginger ale
   Sliced lemons or limes

Combine orange juice with 1½ cans of water for each can of orange juice. Reserve 1 lime and 1 lemon. Squeeze remaining limes and lemons into punch. Add remaining ingredients. Stir well. Pour over ice to serve. Serve with slice of lemon or lime. Yield: 150 servings

Bloody Marys

1 jigger vodka
2 jiggers tomato juice
⅓ jigger lemon juice
   Dash Worcestershire sauce
   Salt and pepper to taste
   Dash Tabasco sauce
½ cup cracked ice

Combine all ingredients in shaker. Shake until thoroughly chilled. Strain into glass. Yield: 1 serving

Sangria

1 cup halved strawberries
2 ripe peaches, peeled and cut into small pieces
1 orange, thinly sliced
1 lime, thinly sliced
   Juice and rind of 1 lemon
¾ teaspoon cinnamon
2 bottles red wine
   Ice cubes

Combine all ingredients in large pitcher. Stir thoroughly, mashing the fruit slightly. Set aside at room temperature for at least 1 hour. Just before serving, add 20 ice cubes and stir until chilled. Yield: Approximately ½ gallon

Irish Coffee

Irish whiskey
Sugar
Hot coffee
Heavy cream

For each serving, pour 1½ ounces of whiskey into large cups. Add sugar to taste. Fill with hot coffee to within ½-inch of the top. Add cream. Do not stir. Yield: 1 serving

Salads and Dressings

Ambrosia

1	cup seedless grapes
1½	cups fresh orange sections
1	cup pineapple chunks
2	medium apples (unpeeled, cored, and cubed)
1	cup maraschino cherries, halved
1	tablespoon sugar
½	cup flaked coconut, toasted
1	cup sour cream
2	tablespoons mayonnaise
1	tablespoon light cream
	Lettuce
½	cup sliced almonds, toasted

*C*ombine fruits, sprinkle with sugar, add coconut and toss lightly. Mix sour cream, mayonnaise and cream; fold into fruit just before serving. Serve on lettuce cups and garnish with almonds. Yield: 6 servings

Variation: Omit sour cream. Mix and saturate fruit with sherry.

Spiced Peach Mold

1	29-ounce jar pickled peaches, juice reserved
1	cup fresh orange juice
1	3-ounce package orange-flavored gelatin
1	8-ounce package cream cheese
½	cup crushed pecans
	Slivers of orange rind
	Lettuce

*R*emove seeds from pickled peaches, tearing as little as possible. Bring peach juice and orange juice to a boil; add gelatin. Soften cream cheese with a little of the hot juice; add pecans. Fill peach hollows with cream cheese mixture. Place each peach in an individual mold and fill with gelatin; chill until firm. Garnish with slivers of orange rind and serve on lettuce. Yield: 8 to 10 servings

Mandarin Salad with Poppy Seed Dressing

2	tablespoons wine vinegar
1	teaspoon Dijon mustard
½	teaspoon salt
⅛	teaspoon cayenne pepper
1	tablespoon honey
6	tablespoons vegetable oil
1½	teaspoons poppy seed
1	small head of lettuce, rinsed, drained and chilled
1	small red onion
1	11-ounce can mandarin oranges, drained

*C*ombine first 7 ingredients and shake well. Tear lettuce into bite-sized pieces. Peel and slice onion into very thin rings. Combine lettuce, onion and oranges. Toss with dressing in large salad bowl. Yield: 4 to 6 servings

For fruit salads, always choose fresh ripe fruit. Cut into equal-sized pieces. Always contrast colors and textures. Do not fix too far ahead or the fruit will become limp and soggy.

Getting a gelatin salad or other food out of a mold can be difficult if you try to run a knife around the inside of the mold or immerse it in hot water. Instead, put the mold on a piece of wood and nail a ¹/₈″ diameter nail through the bottom. Remove the nail and file off the rough edges on the outside of the mold. When filling the mold, cover the hole with heavy masking tape (not cellophane tape). Before unmolding, moisten the serving platter with cold water to help center the mold after it is placed on the plate. Remove the tape from the bottom of the mold and the food will plop out. If it should fail to work, cover the outside of the mold with a warm, damp towel for a few seconds.

Frozen Fruit Salad

1 16-ounce can apricots, chopped
1 16-ounce can pears, chopped
1 bottle maraschino cherries, halved
1 16-ounce can crushed pineapple
1 small can mandarin oranges
2 bananas, sliced
2 eggs, beaten
4 tablespoons vinegar
4 tablespoons sugar
1 small jar marshmallow creme
1 cup chopped pecans
1 6-ounce carton whipped topping

Drain fruits; set aside. Combine eggs, vinegar and sugar in heavy saucepan. Cook until thickened, stirring constantly. Remove from heat. Cool. Add marshmallow creme, pecans and whipped topping. Add fruit and mix well. Pour into individual molds. Freeze for 24 hours. Yield: 9 to 12 servings

Cranberry Raspberry Salad

1   3-ounce package raspberry-flavored gelatin
1   3-ounce package lemon-flavored gelatin
1½ cups boiling water
1   10-ounce package frozen raspberries
1   16-ounce can jellied cranberry sauce
1   7-ounce bottle lemon-lime carbonated beverage

Dissolve gelatin in boiling water. Stir in frozen berries, breaking up large pieces. Break up cranberry sauce with fork. Stir into mixture. Chill until partially set. Carefully pour in soda, stirring gently. Pour into 6-cup ring mold. Chill 5 to 6 hours or overnight. Unmold onto crisp greens. May be garnished with a poached sliced apple. Yield: 8 to 10 servings

Festive Fruit Compote

1½ cups pitted prunes
³/₄ cup orange juice
¹/₃ cup water
2   tablespoons honey
3   tablespoons orange-flavored liqueur
2   teaspoons grated fresh ginger
1   teaspoon grated orange rind
3   grapefruit
2   oranges
    Mint sprigs

In small saucepan combine prunes, orange juice and water. Bring just to boiling. Remove from heat. Gently stir in honey, then the liqueur, ginger and orange rind. Cool, then cover and chill up to 2 days. Several hours before serving, peel and section grapefruits and oranges. Combine citrus fruits with prune mixture. Cover and chill. Garnish with mint. If you wish, serve fruit mixture in grapefruit shell halves with membranes removed. Yield: 6 servings

Note: If fresh ginger is unavailable, substitute 1 teaspoon ground ginger, stirring it into prunes, orange juice and water before bringing to boil.

Shimmering Blueberry Salad

2   envelopes unflavored gelatin
¹/₃ cup sugar
1½ cups boiling water
2   cups rosé wine
2   cups fresh blueberries
1   12-ounce can mandarin oranges, drained

In medium bowl, mix unflavored gelatin with sugar. Add boiling water and stir until gelatin is completely dissolved. Stir in wine. Chill, stirring occasionally, until mixture is consistency of unbeaten egg whites. Fold in blueberries and oranges. Turn into a 5½-cup mold or bowl; chill until firm. Yield: about 10 servings

Southern Potato Salad

4 cups diced cooked potatoes
2 hard-boiled eggs, chopped
1/2 cup chopped celery
1/4 cup chopped pickle
2/3 cup mayonnaise
1 tablespoon vinegar
1 tablespoon instant minced onion
2 teaspoons mixed herbs
1/4 teaspoon white pepper
1 teaspoon dry mustard
1/4 teaspoon crushed fennel seed

Combine potatoes, eggs, celery, and pickle in large bowl. Blend remaining ingredients and gently stir into potato mixture. Chill. Yield: 6 servings

Gazpacho Salad

6 large tomatoes
6 green onions
3 ribs celery
4 cucumbers
2 green peppers
1/2 cup olive oil
1 cup red wine vinegar
1/4 teaspoon freshly ground pepper
1/4 teaspoon salt
1 clove garlic
1/4 teaspoon chopped mint
1/4 teaspoon oregano
Crisp lettuce cups

Chop first five ingredients into bite-sized pieces. Toss and set aside. Combine next 7 ingredients and pour over vegetables. Cover tightly and refrigerate overnight. Remove the garlic before serving. Drain vegetables, reserving dressing to moisten; fill lettuce cups. Yield: 8 servings

Oriental Pea Salad

1 10-ounce package frozen green peas
1 small can water chestnuts, drained and sliced
1 cup shredded carrots
3 ribs celery, sliced
3 green onions, sliced
2 tablespoons salad oil
2 tablespoons wine vinegar
1 tablespoon soy sauce
1 teaspoon sugar
1 teaspoon paprika
2 teaspoons dry mustard
1/2 teaspoon salt
1 small clove garlic, crushed

Place frozen peas in a strainer and run hot water over to thaw. Drain. Combine peas with water chestnuts, shredded carrots, celery and green onions. Combine salad oil, vinegar, soy sauce, sugar, paprika, dry mustard, salt and garlic. Pour over vegetables. Chill at least 1 hour before serving. Yield: 8 servings

Rice Salad

1 6-ounce box chicken-flavored rice
1 6-ounce jar marinated artichoke bottoms
2 to 3 tablespoons minced green onions
12 ripe olives, drained and sliced
1/4 cup mayonnaise
1/2 to 1 teaspoon curry powder
Salt and pepper to taste

Cook rice according to directions on box. Drain and chop artichokes, reserving liquid, add onion, olives and artichokes to rice. Combine mayonnaise with curry powder; add to rice mixture. Slowly add artichoke liquid until salad is desired consistency. Season with salt and pepper. Serve at once or refrigerate and serve chilled. Yield: 8 servings

Salad spinners are excellent for washing and drying greens without bruising them.

*To easily shred cabbage
by hand, pull off
individual leaves, stack,
and slice with a sharp
knife. Keep crisp in
cold water, drain and
pat dry before using.*

Chilled Lima Bean Mold

3 cups cooked baby lima beans, drained
1 cup diced celery
1/4 cup minced parsley
1/4 cup chives
2 teaspoons dill seed
1/2 cup mayonnaise
1/2 cup sour cream
1 teaspoon lemon juice
   Salt, pepper and paprika to taste

*C*ombine lima beans, celery, parsley, chives and
dill seed. Make dressing by combining mayonnaise, sour cream and lemon juice. Carefully fold
in lima bean mixture. Add salt and pepper. Sprinkle with paprika. Chill. May be prepared the night
before serving. Yield: 6 to 8 servings

Layered Party Salad

10 ounces fresh spinach
    Salt and pepper to taste
6 hard-boiled eggs, finely chopped
1/2 pound boiled ham, cut in julienne strips
1 small head iceberg lettuce, shredded
1 10-ounce package frozen tiny peas, thawed
   and patted dry
1 red onion, thinly sliced and separated into
   rings
1 cup sour cream
1 pint mayonnaise
1/2 pound Gruyére cheese, cut in julienne
    strips
1/2 pound bacon, crisply cooked and crumbled

*T*rim and discard tough spinach stems, rinse
leaves well, pat dry, and break into bite-sized
pieces. Arrange spinach in bottom of salad bowl.
Sprinkle with salt and pepper. Add the eggs, ham
and lettuce in layers. Sprinkle with salt and pepper; scatter peas over all. Arrange onion rings on
top. Combine sour cream and mayonnaise until
well blended; spread over salad. Scatter cheese

strips over salad, cover the bowl tightly, and refrigerate overnight. Before serving, sprinkle with
bacon. Do not toss. Yield: 10 servings

Spinach Salad with Sweet and Sour Dressing

1 pound fresh spinach
2/3 cup Bibb lettuce
1 small can water chestnuts, drained and
   sliced
3/4 cup bacon, cooked and crumbled
1/2 cup vegetable oil
1/4 cup sugar
1/4 cup chili sauce
2 tablespoons red wine vinegar
1/2 teaspoon Worcestershire sauce
1 small onion, chopped
1/2 teaspoon dry mustard
1/2 teaspoon salt
1/4 teaspoon cayenne pepper
1 hard-boiled egg, grated

*T*oss first 4 ingredients for salad. Combine remaining ingredients, except egg. Add to salad just
before serving. Sprinkle salad with grated egg.
Yield: 8 servings

Hearts of Palm Salad

1 can hearts of palm
   Spinach leaves, trimmed, washed, and
   patted dry
6 tablespoons vegetable oil
3 tablespoons fresh lemon juice
1/2 teaspoon salt
1/2 teaspoon sugar
1/4 teaspoon paprika
1/2 teaspoon aromatic bitters
1 tablespoon finely minced celery
2 tablespoons finely minced pimiento-stuffed
   green olives
2 tablespoons finely minced scallions (with
   tops)
   Pimiento for garnish

*A*rrange hearts of palm, sliced lengthwise, on spinach leaves. Combine the remaining ingredients except the garnish and pour over the salad. Top with remaining pimiento. Yield: 4 servings

Chicken Salad Supreme

$^3/_4$ cup mayonnaise
$^1/_4$ cup light cream
$^1/_4$ teaspoon curry powder
2   cups cooked and seasoned chicken, sliced
$^1/_2$ cup seedless grapes
$^1/_2$ cup celery, sliced
$^1/_4$ cup capers
1   cup toasted almonds, slivered
    Lemon wedge
    Lettuce leaves
    Parsley

*C*ombine mayonnaise, cream and curry powder. Combine chicken, grapes, celery, capers and $^3/_4$ cup almonds; add mayonnaise mixture. Squeeze lemon juice over salad. Mix; chill for several hours. Serve on lettuce leaves; garnish with remaining almonds and parsley. Yield: 4 servings

Turkey Salad

3   cups diced turkey
1   cup diced celery
1   tablespoon fresh lemon juice
$^1/_2$ teaspoon ground thyme
$1^1/_2$ teaspoons salt
$^1/_8$ teaspoon garlic powder
$^1/_8$ teaspoon ground black pepper
$^1/_3$ cup mayonnaise

*C*ombine all ingredients and mix well. This is excellent served in the center of a Cranberry Raspberry salad. Yield: 6 to 8 servings

Tuna Salad

14 ounces white tuna, rinsed and drained
$^1/_4$ teaspoon lemon juice
6   hard-boiled eggs, chopped
16 pimiento-stuffed olives, chopped
8   green onions, minced
2   apples, chopped
1   cup chopped pecans
1   rib celery, chopped
$^1/_4$ teaspoon sugar
    Salt, pepper and paprika to taste
$1^1/_2$ to 2 cups mayonnaise

*S*prinkle tuna with lemon juice and blend with remaining ingredients to desired consistency. Season to taste. Yield: 8 to 10 servings

Festive Fruit Compote, page 102; Vermont Maple Swirl, page 132

Salmon Salad

6   cups diced cooked potatoes
1½ cups minced celery
1   cup diced cucumber
½   cup sliced green onion
1   1-pound can salmon, drained and flaked
1   tablespoon chopped fresh basil
1½ cups mayonnaise
½   cup sour cream
¼   teaspoon pepper
1   teaspoon salt
2   tablespoons lemon juice or vinegar
      Parsley and tomato "roses"
      Mayonnaise

Combine potatoes, celery, cucumber, onions, salmon and basil. Combine mayonnaise, sour cream, pepper, salt, and lemon juice. Stir into potato-salmon mixture. Pack into a 10-cup mold and chill. When ready to serve, unmold onto cold serving platter and garnish with parsley clusters and tomato "roses". Serve with mayonnaise. Yield: 8 to 10 servings

Note: For how to make a tomato "rose", see page 134.

Seafood Salad in Artichokes

⅓   cup vegetable oil
2   tablespoons vinegar
½   teaspoon salt
⅛   teaspoon pepper
1   pound cooked shrimp, crabmeat, lobster or combination
4   hard-cooked eggs, coarsely chopped
1   cup diced celery
½   cup each: diced radishes and chopped onion
¼   cup finely chopped parsley
6   large California artichokes, cooked and chilled
2   medium tomatoes, cut into sixths
      Parsley sprigs
      Lemon Mayonnaise

Blend oil, vinegar, salt and pepper in large bowl. Add seafood, eggs, celery, radishes, onion and parsley; toss gently. Cover and chill several hours. At serving time, prepare artichokes for stuffing by gently pushing leaves outward; remove fuzzy centers. Fill artichokes with seafood salad, garnish each with tomato wedges and a parsley sprig. Serve with Lemon Mayonnaise. Yield: 6 main-dish servings

Lemon Mayonnaise

Blend ⅔ cup mayonnaise, 1 teaspoon lemon juice and 1 to 2 teaspoons prepared mustard in small bowl. Turn into small serving dish and garnish with a slice of lemon. Use as dressing for salad and as dip for artichoke leaves. Yield: ⅔ cup

Curried Shrimp Salad

¼   cup chopped onions
1   tablespoon vinegar
2   tablespoons vegetable oil
½   teaspoon curry powder
1½ cups cooked rice
1   cup diced celery
¼   cup diced green pepper
2½ cups cooked shrimp
¾   cup mayonnaise
      Salad greens

Combine onion, vinegar, oil and curry powder in a bowl. Stir in rice. Chill at least 2 hours to blend flavors. Just before serving add celery, green pepper, and shrimp. Add mayonnaise and mix lightly. Serve on salad greens. Yield: 6 servings

Taco Salad

1 pound lean ground beef
1 cup chopped onion
1/2 green pepper, chopped
1 tablespoon chili powder
1/2 teaspoon cumin
　Salt and pepper to taste
1 head iceberg lettuce, shredded
2 medium tomatoes, chopped
8 ounces tortilla chips, coarsely crushed
1 small purple onion, chopped
1 avocado, sliced
8 ounces Cheddar cheese, grated

*B*rown beef with onion and pepper; drain. Season with chili powder, cumin, salt and pepper. Keep warm. Mix remaining ingredients except cheese. Add meat mixture; cover with cheese. Set aside until cheese melts slightly. Toss and serve immediately. Yield: 6 to 8 servings

Southern Green Salad

　Chopped endive
　Lettuce and parsley
　Chopped celery
　Green pepper rings
1 small onion, chopped
2 small tomatoes, chopped
1/4 cup vinegar
1/2 cup catsup
1/3 cup mayonnaise
1/2 teaspoon steak sauce
2 tablespoons pickle relish
　Dash dry mustard
2 hard-boiled eggs, chopped

*T*oss together endive, lettuce, parsley, celery, and green pepper. Soak onion and tomatoes in vinegar a few minutes. Add catsup, mayonnaise, steak sauce, relish, and mustard; mix well. Spoon dressing over salad greens and garnish with eggs. Yield: 6 to 8 servings

Avocado Salad Dressing

2 ripe avocados
　Juice of 1 lemon
1 tablespoon mayonnaise
1 teaspoon grated onion
　Salt and pepper to taste
3/4 cup vegetable oil
1/4 cup white wine vinegar

*M*ash avocados until smooth. Add the lemon juice, mayonnaise, onion, and salt and pepper to taste. Mix thoroughly. In a separate bowl, blend oil with white wine vinegar. Stir into the avocado mixture. Serve over peeled and sliced tomatoes or toss with a green or seafood salad. Yield: Approximately 1 1/2 cups

French Dijon Salad Dressing

4 teaspoons Dijon mustard
4 teaspoons red wine vinegar
1 egg yolk
1/2 teaspoon Worcestershire sauce
　Hot sauce
1/2 cup olive oil
　Salt and pepper to taste
4 teaspoons whipping cream
　Lemon juice, optional

*P*lace the mustard, vinegar, egg yolk, Worcestershire sauce, and a dash of hot sauce in a salad bowl. Use a wire whisk and start beating the mixture rapidly. Gradually add the oil, beating constantly. The mixture should be like a thin mayonnaise. Add salt and pepper to taste, then add cream. If you wish a thinner dressing, beat in a little water. If desired, add a little fresh lemon juice to taste. Yield: Approximately 1 1/4 cups

Salad dressings are even more flavorful when made with fresh herbs. If you only have dried herbs on hand, remember to use only half as much of the specified amount of fresh herbs.

Sour Cream Dressing

¹/₂ small onion
4   heaping tablespoons sour cream
6   tablespoons vegetable oil
1   tablespoon vinegar
1¹/₂ tablespoons milk
1¹/₂ tablespoons sugar
     Salt and pepper to taste

*G*rate or mince onion; add sour cream, oil, vinegar and milk. Stir until smooth and creamy. Mix in the sugar, salt and pepper. Chill for 30 minutes before serving. Best served over Boston or Bibb lettuce, plain, or with tomato. Yield: 1 cup

Seafood Salad in Artichokes, page 106.

Poppy Seed Dressing

1¹/₂ cups sugar
2   teaspoons dry mustard
2   teaspoons salt
²/₃ cup vinegar
1¹/₂ teaspoons onion juice
2   cups vegetable oil
3   tablespoons poppy seed

*C*ombine sugar, mustard, salt and vinegar. Add onion juice and blend thoroughly. Add oil slowly, beating constantly until thick. Add poppy seed and continue beating. Store in refrigerator. Yield: 3¹/₂ cups

Roquefort Dressing

¹/₃ cup Roquefort or Blue cheese
¹/₂ teaspoon Beau Monde seasoning
¹/₄ teaspoon salt
¹/₈ teaspoon garlic powder
¹/₄ teaspoon prepared mustard
¹/₂ cup mayonnaise
¹/₂ cup light cream

*B*lend cheese with seasonings. Add mayonnaise alternately with cream. Whip until smooth. Yield: 1¹/₃ cups

Louis Dressing

2   cups mayonnaise
¹/₂ cup heavy cream, whipped
¹/₂ cup chili sauce
¹/₄ cup chopped green onions
     Salt and pepper to taste
1   tablespoon lemon juice

*C*ombine all ingredients in a jar and shake well to mix thoroughly. Set aside for at least 1 hour to allow the flavors to blend. Can be stored in the refrigerator for several days. Yield: 3¹/₂ cups

Soups

Carrot Vichyssoise

3 cups chicken stock
2 cups peeled, diced boiling potatoes
1¼ cups sliced carrots
1 leek, sliced
1 cup light cream
1 teaspoon salt
¼ teaspoon white pepper
¼ teaspoon nutmeg
  Shredded raw carrot for garnish

*P*lace stock, potatoes, carrots and leek in a saucepan; bring to a boil and simmer until vegetables are tender, about 25 minutes. In food processor or blender, purée mixture, a small portion at a time. Pour into a bowl and add cream and seasonings. Chill. Serve cold. Garnish with shredded carrot. Yield: 4 servings

Chilled Cucumber Yogurt Soup

3 to 4 cucumbers
4 cups chicken stock
2 tablespoons minced green onion
½ cup chopped celery
½ teaspoon dried dill weed
½ teaspoon dried mint leaves
1 teaspoon grated lemon rind
2 cups plain yogurt
  Minced parsley

*P*eel cucumbers. Cut into halves and remove seeds. Dice enough to measure 3 cups. Bring chicken stock to a boil, add cucumbers, green onion, celery, dill weed and mint. Simmer for 10 minutes. Cool, then puree in blender or food processor until smooth. Stir in lemon rind and yogurt. Chill for several hours. Sprinkle each serving with fresh minced parsley. Yield: 6 servings

Cold Pea Soup with Mint

1 10-ounce package frozen small green peas
1 medium onion, thinly sliced
1 cup water
1 tablespoon minced fresh mint
3 cups chicken stock
2 tablespoons all-purpose flour
½ cup heavy cream
  Salt and freshly ground pepper to taste
  Sour cream
  Mint sprigs

*C*ook green peas and onion in 1 cup water until tender. Add mint and purée in a blender or food processor until smooth. Set aside. In a saucepan, blend ½ cup of chicken stock with the flour until smooth. Add rest of stock and cook, stirring until thickened. Add puréed peas and bring to a boil. Add cream, salt and pepper. Chill thoroughly. Garnish soup with a dollop of sour cream and a sprig of mint before serving. Yield: 4 servings

Garnishes for soups are easy and attractive. Just before serving, top soup with chopped herbs or parsley, grated cheese, sour cream, croutons, or a sprinkling of paprika.

Sweet Potato and Bourbon Soup

3   tablespoons butter
4   medium sweet potatoes, peeled and sliced
6   cups chicken stock
¼ to ⅓ cup bourbon
½   teaspoon salt
    Freshly ground black pepper

*H*eat the butter in a large skillet or heavy saucepan. Add a layer of sweet potatoes and brown on both sides. Repeat the layering and browning until all potatoes are browned. Add 5 cups of chicken stock. Cook, covered, until potatoes are tender. When tender remove potatoes and mash to a chunky texture. Blend in remaining cup of chicken stock and stir until soup becomes a medium thick consistency. Add bourbon and bring to a boil. Season with salt and pepper. Yield: 4 to 6 servings

Cold Tomato Soup

12 large fresh tomatoes, peeled and seeded
3   medium onions, chopped
⅓   cup chopped celery
2   teaspoons salt
1   teaspoon pepper
1   teaspoon sugar
½   teaspoon dried basil
6   tablespoons butter
1   pint sour cream
    Fresh basil or dill for garnish

*S*auté tomatoes, onion, celery, salt, pepper, sugar and dried basil in butter until soft, about 30 minutes. Pour into blender or food processor and purée. Chill before serving. When ready to serve stir in sour cream. Garnish with fresh basil or dill. Yield: 10 to 12 servings

Chicken and Avocado Soup

6   cups chicken broth
1   whole chicken breast, skin on
2   onions, sliced
½   teaspoon oregano
1   bay leaf
½   teaspoon salt
¼   teaspoon freshly ground black pepper
1   ripe avocado

*P*lace chicken broth, chicken breast, onion, and seasonings in a large saucepan. Bring to a boil; reduce heat. Cover and cook for 20 minutes. Remove the chicken breast and set aside to cool. Strain the stock into a saucepan and set aside. Discard onion. When chicken is cool, remove and discard the skin and cut chicken into small strips. Just before serving, stir the strips into the soup and heat. Peel the avocado; cut into slices and add to the soup. The slices will float on top. Yield: 6 servings

Cold Peach Soup

4   large ripe peaches
2   cups dry white wine
1   cup water
3   tablespoons sugar
¼   teaspoon cinnamon
⅛   teaspoon nutmeg
¼   teaspoon curry powder
3   cloves
    Sour cream for garnish
    Orange slices for garnish

*D*rop peaches in boiling water for 1 minute. Peel and halve. Purée in blender or food processor. Pour purée into saucepan; add wine, water, sugar and spices. Bring to a boil and simmer 10 minutes, stirring occasionally. Remove cloves and chill 3 to 4 hours before serving. Serve with a dollop of sour cream and an orange slice. Yield: 4 to 5 servings

Artichoke Cream Soup

1 14-ounce can artichoke hearts
2 tablespoons chopped onion
4 tablespoons butter
2 tablespoons all-purpose flour
1/2 cup cold milk
2 to 3 cups chicken consommé
3 egg yolks
1/2 cup heavy cream
1/4 teaspoon nutmeg
1 teaspoon lemon juice
   Salt to taste

*D*rain and chop artichoke hearts, reserving liquid. Set aside. In a 3-quart saucepan, sauté onion in butter until transparent. Blend in flour and milk, stirring constantly. Add reserved artichoke liquid and consommé. Bring to a boil. Remove one cup of hot liquid. Combine egg yolks and cream, stir into cup of hot liquid. Return mixture to saucepan, stirring well. Add chopped artichoke hearts, nutmeg, lemon juice and salt. Yield: 6 to 8 servings

Cream of Wild Rice Soup

1 4.4-ounce package long grain and wild
   rice mix
1 1/2 tablespoons butter
1 cup chopped onion
1 1/2 tablespoons all-purpose flour
1 teaspoon salt
   Black pepper to taste
3 10 3/4-ounce cans chicken broth
1 pint light cream
1/4 cup dry white wine
   Sour cream or parsley to garnish

*P*repare rice mix according to package directions. Melt butter in a Dutch oven; add onion and sauté, stirring until tender, about 8 minutes. Stir in flour, salt and pepper until smooth. Add cooked rice, chicken broth, light cream and wine. Heat, stirring just until mixture reaches the boiling point. Remove from heat. Ladle about 1 1/2 cups into blender and process until smooth. Pour into large bowl. Repeat until all soup is blended. Return to Dutch oven and heat, stirring occasionally until heated through. Garnish with sour cream and serve. Yield: 2 1/2 quarts

Cream of Corn Soup

2 strips bacon, finely chopped
2 tablespoons chopped onion
2 cups fresh or frozen corn
2 tablespoons butter
2 tablespoons all-purpose flour
2 cups milk
1 teaspoon salt
1/2 teaspoon pepper
2 cups light cream

*F*ry bacon until crisp; add onion and sauté until soft. Process corn in a food chopper or processor. Add to onion and bacon. Cook until mixture begins to brown. Add butter, then flour. Cook slowly for 3 minutes. Add milk, salt and pepper; cook until thickened. Add cream and heat, stirring until smooth. Serve with corn muffins or crackers. Yield: 6 servings

To make croutons, cube bread and toast or sauté in butter or oil until golden brown.

If the soup is too salty, add a small peeled raw potato and simmer over low heat for 10 to 15 minutes. Remove and discard potato.

Oyster Soup

¹/₄ **pound butter**
1 **cup finely chopped celery**
1 **cup finely chopped green onions and tops**
1 **clove garlic, pressed**
1 **tablespoon all-purpose flour**
6 **cups liquid, oyster liquor plus clam juice and/or white wine**
2 **dozen oysters, drained, liquor reserved**
2 **bay leaves**
   Salt, black pepper, cayenne pepper and hot sauce to taste
   Minced parsley

Melt butter in heavy skillet and sauté vegetables and garlic until tender. Blend in flour and cook 5 minutes, stirring over low heat. Add liquids slowly; stir constantly. Add oysters and seasonings; simmer 20 minutes. Remove bay leaves and sprinkle with parsley. Yield: 1¹/₂ quarts

Cheese Soup

4 **tablespoons butter**
¹/₄ **cup finely chopped onion**
¹/₂ **cup finely chopped green pepper**
¹/₂ **cup finely chopped carrots**
5 **tablespoons all-purpose flour**
3 **10³/₄-ounce cans chicken broth**
³/₄ **pound sharp Cheddar cheese, grated**
2 **cups milk**
¹/₄ **teaspoon salt**
¹/₈ **teaspoon pepper**
   Parsley

In a large saucepan, sauté onion, green pepper, and carrots in butter for 10 minutes, stirring occasionally. Remove from heat. Blend in flour and cook one minute, stirring constantly. Transfer to a double boiler. Stir in broth, and heat to the boiling point. Add 1 cup of cheese at a time and stir until melted. After all cheese is melted, add milk, salt and pepper. Heat until boiling. Add parsley to garnish before serving. Yield: 6 to 8 servings

Peanut Butter Soup

1 **tablespoon butter or margarine**
2 **tablespoons all-purpose flour**
1 **small onion, finely chopped**
1 **quart hot chicken stock or milk**
¹/₄ **cup finely chopped celery**
1 **cup peanut butter**

Melt butter in the top part of a double boiler placed over direct heat. Add flour and brown lightly, stirring constantly. Add onion, cooking until soft. Add chicken stock, celery, and peanut butter and place double boiler over boiling water. Stir until smooth and heated through. Yield: 4 servings

Hot Potato Soup

¹/₄ **cup bacon drippings**
1 **cup chopped onion**
¹/₂ **cup chopped celery**
1 **cup sliced mushrooms**
¹/₃ **cup all-purpose flour**
3 **cups chicken broth**
3 **cups milk**
4 **cups diced, peeled new potatoes**
1¹/₂ **cups grated Swiss cheese**
2 **teaspoons salt**
¹/₈ **teaspoon pepper**
   Chopped chives

Heat bacon drippings in a large saucepan. Add onion, celery, and mushrooms; sauté until soft. Blend in flour over medium heat until golden brown. Stir in chicken broth and milk. Add potatoes, stirring until soup comes to a slight boil and thickens slightly. Simmer 10 to 15 minutes or until potatoes are tender. Stir in cheese, a small amount at a time until melted and smooth. Season with salt and pepper. Garnish with chives. Yield: 6 to 8 servings

Summer Blueberry Soup

1   envelope unflavored gelatin
¼   cup sugar
2½   cups water
2   tablespoons lemon juice
2   cups fresh blueberries
½   teaspoon ground cinnamon
1   cup light cream

*I*n medium saucepan, mix unflavored gelatin with sugar; blend in 1 cup water. Let stand 1 minute. Stir over low heat until gelatin is completely dissolved, about 5 minutes. Stir in remaining water, lemon juice, blueberries and cinnamon. Simmer, stirring frequently and crushing berries slightly, 15 minutes or until blueberries are tender. Cool completely; stir in cream. Chill 4 hours or overnight. Garnish, if desired, with lemon slices and additional blueberries. Yield: about 1 quart soup

Note: Soup will thicken upon chilling.

Ham and Bean Soup

1   pound dried great northern beans
6   cups of water
1½   pounds ham or ham hock, cooked and
     cubed
2   teaspoons salt
3   cloves garlic, minced
2   cups water
4   medium potatoes, peeled and quartered
3   carrots, cut into ½-inch slices
1   medium onion, finely chopped

*S*ort and wash beans; place in a Dutch oven. Cover with water 2 inches above beans. Soak overnight. Drain. Combine beans, six cups of water, ham, salt and garlic in a large Dutch oven. Bring to a boil. Cover, reduce heat and simmer 1½ hours. Add 2 cups water and vegetables to beans. Cover and simmer about 30 minutes or until vegetables are tender. Yield: About 1 gallon

Ranchero Chowder

2   slices bacon, chopped
1   medium onion, chopped
½   pound ground beef
1   can tomatoes
3   teaspoons instant beef bouillon
3   cups water
½   teaspoon salt
⅛   teaspoon pepper
1   teaspoon chili powder
1   can red kidney beans
3   cups hot, cooked rice

*C*ook bacon until crisp in heavy Dutch oven. Drain and reserve. Sauté onion in drippings. Add beef; cook until evenly browned. Stir in tomatoes, beef broth, water, salt, pepper, chili powder and kidney beans. Cover; simmer for 15 minutes. Place ½ cup rice into serving bowls. Ladle in chowder. Sprinkle with bacon. Yield: 6 servings

Summer Blueberry Soup, this page; Berry Blueberry Jam, page 167; Shimmering Blueberry Salad, page 102; Blueberry Ice Cream, page 156; Fresh Blueberry Cheesecake, page 75.

Chili-Potato Soup

7 large potatoes, peeled and diced
1 10³/₄-ounce can cream of mushroom soup
1 large onion, diced
2 13-ounce cans chili beans
¹/₂ teaspoon garlic salt
¹/₂ teaspoon pepper
¹/₂ cup Cheddar cheese

Cook potatoes until tender. Drain potatoes, leaving 2 cups of liquid in the pot. Add soup, onion, and chili beans; simmer about 30 minutes. Add cheese and serve. Yield: 6 to 8 servings

Creamy Corn Chowder

¹/₄ pound bacon, diced
1 cup chopped onion
1 green pepper, chopped
2 tablespoons bacon drippings
2¹/₂ cups chicken broth
2 cups diced potatoes
1 15-ounce can creamed corn
1 teaspoon paprika
¹/₂ teaspoon pepper
¹/₄ teaspoon sage
Salt to taste
2 cups milk or light cream

Brown bacon in Dutch oven and drain, reserving 2 tablespoons of drippings. Sauté onion and green pepper in drippings until soft. Add chicken broth and diced potatoes. Bring to a boil and simmer until potatoes are cooked. Add creamed corn, seasonings, bacon and milk. Heat through. Yield: 6 servings

Split Pea Soup

1 ham bone
1 small package split peas
2 large onions, chopped
1 clove garlic
1 bay leaf
Salt and pepper
Grated celery and carrots, optional

Cover ham bone with water; cook for 1 hour. Remove bone and cool. Add split peas to ham liquid. Add onion, garlic, bay leaf, salt, and pepper to taste. Simmer for 1 hour. Add water to thin. Add ham pieces from the bone. Add grated celery and carrots if desired. Store in refrigerator. Yield: 1 quart

Vegetables

Scalloped Artichokes

1 small onion, finely chopped
1/2 medium green pepper, finely chopped
2 tablespoons vegetable oil
8 cooked artichoke hearts, fresh, frozen or canned
1 egg
3/4 cup sour cream
1/4 teaspoon salt
Dash of hot sauce
1/8 teaspoon each: thyme and sweet basil or rosemary
10 Ritz crackers

Cook onion and green pepper in oil until soft, but not browned. Turn into 1 1/2 to 2-quart casserole and add artichoke hearts. Beat egg slightly and combine with sour cream. Add seasonings. Pour over artichoke hearts. Crush crackers and sprinkle on top. Bake in a 350 degree oven for 20 to 25 minutes. Yield: 4 servings

Artichoke and Asparagus Casserole

2 15-ounce cans artichoke hearts
2 14-ounce cans giant green asparagus
2 small cans water chestnuts
1/2 pound butter
1 cup all-purpose flour
2 cups New York State sharp grated cheese
1/2 cup sherry
1/8 teaspoon nutmeg
1/8 teaspoon each: salt, pepper, and Ac'cent
Toasted almonds

Drain vegetables and reserve liquids. Melt butter. Brown flour slowly in butter. Add liquid from vegetables. If needed, add a little water. Sauce should be thick. Add grated cheese and sherry. Add seasonings. Layer vegetables in casserole dish. Top with sauce. Bake in a 350 degree oven for 20 to 25 minutes or until bubbly and hot throughout. Sprinkle with almonds before serving. Yield: 6 servings

Asparagus with Orange and Cashews

2 1/2 pounds fresh asparagus
4 tablespoons butter
3 tablespoons all-purpose flour
2 cups light cream
Salt
White pepper
1 orange, sectioned
1/2 cup chopped cashews
Grated orange rind for garnish

Steam the asparagus until tender. Make a cream sauce by melting the butter in a small saucepan and stirring in the flour. Stir over low heat for two minutes, then gradually add the cream and cook until thick, stirring constantly. Season to taste with salt and white pepper. Cut the orange sections into large pieces. Add to the cream sauce. Arrange the asparagus on a heated serving platter and salt lightly. Pour the sauce over the asparagus and sprinkle with the cashew nuts and grated orange rind. Serve immediately. Yield: 8 servings

In menu planning, it is wise to remember that asparagus and artichokes do not go well with wine. The combination produces a metallic taste.

Store unwashed fresh vegetables in refrigerator until ready to use. Wash before cooking. Most fresh vegetables should be used within a day or two.

French Green Bean Casserole

3 packages frozen French-cut green beans
1 large onion, chopped
1/2 cup sliced mushrooms
1/2 cup butter
2 10³/4-ounce cans cream of mushroom soup
1/2 pound grated sharp Cheddar cheese
    Juice of 1 lemon
1/4 cup sherry
1 can French-fried onions

*C*ook green beans according to directions on package. Cook onion and mushrooms in butter until transparent. Combine with green beans and remaining ingredients, except onion rings. Blend well. Pour into greased casserole and top with French-fried onions. Bake in a 350 degree oven for 10 to 12 minutes. Yield: 10 to 12 servings

Green Beans in Sour Cream

1¹/2 pounds green beans
    Salt
3 tablespoons butter
1/2 pound mushrooms, sliced
1 cup sour cream
    Salt to taste
1/2 teaspoon white pepper

*S*tring the beans and break into bite-sized pieces. When ready to cook beans, fill a large, heavy saucepan with water and bring to a boil. Add beans to the boiling water with a little salt and cook until tender, about 1¹/2 hours. Prepare sauce while beans are cooking. Melt the butter in a heavy skillet and sauté the mushrooms, tossing them with a wooden spoon over high heat. Reduce heat and stir in the sour cream, salt and white pepper. Do not boil. Drain the beans well, return to the pan and add the sour cream and mushroom sauce. Heat through, but do not boil. Serve immediately. Yield: 4 to 6 servings

Wonderful Baked Beans

2 1-pound cans pork and beans
1 1-pound, 3-ounce can chili without beans
1/3 cup dark brown sugar
1 tablespoon Worcestershire sauce
2 cloves garlic, chopped
3 medium onions, chopped
1/2 green pepper, chopped
1/2 rib celery, chopped
1 tablespoon prepared mustard
1 tablespoon chili powder
1/2 of a 14¹/2-ounce bottle of catsup
6 strips of bacon

*C*ombine all ingredients, topping with bacon slices. Bake in a 275 to 300 degree oven for 2¹/2 hours. Yield: 6 servings

Beets with Orange Sauce

 1/4 cup firmly packed brown sugar
 1 1/2 tablespoons all-purpose flour
 1 tablespoon butter
 3/4 cup orange juice
   Sliced orange rind to taste
   Salt and pepper to taste
 2 1/2 cups sliced, cooked beets

*C*ombine brown sugar and flour. In a saucepan, melt butter and add brown sugar-flour mixture, stirring until well blended. Add orange juice and orange rind, stirring and cooking until thickened. Add seasonings and well-drained beets. Heat thoroughly. Yield: 4 to 5 servings

Broccoli Casserole

 2 10-ounce packages frozen chopped broccoli, cooked and drained
 1 roll garlic cheese
 1 10 3/4-ounce can cream of potato soup
 1 small can water chestnuts, sliced
 1/2 cup cracker crumbs
 2 tablespoons butter

*C*ombine cooked broccoli, garlic cheese and potato soup over medium heat until cheese and soup are melted. Add sliced water chestnuts. Pour into a greased 3-quart casserole. Top with cracker crumbs and butter. Bake in a 350 degree oven until heated through. Yield: 6 servings

Carrot Soufflé

 3 cups grated carrots
 1 cup grated cheese
 3 eggs
 1/3 cup sugar
 1 cup milk
 1 teaspoon salt
 1/2 teaspoon nutmeg

*M*ix all ingredients. Place in buttered 2-quart dish and bake in a 350 degree oven for 1 hour. Yield: 6 to 8 servings

Cauliflower Au Gratin

 1 medium head cauliflower
   Salt and pepper, to taste
 1 cup sour cream
 1 cup grated sharp Cheddar cheese
 1 teaspoon sesame seed

*S*eparate cauliflower into flowerets. Cook in small amount of boiling salted water 10 to 12 minutes or until tender. Drain. Place half of cauliflower into a 2-quart casserole. Season with salt and pepper. Spread half the sour cream, half the cheese, and half the sesame seed over cauliflower. Repeat layers. Bake in a 350 degree oven for 15 minutes or until cheese melts. Yield: 4 servings

Corn Pudding

 2 1/2 cups cream-style corn
 5 tablespoons all-purpose flour
 1 tablespoon sugar
 1 teaspoon salt
 1/4 cup butter, melted
 3/4 cup milk
 3 eggs, beaten

*M*ix corn and flour with a wire whisk. Add remaining ingredients and mix well. Bake in a greased 2-quart casserole dish in a 325 degree oven for 1 hour. Yield: 4 to 6 servings

Never husk corn until ready to use. The sugar begins conversion to starch as soon as it is picked and the husks will slow the process somewhat. It is best to cook corn as soon as possible after picking. If you grow your own corn, have the water boiling when you go out to pick the corn.

Never wash mushrooms. Wipe them with a dampened paper towel and set aside to dry. Trim ends, but do not peel.

The best method of reheating vegetables is in the top of a double boiler or in a microwave.

Eggplant and Tomato Parmesan

1   medium eggplant, peeled and cut crosswise
    into 1/2 inch slices
2   tablespoons lemon juice
1/4 cup vegetable oil
1   large tomato or two medium tomatoes,
    sliced
1/2 cup freshly grated Parmesan cheese

Brush each slice of eggplant on both sides with lemon juice to prevent it from turning brown. Place slices on baking sheet, brush with oil, and bake 5 to 8 minutes. Turn slices and repeat the process. Top eggplant with a slice of tomato, and sprinkle generously with cheese. Yield: 4 servings

Mushrooms Baked In Cream

1/2   cup softened butter
1 1/2 teaspoons chopped parsley
1 1/2 teaspoons chopped chives
1 1/2 teaspoons chopped green onions
1/8   teaspoon nutmeg
      Salt to taste
16   to 20 large mushroom caps
3/4   cup heavy cream
      Paprika

Combine butter, parsley, chives, onion, nutmeg, and salt; mix well. Wipe mushroom caps with a dampened paper towel. Stuff caps with seasoned butter and place in a shallow baking dish. Pour heavy cream over mushrooms and sprinkle lightly with paprika. Bake in a 450 degree over for 10 minutes. Yield: 4 to 6 servings

Fried Okra

1   pound okra
1/2 cup corn meal
1/2 teaspoon salt
1/4 teaspoon pepper
2 to 3 tablespoons vegetable oil

Slice okra into 1/2-inch rounds. In a paper bag, combine corn meal, salt and pepper; add okra and shake. Fry in hot oil until okra is browned. Drain on paper towels. Season with salt and pepper before serving. Yield: 4 servings

Twice Baked Potatoes

6   baking potatoes
6   tablespoons butter
1 1/2 teaspoons salt
1/2   teaspoon hot sauce
2   eggs, beaten
1   cup grated sharp Cheddar cheese

Bake potatoes in a 450 degree oven for 1 hour. Immediately cut slice from top of each and scoop out potato. Mash well. Add butter, salt, hot sauce, eggs and half the cheese. Beat until smooth and creamy. Spoon into shells and top with remaining cheese. Bake in a 425 degree oven for 20 minutes. Yield: 6 servings

Sweet Potatoes and Apricots

1   1-pound can whole sweet potatoes, halved
      lengthwise
1 1/4 cups brown sugar
1 1/2 tablespoons cornstarch
1/4   teaspoon salt
1/4   teaspoon cinnamon
1   teaspoon grated orange rind
1   1-pound can apricot halves
2   tablespoons butter
1/2   cup pecan halves

Place sweet potatoes in greased 2-quart baking dish. In saucepan, combine brown sugar, cornstarch, salt, cinnamon and orange rind. Drain apricots, reserving syrup. Stir 1 cup apricot syrup into cornstarch mixture. Cook and stir over medium heat until boiling. Boil 2 minutes. Add apricots, butter and pecan halves. Pour over potatoes. Bake in a 375 degree oven for 25 minutes. Yield: 6 servings

Party Squash

- 1 pound yellow squash, sliced
- 1 teaspoon sugar
- 1/2 cup mayonnaise
- 1/2 cup minced onion
- 1/4 cup finely chopped green pepper
- 1/2 cup chopped pecans
- 1 egg, slightly beaten
- 1/2 cup grated Cheddar cheese
  Salt and pepper to taste
  Bread or cracker crumbs
- 1/4 cup butter

Cook squash, drain and mash. Add remaining ingredients except crumbs and butter. Pour into a 2-quart casserole. Top with crumbs; dot with butter. Bake in a 350 degree oven for 35 to 40 minutes. Yield: 6 servings

Candied Yams and Cranberries

- 6 medium yams
- 1/2 cup butter or margarine
- 3/4 cup packed light brown sugar
- 2 cups fresh cranberries
- 1 teaspoon salt
- 1/8 teaspoon pepper

Place yams in a large saucepan with water to cover. Bring to a boil; cover and reduce heat. Simmer 20 to 30 minutes or until yams are fork tender. In a medium saucepan, melt butter. Add sugar, cranberries, salt and pepper. Cook, stirring constantly, over medium heat until cranberries pop and sugar is dissolved. Remove from heat. Peel cooked yams and cut into quarters; place in a 2-quart casserole. Pour cranberry sauce over yams. Cover and bake in a 350 degree oven for 30 minutes. Yield: 6 servings

Yam Pudding

- 6 large yams
- 1/4 cup butter or margarine
- 1/4 cup and 1/3 cup packed brown sugar, divided
- 2 teaspoons grated fresh lemon rind
- 1 tablespoon fresh lemon juice
- 1/2 teaspoon salt
- 1/2 cup slivered almonds

To prepare yams, wash and bake in a 350 degree oven for 40 minutes, or cook in boiling water to cover for 20 minutes or until soft. Cool, peel and place in large bowl. Mash until smooth. Add butter, 1/4 cup brown sugar, lemon rind, lemon juice and salt; mix well. Turn into a greased 1 1/2-quart baking dish. Sprinkle remaining 1/3 cup brown sugar and almonds in ring on top of yams. Bake in a 350 degree oven for 40 to 50 minutes. Yield: 6 to 8 servings

Vegetable Casserole

- 1 small cauliflower
- 8 small new potatoes
- 8 small carrots
- 10 small onions
- 1 cup canned or frozen green peas
- 4 tablespoons butter
- 4 tablespoons all-purpose flour
- 2 cups milk
- 1 teaspoon salt
- 1 teaspoon pepper
- 1/2 pound sharp cheese, grated

Separate cauliflower into flowerets. Add next 3 ingredients; cook in water until tender. Drain well. Add drained peas. Place in a 2-quart casserole. Melt butter in a saucepan, add flour, cook until smooth, add milk, salt and pepper and cook until thickened, stirring constantly. Add cheese, stir until melted. Pour over vegetables. Bake uncovered in a 375 degree oven for 15 minutes. Yield: 6 to 8 servings

To make a bouquet garni, tie the following securely in cheesecloth: 4 peppercorns, 2 bay leaves, parsley sprigs, fresh thyme and basil, and 4 celery tops.

Wash and dry yams. Place in shallow pan and bake in a 350-degree oven for 40 minutes or until soft. Cut tops from yams, carefully scoop out centers and mash in large bowl. Add butter, milk, egg, salt and oregano; beat until smooth. Add sausage, mix well. Pile into yam shells and bake in a 400 degree oven for 15 minutes. Yield: 6 servings

Wild Rice Casserole

1½ cups boiling water
1   4.4-ounce package Wild Rice and Herbs
1   10¾-ounce can chicken with rice soup
1   small can mushrooms and liquid
½   cup water
1   teaspoon salt
1   bay leaf
¼   teaspoon each: celery salt, garlic powder, pepper, onion salt and paprika
3   tablespoons chopped onion
3   tablespoons vegetable oil
¾   pound lean ground beef

Pour boiling water over rice and herbs. Simmer, covered, 15 minutes. Place rice in a 2-quart casserole. Add soup, mushrooms and liquid, water and seasonings. Mix and set aside. Sauté onion in oil until transparent and add to casserole. Brown meat in frying pan and add to rice mixture. Chill. When ready to bake, cover and bake in a 325 degree oven for 30 to 45 minutes. Yield: 4 to 6 servings

Candied Yams and Cranberries, page 119; Sausage Stuffed Yams, this page; Yam Pudding, page 119.

Sausage Stuffed Yams

6   medium yams
2   tablespoons butter or margarine
2   tablespoons milk
1   egg
1   teaspoon salt
¼   teaspoon dried leaf oregano
4   ounces link sausages, cooked and sliced

Cheese, Eggs and Pasta

Savory Herbed Baked Brie

1 wheel Brie, about 8 inches in diameter
¼ cup chopped fresh parsley
1 small clove garlic, minced
1 teaspoon dried rosemary, crushed
1 teaspoon dried leaf thyme, crushed
1 teaspoon dried leaf marjoram, crushed
8 very thin slices hard salami, finely chopped
1 sheet Pepperidge Farm Frozen Puff Pastry
1 egg, lightly beaten

Place Brie in freezer 30 minutes. Combine parsley, garlic, rosemary, thyme and marjoram. Remove Brie from freezer, slice in half lengthwise with a long, thin-bladed knife. Spread herb mixture over cut side of Brie. Sprinkle with chopped salami. Press Brie halves back together. Thaw pastry sheet 20 minutes at room temperature; gently unfold. Roll pastry out on floured surface to a 12x18-inch rectangle. Place Brie in center of pastry. Bring edges of pastry over top; cut off excess. Seal corners by brushing with egg and pressing pastry together. To bake, place Brie seam-side down on lightly greased jelly-roll pan. Brush with egg and make 4 holes in top. Bake in a 350 degree oven for 30 minutes or until pastry is golden and puffed. (Cheese inside should be runny.) Set aside at least 15 minutes before serving. Serve with crackers. Yield: 15 to 20 servings

Note: A design may be made for the top from the excess pastry dough. It should be brushed with egg and pressed to seal.

Savory Herbed Baked Brie, this page.

Save time by grating cheese all at once. Store in jars or plastic containers for later use. Grating is a good way to use up older hardened cheeses.

Cheese Soufflé

2 tablespoons butter
2 tablespoons all-purpose flour
2 cups milk
1/4 teaspoon salt
1/8 teaspoon dry mustard
1/8 teaspoon baking soda
1/8 teaspoon paprika
1 cup grated Cheddar cheese
2 eggs yolks
2 egg whites, stiffly beaten

Melt butter; stir in flour. When smooth and bubbly, add milk and dry ingredients. Stir until thickened. Add cheese, stirring until melted. Beat yolks in a bowl and pour hot mixture over yolks, stirring constantly. When blended, gently fold in stiffly beaten egg whites. Pour into a buttered soufflé dish, place dish in pan of hot water. Bake in a 325 degree oven for 45 to 50 minutes or until firm. Yield: 2 to 3 servings

Welsh Rabbit

2 tablespoons butter
1 pound sharp Cheddar cheese, cubed
1/2 teaspoon salt
1 teaspoon dry mustard
   Cayenne pepper
1 cup beer
2 egg yolks, beaten
1 teaspoon Worcestershire sauce
4 slices toast

Melt butter in saucepan. Add cheese, salt, mustard, and cayenne pepper to taste. Stir until cheese melts. Continue stirring while gradually adding the beer. Remove from heat; add egg yolks while stirring vigorously. Cook mixture until thickened and smooth. Do not overcook. Stir in Worcestershire sauce and serve hot over toast. Yield: 4 servings

Cheese Garlic Grits Casserole

1 cups grits
5 cups boiling water
1 teaspoon salt
1 roll garlic cheese
1/2 cup butter
3 egg whites, stiffly beaten

Stir grits into boiling water; add salt. Simmer for 25 minutes. Remove from heat and add cheese and butter. Cover and set aside until cool. Fold in egg whites. Place in greased casserole and bake in a 350 degree oven for 25 minutes. Yield: 8 servings

Quiche Lorraine

1 cup grated Swiss cheese
1 cup grated Mozzarella cheese
6 slices bacon, cooked and crumbled
1 frozen 9-inch pie crust
3/4 cup light cream
2 eggs beaten
1/4 teaspoon salt
1/8 teaspoon pepper
1 1/2 teaspoons basil
1 tablespoon Parmesan cheese

Place cheeses and bacon in crust. In a mixing bowl, blend cream, eggs, salt, pepper and basil. Pour over cheese and bacon. Sprinkle with Parmesan cheese. Bake in a 375 degree oven for 30 to 35 minutes. Yield 4 to 6 servings

Oven Omelet

8 eggs
1 cup milk
1 3-ounce package thin-sliced corned beef
1/4 cup mushrooms
1 cup grated Cheddar cheese
1 tablespoon onion

CHEES

drain
rooms
and or
juice,
salt, ar
simme
other
cup Pa
a grea
with I
sauce
rella
Mozz
chees
oven
ing N
utes
servi

Sal

12
1
1
2
2
¹/₄
¹/₄
1
¹/₂

6

dra
kee
ricc
salt
squ
hea
cas
30
wh
ove
Di

*B*eat eggs and milk. Chop beef and mushrooms and add to egg mixture. Pour into an 8x8x2-inch baking dish. Bake, uncovered, in a 350 degree oven for 40 to 45 minutes or until golden brown. Yield: 4 servings

Huevos Rancheros

1   medium onion, chopped
1   clove garlic, crushed
2   tablespoons butter
¹/₂ pound ground chuck
1   green pepper, chopped
1   fresh tomato, chopped
¹/₄ teaspoon chili powder
¹/₄ teaspoon oregano
1   tablespoon all-purpose flour
¹/₂ cup beef broth
    Salt
    Pepper
6   eggs
    Butter
    Tortillas

*S*auté onion and garlic in butter. Stir in ground chuck and pepper. Add tomato, chili powder, and oregano. Stir in flour and add beef broth. Salt and pepper to taste. Simmer 10 minutes. Fry eggs in butter. Place on large plate and spoon beef mixture over eggs. Serve with tortillas. Yield: 6 servings

Eggs Sardou

2 tablespoons butter
2 tablespoons all-purpose flour
1 cup milk
1 package frozen chopped spinach, cooked
  and drained
6 large artichokes
6 eggs
  Hollandaise Sauce

*M*elt butter, add flour and cook 2 minutes. Add milk; heat, stirring constantly until thickened. Add spinach; set aside and keep warm. Boil artichokes in salted water; drain and remove choke and leaves. Fill with creamed spinach. Poach eggs and place on top of spinach. Cover with Hollandaise Sauce. Yield: 4 to 6 servings

Hollandaise Sauce

¹/₂ cup butter
3   egg yolks
    Juice of 1 lemon
    Salt, pepper

*I*n double boiler, gradually add melted butter to egg yolks and lemon juice, stirring constantly until thick. Season to taste. Yield: 4 to 6 servings

Eggs Benedict

*S*auté six slices Canadian bacon in butter. Place each on a toasted English muffin half and top each with poached egg. Cover with Hollandaise Sauce. Yield: 3 to 6 servings

Daisy's Brunch Casserole

9 hard-boiled eggs
1 pound bacon, cooked
3 cups White Sauce (Recipe is on page 124)
2 cups grated Cheddar cheese
  Bread crumbs

*G*rate eggs and crumble bacon. Alternate layers of White Sauce, eggs, bacon and cheese in a 2-quart casserole. Add extra white sauce and bread crumbs on top. Bake for 30 minutes in a 350 degree oven. Yield: 6 to 8 servings

Eggs will keep for 4 to 5 weeks in the refrigerator. For cooking, use eggs at room temperature, unless separating the whites and yolks.

Curdled Hollandaise sauce can be rescued by processing in a blender or it can be reconstituted by beating a fresh egg yolk and gradually adding the sauce.

Chees
be ad
so the
tough
string

If you have leftover pasta, rinse it in cool water, drain, and store up to 3 days in refrigerator in a covered container.

Dill Sauce

1½ tablespoons butter
1½ tablespoons all-purpose flour
¼ teaspoon salt
⅛ teaspoon pepper
1½ cups milk
3 tablespoons finely snipped fresh dill or 2 teaspoons dried dill weed
1 tablespoon lemon juice

Pasta yields 4 servings per pound as a main dish and 6 to 8 servings per pound if used as a side dish.

*M*elt butter in small saucepan over medium heat; stir in flour, salt and pepper. Remove saucepan from heat; gradually add milk, stirring until mixture is smooth. Return to medium heat; bring to boiling, stirring constantly. Reduce heat, simmer 1 minute. Remove from heat; stir in dill and lemon juice.

To k
mac
over,
of c
pot.

Scallops and Shells

1 8-ounce package large shells, uncooked
2 tablespoons butter
½ pound sliced fresh mushrooms
½ cup chopped green onion
1 clove garlic, minced
1 pound fresh bay or sea scallops

¼ cup dry white wine or sherry
½ teaspoon salt
¼ teaspoon thyme
⅛ teaspoon pepper
3 tablespoons butter
2 tablespoons all-purpose flour
1 cup light cream
¼ cup chopped fresh parsley
2 tablespoons chopped pimiento

*C*ook shells according to package directions; drain. Cover to keep hot. Meanwhile, melt 2 tablespoons butter in skillet; add mushrooms, onion and garlic. Sauté until tender. Add scallops, wine, salt, thyme and pepper; cover and simmer 5 minutes, or until scallops are tender. Melt 3 tablespoons butter in medium saucepan over low heat; add flour stirring until smooth. Cook 1 minute, stirring constantly. Gradually add light cream; cook over medium heat, stirring until mixture is thickened and bubbly. Drain scallops, reserving liquid. Return scallops to skillet; add chopped parsley and pimiento. Cover to keep hot. Add scallop liquid to cream mixture stirring to blend well; heat to boiling. Pour cream sauce over shells; toss. Arrange on serving platter. Top with scallop-mushroom mixture. Yield: 4 to 6 servings

O
St
pe
Sh

Breads

Country Biscuits

2   cups all-purpose flour
3   teaspoons baking powder
1   teaspoon salt
¹/₄ cup shortening
³/₄ cup milk

*S*ift the dry ingredients together and cut in the shortening. Add milk, stirring until all flour is moistened. Turn out on lightly floured board. Knead dough about 20 seconds, then roll to about ¹/₂-inch thickness. Cut biscuits and place on ungreased baking sheet. Bake in a 450 degree oven for 8 to 10 minutes. Yield: 12 two-inch biscuits

Beaten Biscuits

4 cups all-purpose flour
1 teaspoon salt
1 teaspoon baking powder
1 tablespoon sugar
4 tablespoons chilled shortening
  Equal parts chilled milk and ice water
  Melted butter

*S*ift together the dry ingredients. Cut in shortening until mixture is the consistency of corn meal. Add the milk and water to make a stiff dough. Beat the dough until very thin. When dough is thin, roll to ¹/₂-inch thickness. Cut with biscuit cutter. Spread tops with melted butter. Pierce top of biscuits with a fork. Bake in a 325 degree oven for 30 minutes. Yield: 24 biscuits

Cornbread

1   egg
1   cup buttermilk
1   cup corn meal
1   teaspoon salt
¹/₂ teaspoon baking soda
2   teaspoons baking powder
2   tablespoons bacon drippings

*B*eat egg into buttermilk. Combine dry ingredients with liquid. Add drippings to mixture. Bake in a 450 degree oven for 15 to 20 minutes. Yield: 6 servings

Hush Puppies

1   egg
2   cups buttermilk
2   cups corn meal
1¹/₂ teaspoons baking soda
1   tablespoon salt
2   tablespoons all-purpose flour
1   tablespoon baking powder
6   tablespoons chopped onion
    Vegetable oil or shortening

*B*eat egg and buttermilk together. Combine dry ingredients and add chopped onion. Blend in egg-buttermilk mixture. Heat oil to 370 degrees. Drop hush puppies into hot oil. Fry until evenly browned. Drain on paper towels and serve at once. Yield: 12 to 14 hush puppies

To freshen stale bread, wrap tightly in foil and place in a 450° oven for 5 to 10 minutes.

Biscuits are done when golden brown and springy to the touch. Muffins are ready when brown and they begin to pull away from the sides of the pan.

Make muffins and biscuits, bag them, and freeze. Take a few directly from the freezer and arrange in a circle on a paper towel in the microwave. Heat a few seconds, turning upside down once. They will seem just like they are freshly baked if served at once.

Cracklin' Bread

2   cups yellow corn meal
1/2 teaspoon baking soda
1/2 teaspoon baking powder
1/2 teaspoon salt
1   cup cracklings
1 1/2 cups buttermilk
    Butter

Sift the corn meal, soda, baking powder and salt into a mixing bowl. Stir in the cracklings and mix well. Add the buttermilk and beat well with a wooden spoon. Place a large pat of butter in a 9-inch skillet and place in 400 degree oven. When the skillet is piping hot, spread the butter evenly over the bottom. Spread the stiff batter into the skillet and bake in a 400 degree oven for about 25 minutes, or until the bread is lightly browned. The bread will be crumbly and chewy. Slice into wedges and serve immediately. Yield: 6 to 8 servings

Spoon Bread

1 cup corn meal
1 teaspoon salt
1 tablespoon shortening
2 cups boiling water
1 cup milk
2 eggs, separated and beaten

Combine corn meal, salt and shortening; add boiling water, stir until cool. Add milk and beaten egg yolks. Mix well. Fold in stiffly beaten egg whites. Pour into greased baking dish. Bake in a 400 degree oven for 30 to 40 minutes. Yield: 6 to 8 servings

Gingerbread

1   cup shortening
1   cup sugar
2   eggs
1   cup dark corn syrup
2 1/2 cups all-purpose flour
1   teaspoon salt
2   teaspoons powdered ginger
1   teaspoon baking soda
1   cup boiling water
    Whipped cream for topping

Cream the shortening and sugar together. Add the eggs, one at a time, and beat well with a wooden spoon. Add the corn syrup and mix thoroughly. Sift the flour, salt and powdered ginger together and fold into the creamed mixture. Dissolve the soda in the boiling water; add and beat well. Pour into a greased 13x9x2-inch square pan or a large loaf pan and bake in a 350 degree oven for 30 to 40 minutes. Yield: 12 to 16 servings

Sally Lunn Bread

1 cake yeast
1 tablespoon sugar
2 cups lukewarm milk
4 tablespoons melted butter
4 cups sifted all-purpose flour
2 eggs, beaten
1 teaspoon salt

In a mixing bowl, dissolve the yeast and sugar in milk. Stir in the melted butter. Sift the flour into the mixture and stir well. Add the beaten eggs. Add salt and beat with a wooden spoon until smooth. Pour the batter into a greased 8x12-inch baking pan, cover with a cloth and set aside to rise in a warm place until doubled in size, about 1 1/2 hours. Bake the bread in a 375 degree oven for about 30 minutes, or until lightly browned. Yield: 10 to 12 servings

Zucchini Bread

3   eggs
1   cup vegetable oil
1¹/₂ cups sugar
2   cups grated, well-drained zucchini
2   teaspoons vanilla
2   cups sifted all-purpose flour
¹/₄ teaspoon baking powder
2   teaspoons baking soda
3   teaspoons ground cinnamon
1   teaspoon salt
1   cup raisins
1   cup chopped walnuts or pecans

Beat eggs lightly in large bowl. Stir in oil, sugar, zucchini, and vanilla. Sift flour, baking powder, soda, cinnamon and salt onto waxed paper. Stir into egg mixture until well-blended; stir in raisins and nuts. Spoon batter into two well-greased 8x5x3-inch loaf pans. Bake in a 375 degree oven for 1 hour or until the center springs back when lightly pressed with finger. Cool on wire rack 10 minutes. Remove from pans and cool completely. Yield: 2 loaves

Variation: Omit raisins and add one-half teaspoon grated lemon peel.

Banana Nut Bread

4   ripe bananas
2   large eggs
1   teaspoon lemon juice
¹/₂ cup bran cereal
    Grated rind of one lemon
1¹/₂ cups sifted all-purpose flour
³/₄ cup sugar
1   teaspoon salt
1   teaspoon baking soda
¹/₄ cup wheat germ
¹/₂ cup chopped walnuts or pecans

Beat bananas, eggs, lemon juice, and rind in large mixing bowl. Add bran and set aside to soften for 5 minutes. Mix well. Sift flour, sugar, salt and soda. Add to banana mixture and beat well. Stir in wheat germ and nuts. Grease and flour one 9x5-inch loaf pan or three 5³/₄x3¹/₄-inch miniature loaf pans. Pour batter into pan and bake in a 350 degree oven for 50 to 60 minutes or until a wooden skewer inserted in center comes out clean. May be frozen. Yield: 1 large loaf or 3 miniature loaves

Cranberry Nut Muffins

1¹/₃ cups all-purpose flour
1   teaspoon baking soda
1¹/₄ teaspoons baking powder
¹/₂ teaspoon salt
³/₄ cup sugar
    Rind of 1 medium orange
6   tablespoons butter
1   teaspoon lemon juice
2   eggs
¹/₄ cup orange juice
1¹/₄ cups fresh cranberries
1   cup chopped pecans

Mix together flour, soda, baking powder, and salt; set aside. Place sugar and orange rind in bowl of food processor and process with metal blade until finely chopped. Add butter and lemon juice and with off/on motion combine until well mixed. Add eggs and orange juice and process until smooth. Add cranberries and nuts; combine with off/on motion. Add flour mixture and combine just until flour disappears. Spoon into well-greased tiny muffin tins. Bake in preheated 350 degree oven until golden brown, approximately 20 minutes. Remove from tins to cool. May be frozen. Serve with cream cheese and marmalade spread. Muffins may be made just as successfully with electric mixer, using grated orange rind and finely chopped cranberries. Yield: 36 tiny muffins

For quick garlic bread, slash a loaf of French bread diagonally. Spread butter mixed with crushed garlic in the cuts or spread with butter and sprinkle with garlic salt. Wrap in foil, bake in a hot oven for 10 minutes.

When baking muffins, never fill cups more than ²/₃ full to allow room for rising during baking.

Williamsburg Sweet Potato Muffins

¹/₂   cup butter or margarine
1¹/₄ cups sugar
2   eggs
1¹/₄ cups mashed sweet potatoes or canned yams
1¹/₂ cups all-purpose flour
2   teaspoons baking powder
¹/₄   teaspoon salt
1   teaspoon cinnamon
¹/₄   teaspoon nutmeg
1   cup milk
¹/₄   cup chopped pecans
¹/₂   cup chopped raisins
      Sugar

*C*ream butter and ¹/₂ cup sugar; add eggs, mixing well. Blend in potatoes. Sift remaining sugar, dry ingredients and spices, and add alternately with the milk. Do not overmix. Fold in pecans and raisins. Fill greased muffin tins ²/₃ full. Sprinkle with extra sugar. Bake in a 400 degree oven for 25 minutes. Turn out of tins and cool. Yield: 2 dozen

Blueberry Buttermilk Muffins, this page.

Pumpkin Bread for Finger Sandwiches

1   cup water
1   cup vegetable oil
1   can pumpkin pie filling or 1 can plain pumpkin
3   cups sugar
3   eggs
1   cup chopped black walnuts
1¹/₂ cups chopped dates
3¹/₂ cups self-rising flour
1   teaspoon each: nutmeg, ginger, and salt
¹/₂   teaspoon cloves
¹/₂   teaspoon baking powder
2   teaspoons cinnamon
2   teaspoons baking soda

*M*ix first seven ingredients in large mixing bowl. Sift together remaining ingredients. Combine with pumpkin mixture. Pour into 2 large greased 9x5-inch loaf pans. Bake in a 325 degree oven for 1¹/₂ hours. Yield: 2 loaves

Blueberry Buttermilk Muffins

2¹/₂ cups all-purpose flour
2¹/₂ teaspoons baking powder
1   cup sugar
¹/₄   teaspoon salt
1   cup buttermilk
2   eggs, beaten
¹/₂   cup butter
1¹/₂ cups fresh or dry-pack frozen blueberries, rinsed and drained

*S*ift dry ingredients together into large bowl. Make a well, add buttermilk, eggs and butter which has been melted and browned slightly. Mix well. Fold in blueberries. Pour into well-greased muffin tins. Bake for 20 minutes in a 400 degree oven. Serve warm with butter. Yield: 24 small muffins

Blueberry Muffins

1³/₄ cups self-rising flour
³/₄ cup sugar
1   egg
³/₄ cup milk
¹/₃ cup vegetable oil
³/₄ cup blueberries

Combine all ingredients, except blueberries; mix well. Stir in blueberries. Drop from tablespoon to fill greased muffin cups ²/₃ full. Bake in a 400 degree oven for 25 minutes. Yield: 1 dozen

Sour Cream Pecan Coffee Cake

1   cup butter or margarine
2   cups sugar
2   eggs
2   cups all-purpose flour, sifted
1   teaspoon baking powder
¹/₄ teaspoon salt
¹/₂ teaspoon vanilla
1   cup sour cream
3   tablespoons brown sugar
¹/₂ teaspoon cinnamon
¹/₂ cup chopped pecans
    Confectioners' sugar

Cream butter and sugar; add eggs and beat. Sift dry ingredients and add to creamed mixture, fold in vanilla and sour cream and mix gently. Combine brown sugar, cinnamon and pecans. Spoon half the pecan mixture into a greased and floured bundt or tube pan. Cover with half the batter. Spoon on remaining pecan mixture and cover with batter. Bake in a 350 degree oven for 55 to 60 minutes or until wooden skewer inserted in center comes out clean. Do not overbake. Set aside for 10 minutes. Run sharp knife around edge. Invert onto plate. Sprinkle with confectioners' sugar when cool. Hint: this cake keeps well several days when wrapped in plastic. Yield: 12 to 15 servings

Cream Cheese Coffee Cake

1   3-ounce package cream cheese, softened
4   tablespoons butter or margarine
2   cups packaged biscuit mix
¹/₃ cup milk
¹/₂ cup fruit preserves
1   cup confectioners' sugar, sifted
1 to 2 tablespoons milk
¹/₂ teaspoon vanilla

Cut cream cheese and butter into biscuit mix until crumbly. Blend in ¹/₃ cup milk. Turn onto floured surface; knead 8 to 10 strokes. Roll dough on waxed paper to form a 12x8-inch rectangle. Turn onto greased baking sheet; remove paper. Spread preserves down center of dough. Make 2¹/₂-inch cuts at 1-inch intervals on long sides. Fold strips over filling. Bake in a 425 degree oven for 12 to 15 minutes. Combine sugar, remaining milk, and vanilla. Drizzle on top. Very easy! Yield: 10 to 12 servings

Line baskets with napkins or linen serving towels to keep breads hot during serving.

Assorted breads; Lemon Tea Cookies, page 159.

When making rolled sandwiches, steam the bread in a colander over boiling water for a minute or two and it will roll easily without breaking.

Vermont Maple Swirl

$3^{1}/_{2}$ to 4 cups all-purpose flour, divided
$^{1}/_{4}$ cup sugar
1 package active dry yeast
$^{1}/_{2}$ teaspoon salt
$^{1}/_{2}$ cup milk
$^{1}/_{3}$ cup butter, softened
4 eggs
    Prune-Walnut Filling
    Maple Icing
    Halved pitted prunes and walnut halves

In large bowl of electric mixer combine $^{3}/_{4}$ cup of the flour, the sugar, yeast and salt; mix to blend thoroughly. In small saucepan combine milk and butter. Heat over low heat until very warm, 120 to 130 degrees. Butter need not melt completely. Beating at medium speed, gradually add milk mixture to yeast mixture. Beat 2 minutes, scraping bowl as needed. Add 3 of the eggs, then 1 more cup of the flour. Beat at high speed 2 minutes. Mix in enough additional flour to make a stiff dough, about $1^{1}/_{2}$ cups. Turn out onto floured board. Knead 8 to 10 minutes, working in as much of the remaining flour as needed to make a smooth, non-sticky dough. Place in greased bowl, turning to grease top. Cover with plastic wrap and towel. Set aside to rise in warm place until doubled in size, about $1^{1}/_{2}$ hours. Punch dough down. On lightly floured board, stretch and roll out dough into a rectangle 12x16 inches. Spread evenly with Prune-Walnut Filling to within $^{1}/_{2}$-inch of edges. Starting from long end, roll up jelly-roll style.

Moisten edge with water and pinch seam to seal completely. Tuck ends under and pinch to seal. Gently place diagonally, seam-side down, on greased baking sheet. Cover with towel and let rise in warm place until almost doubled, about 1 hour. Brush generously with remaining egg, beaten. Bake in middle of preheated 350 degree oven 25 to 35 minutes until evenly browned and loaf sounds hollow when tapped. Remove to rack to cool. Drizzle with Maple Icing and garnish with prune and walnut halves. To serve, cut into diagonal slices. Yield: 12 servings

Prune-Walnut Filling

Combine $1^{1}/_{2}$ cups (about 9 ounces) pitted prunes, $^{1}/_{2}$ cup water and $^{1}/_{2}$ teaspoon maple flavoring in container of electric blender. Blend until almost smooth, turning on and off and scraping sides of container as needed. Transfer to bowl; mix thoroughly with 1 cup chopped walnuts.

Maple Icing

In small bowl mix 1 cup confectioners' sugar, 1 to 2 tablespoons milk and $^{1}/_{4}$ teaspoon maple flavoring until smooth and consistency desired for drizzling.

Entreés

Lemon Barbecued Chicken

Meaty pieces of 2 skinned chickens, or breasts only
1 cup vegetable oil
½ cup fresh lemon juice
1 tablespoon salt
1 teaspoon paprika
2 teaspoons onion powder
2 teaspoons basil
½ teaspoon thyme
½ teaspoon garlic powder

*P*lace chicken in shallow pan. Mix remaining ingredients and pour over. Cover and refrigerate overnight. Bring to room temperature one hour before grilling. Grill 10 to 12 minutes per side, basting often. Yield: 6 servings

Creole Chicken

½ cup butter
1 broiler-fryer, cut in serving pieces
1 large onion, chopped
1 green pepper, chopped
1 cup chopped celery
2 16-ounce cans tomatoes
1 3-ounce can mushrooms
1 tablespoon Worcestershire sauce
1 tablespoon sugar
⅛ teaspoon hot sauce
1 tablespoon parsley flakes
1 teaspoon oregano
Salt and pepper to taste

*M*elt butter in large skillet. Sauté chicken pieces. Remove chicken and sauté onion, pepper, and celery. Add tomatoes, mushrooms, and seasonings. Place chicken in the sauce, cover tightly, and simmer 30 minutes or until done. Yield: 4 servings

Curried Orange Chicken

6 chicken breasts, boned
1 to 2 tablespoons curry powder
½ cup orange juice
¼ cup honey
2 tablespoons mustard
2 teaspoons cornstarch
2 tablespoons water
Salt to taste

*S*prinkle chicken breasts with curry powder and rub in well. Arrange chicken breasts in a flat baking dish. Combine orange juice, honey and mustard. Pour over chicken. Bake, uncovered, in a 375 degree oven for one hour, basting several times while cooking. Combine cornstarch and water, blending well. Drain pan juices, add to cornstarch mixture and cook over low heat until thickened. Add salt, if necessary. Pour over chicken when ready to serve. Yield: 4 to 6 servings

Making Garnishes

Tomato Rose
Immerse a small tomato in boiling water for one minute, then remove and cool. Working from the bottom, use a paring knife to peel off the skin in one long, thin spiral. Wind the skin loosely around a wooden skewer, folding back the edges as you wind to simulate petals. Slip out the skewer and refrigerate the rose.

Fruit Rose
Follow directions for tomato rose, but use an orange, lemon, or lime.

Carrot Curl
Shave lengthwise a strip of carrot with a vegetable parer. Curl the shaving around your finger and fasten with a toothpick. Refrigerate in ice water for one hour. Drain and remove the toothpick.

Celery Curl
Using a piece of celery stalk 1¹/₂-inches long, cut very thin slices ¹/₂-inch deep at each end, thus leaving ¹/₂ inch unsliced in the center. Refrigerate at least one hour in a covered container of ice water. Slices will curl. Drain before using.

Cucumber Lily
Cut a 1¹/₂-inch-thick slice of cucumber and scoop out the seeds.

Chicken with Apples

- 2 to 3 apples, sliced
- ¹/₄ cup raisins
- 2 tablespoons sugar
- ¹/₄ teaspoon cinnamon
- 1¹/₂ pounds chicken breasts
  Seasoned salt to taste
- ¹/₄ cup white wine
- 2 tablespoons sugar
  Juice and grated rind of ¹/₂ orange

*I*n buttered casserole, place apples, raisins, sugar and cinnamon. Season chicken breasts with seasoned salt and set aside to dry for 30 minutes. Place chicken on top of apples. Bake, uncovered, for one hour in a 325 degree oven. Meanwhile, combine remaining ingredients and simmer for 15 minutes. Glaze chicken. Bake 30 minutes longer. Yield: 6 servings

Chicken with Wild Rice

- 2 3-pound whole fryers
- 1 cup water
- 1 cup dry sherry
- 1¹/₂ teaspoons salt
- ¹/₂ teaspoon curry powder
- 1 medium onion, sliced
- ¹/₂ cup chopped celery
- 1 pound fresh mushrooms
- ¹/₄ cup butter or margarine
- 2 4.4-ounce packages long grain and wild rice with seasonings
- 1 cup sour cream
- 1 10³/₄-ounce can cream of mushroom soup

*P*lace chicken in a deep kettle; add water, sherry, salt, curry powder, onion and celery. Cover and bring to a boil; reduce heat and simmer for one hour. Remove from heat; strain broth. Refrigerate chicken and broth at once, without cooling. When chicken is chilled, remove meat from bones and cut meat into bite-sized pieces. Wipe mushrooms with dampened paper towel. Reserve 6 whole mushrooms; slice and sauté all mushrooms in butter for about 5 minutes, stirring constantly. Measure chicken broth; use as part of the liquid for cooking rice, following package directions for firm rice. Combine chicken, mushrooms and rice in a 3¹/₂ or 4-quart casserole dish. Blend in sour cream and mushroom soup. Arrange reserved mushroom caps in a circle over the top of the casserole. Cover; refrigerate overnight, if desired. To heat, bake, covered, in a 350 degree oven for 1 hour. The casserole may be completely prepared and frozen ahead of time. Yield: 8 to 10 servings

Chicken Tetrazzini

- ¹/₂ pound spaghetti
  Chicken broth
- 1 cup sliced mushrooms
- 6 tablespoons butter
- 3 tablespoons all-purpose flour
- 2 cups chicken broth
- 1 cup heavy cream
  Salt and pepper
- 3 cups cubed, cooked chicken
- ¹/₂ cup grated American, Parmesan, or Swiss cheese
- ¹/₃ cup toasted slivered almonds

*C*ook spaghetti in chicken broth until tender; drain and keep warm. Sauté mushrooms in 3 tablespoons of butter. Melt remaining 3 tablespoons butter, add flour, and slowly stir in 2 cups broth. Heat cream and add to sauce along with salt and pepper. Pour ¹/₂ the sauce over chicken. Add remaining sauce to the spaghetti and mushrooms. Place ¹/₂ the spaghetti in shallow baking dish, add layer of chicken, and sprinkle with ¹/₂ the cheese. Repeat. Top with almonds. Bake in 350 degree oven until lightly browned, about 12 to 15 minutes. Yield: 8 servings

Bourbon Chicken

8 chicken breasts, boned and halved
   Flour, salt, pepper, and paprika
1/2 cup butter
1 pound fresh mushrooms, sliced
2 ounces bourbon
2 10³/₄-ounce cans cream of chicken soup
3/4 teaspoon curry powder
   Parsley
   Slivered almonds

*D*ust chicken with flour, salt, pepper and paprika. Sauté in hot butter. Brown and place in casserole. In same butter, sauté mushrooms and add to chicken. Add bourbon to skillet, then stir in undiluted soup and curry powder. Stir to form a smooth thick sauce. Check seasonings. Pour over chicken and mushrooms. Sprinkle with parsley and almonds. Bake in a 350 degree oven for 1 hour. Yield: 8 servings

Chestnut Stuffing

1¹/₂ cups finely chopped onion
1¹/₂ cups finely chopped celery
5 tablespoons butter
8 cups dry bread cubes
1 cup chopped water chestnuts
1¹/₂ teaspoons salt
1/8 teaspoon pepper
1/2 teaspoon poultry seasoning
1/2 teaspoon sage
1/4 cup water
1 egg, well beaten

*C*ook onion and celery in butter until tender. Add mixture to bread cubes and place in a large pan. Add chestnuts and sprinkle with seasonings. Combine. Add water and egg. Toss together with forks. Stuff bird immediately and roast. Yield: Enough for a 12-pound bird

Cut the rim into deep points. With the tip of the knife carefully pull back the green skin of each point almost to the bottom of the slice. Place a sprig of parsley in the center.

Radish Rose
Cutting away from the pointed end, make five or six thin slices almost to the base of the radish. These will open out when refrigerated in ice water.

Roast Duckling with Apple Cornbread Stuffing, page 136; Apple Cranberry Cobbler, page 156.

Bacon Curl
Cook bacon until brown, but still limp. Roll around a fork, secure with a toothpick, and drain on a paper towel. As the bacon cools, it will set in a curl. Remove the toothpick.

Spring Onion Curl
Trim the green top of an onion to 3 inches. Slit tops down to the white part three or four times. They will curl up when placed in ice water.

Frosted Fruit, Leaf, or Flower
Dip small bunches of grapes, cherries with stems, mint leaves, or violet flowers in slightly beaten egg white, then in sugar. Chill.

Flavored Butter
Soften butter and mix with chopped parsley, finely grated lemon rind, or paprika. On squares of waxed paper, form the butter into decorative shapes. Refrigerate until firm.

Chocolate Leaves
Melt semi-sweet chocolate bits in a pan over hot water. Use gardenia, rose, violet, nasturtium, or lemon leaves from a florist. (Do NOT use English ivy, azalea, laurel, or poinsettia leaves as they are poisonous.) Wash the leaves in warm, soapy water,

Cornbread and Grits Dressing

1　cup chopped onion
1　cup chopped celery
1/4　cup fat or shortening
1　cup day-old or stale bread cubes
5　cups crumbled egg cornbread
1　cup coarse cracker crumbs
1 1/2　cups cooked grits
3 to 4 cups broth
1/4　cup melted fat or butter
3　eggs
　　Salt, pepper, and poultry seasoning to taste

*S*auté onion and celery in 1/4 cup fat. Combine all ingredients, using enough broth to make a thick custard-like consistency. Bake in a greased 9x12-inch pan in a 425 degree oven until brown and firm. This is a moist and very delicious dressing. Yield: 8 to 10 servings

Oyster and Celery Dressing

3/4　cup fat or shortening
2　tablespoons chopped onion
3　tablespoons chopped parsley
1 1/2　cups chopped celery
6　cups soft bread crumbs
1　pint oysters, chopped
　　Salt and pepper to taste

*M*elt fat. Add onion, parsley, and celery, and cook until tender. Add bread crumbs and heat through. Add oysters and seasonings and mix lightly but thoroughly. Yield: 8 cups stuffing—enough for a 10-pound bird

Turkey Dressing

1　cup diced celery
2　medium onions, diced
1/2　cup butter or margarine
21　cups cubed bread, measured after cubing

1　tablespoon salt
1/2　teaspoon pepper
1　tablespoon poultry seasoning
1　teaspoon sage
　　Cooked giblets, finely chopped, optional
1　cup liquid from cooked giblets
3　eggs, beaten

*S*lowly simmer celery and onions in butter until soft but not brown. Pour over bread cubes. Add seasonings, and giblets. Add giblet liquid and eggs, gently folding into dressing. Stuff into turkey. Yield: About 10 cups stuffing—enough for a 15 to 18-pound turkey

Roast Duckling with Apple Cornbread Stuffing

2 ducklings, about 5 pounds each
Apple Cornbread Stuffing

*W*ash ducklings inside and out; pat dry. Remove fat; set over low heat to melt. Cover giblets with cold water; bring to boil; simmer to make broth. Prepare stuffing. Just before roasting, stuff and truss ducklings; place on rack in large roasting pan. Do not add water; do not cover. Roast in a 350 degree oven for about 2 1/2 hours or until thoroughly cooked (25 to 30 minutes per pound). Yield: 8 servings

Apple Cornbread Stuffing

1/3　cup minced onion
3/4　cup melted fat, from ducklings or butter
6　cups crumbled cornbread
2　tablespoons minced parsley
1 1/2　cups finely diced unpeeled red apples
1　teaspoon powdered sage
1/8　teaspoon pepper
3/4　cup hot giblet stock
　　Salt to taste

Cook onion in fat until golden brown. Combine with remaining ingredients; mix thoroughly. Yield: enough stuffing for 2 five-pound ducklings

Duck in Raisin Sauce

2   ducks
     Salt
2   celery ribs and tops
1   apple, chopped
     Pepper
     Bacon
1   cup apple cider or juice
1½   cups rosé wine
1   cup raisins
3   tablespoons currant jelly
1   tablespoon all-purpose flour
2   tablespoons water

Wipe ducks; salt cavities. Place chopped celery and apple in cavities. Salt and pepper breasts and cover with bacon strips. Place in baking pan. Pour in cider, wine and raisins. Bake in a 375 degree oven for 1 hour. Stir jelly and flour blended with water into pan juices; heat and stir until gravy is smooth and thickened. Yield: 6 servings

Sherried Pork Roast

⅔   cup pitted prunes
¾   cup sherry
1   3-pound lean, boned pork loin roast
2   ounces crystallized ginger
¼   cup honey
2½   tablespoons soy sauce
¼   cup onion, grated
     Salt and pepper to taste
     Parsley sprigs, for garnish

Plump prunes in sherry 1 to 2 hours or overnight; drain, reserving sherry and prunes. Make a slit lengthwise about 2½ inches deep in boned side of pork roast; fill with drained prunes, dividing equally. Tie roast securely to enclose prunes. Chop 1 ounce of the ginger; combine with reserved sherry, honey, soy sauce, onion, salt and pepper; blend well. Marinate pork in sherry mixture 2 to 4 hours; drain and reserve marinade. Roast pork in a 350 degree oven, basting frequently with reserved marinade for 1½ to 2 hours, until meat thermometer registers 160 degrees. (Cover roast with foil as needed to prevent overbrowning). Slice remaining ginger. Garnish roast with ginger and parsley.

Sweet and Sour Pork

1½   pounds lean pork shoulder, cubed
2   tablespoons vegetable oil
¼   cup water
1   1-pound can pineapple chunks
¼   cup brown sugar
2   tablespoons cornstarch
¼   cup vinegar
1   tablespoon soy sauce
½   teaspoon salt
½   cup green pepper strips
¼   cup thinly sliced onions
     Rice or chow mein noodles

Brown pork in oil. Add water, cover, and simmer 1 hour. Drain pineapple, reserve juice. Combine juice, brown sugar, cornstarch, and pork and set aside for 10 minutes or more (may be put in refrigerator at this point and reheated before serving). Add vinegar, soy sauce, salt, green pepper, onion and pineapple chunks. Cook until hot, 3 to 4 minutes. Serve over rice or chow mein noodles. Yield: 3 to 4 servings

rinse, dry, and lightly coat with vegetable oil on the underside. Using a pastry brush, spread chocolate on oiled surface and refrigerate about 30 minutes until firm. Carefully peel chocolate from the leaves and store in a box, separating layers with waxed paper.

Chocolate Curls
Hold a bar of chocolate that has been chilled until firm on a chopping board and pull a vegetable peeler down the full length of the bar at a 30-degree angle. The chocolate will come off in curls. Use a toothpick to lift the curl.

Ribs with Apricot-Curry Glaze, this page.

Ribs with Apricot-Curry Glaze

  2 tablespoons vegetable oil
  1 cup chopped onion
  1 clove garlic, minced
  4 teaspoons curry powder
  1 cup apricot nectar
  3 tablespoons honey
  3 tablespoons cider vinegar
  $^1/_2$ teaspoon Tabasco sauce
  4 pounds pork spareribs, baby back ribs or beef ribs

*H*eat oil; sauté onion and garlic until golden. Stir in curry powder; cook 1 minute. Stir in apricot nectar, honey, vinegar, and Tabasco sauce. Simmer 10 minutes, stirring often to prevent sticking. Arrange ribs on grill in a single layer over low heat. Position grill rack as far from coals as possible. For pork ribs, grill 15 minutes per side. Brush with apricot glaze. Grill 45 minutes longer or until meat is cooked through; turn meat often brushing each time with glaze. For beef ribs, grill 5 minutes per side; continue ·basting and turning 35 minutes longer or until meat is cooked to desired degree of doneness. Yield: 4 servings

Savory Pork Pub Pie

  $1^1/_2$ cups all-purpose flour
  $1^1/_2$ teaspoons baking powder
  2 teaspoons crumbled sage
  $^1/_4$ teaspoon salt
  $^1/_2$ teaspoon pepper
  5 tablespoons cold butter or margarine, cubed
  3 tablespoons finely chopped parsley
  $^1/_4$ cup cold water
  3 slices bacon, cut in 1-inch pieces
  3 cups sliced onions
  2 pounds lean pork shoulder or loin, cut in 1-inch cubes
  $^1/_4$ cup *each:* all-purpose flour and vegetable oil
  1 cup (about 6 ounces) pitted prunes, halved
  $1^1/_4$ cups chicken bouillon or broth
  $1^1/_2$ teaspoons *each* salt and ground allspice
  2 tablespoons cider vinegar
  1 egg, beaten

*I*n large bowl, combine flour, baking powder, $^1/_2$ teaspoon sage, salt and $^1/_8$ teaspoon pepper; mix. With pastry blender work in butter until mixture resembles coarse meal. Add parsley and water;

When testing meat for doneness, insert thermometer before roasting in center of thickest part of meat. Be sure not to touch the bone. For rare roast beef, the internal temperature should register 120°. For medium rare, 140°. For medium, 145° to 150°. Well done should be 155° to 165°. Lamb should be roasted only until medium rare at 140° to 145°.

toss. Gather into a ball, wrap and chill at least 30 minutes. In large skillet cook bacon over medium heat, stirring occasionally, until crisp. Transfer with slotted spoon to shallow 2-quart baking dish. Add onions to skillet; cook and stir 5 minutes. Transfer to baking dish. Dredge pork in flour. Add 2 tablespoons of the oil to skillet; increase heat to high. Add half of the pork; toss until lightly browned; transfer to baking dish. Repeat with remaining pork. Add prunes and toss contents of baking dish. Reduce heat to medium; add bouillon, salt, allspice, remaining sage and pepper to skillet. Cook and stir about 5 minutes until mixture comes to boil and brown particles are loosened. Stir in vinegar; pour into baking dish. Roll out pastry to cover top of baking dish with 1-inch overhang. Lay pastry over baking dish and fold edge under. Crimp edges, pressing against rim. Brush generously with egg. Prick crust several times with fork. Place on baking sheet and bake in a 375 degree oven for 1 hour and 15 minutes. After about 1 hour lay a piece of foil over pie if top is deeply browned. Yield: 6 to 8 servings

Ham Loaf

1 pound lean ground pork
1 pound ground ham
2 eggs, beaten
$^{1}/_{2}$ cup bread crumbs
$^{1}/_{2}$ cup milk
  Salt
$^{1}/_{2}$ of a 10$^{3}/_{4}$-ounce can tomato soup

Mix all ingredients except soup and form into a loaf. Place in a greased pan and pour tomato soup on top. Bake in a 375 degree oven for 1$^{1}/_{2}$ hours. Yield: 6 servings

Country Ham

Boiling Country Ham. Cut off hock, clean whole ham thoroughly with a brush and rough cloth. Trim off any dark, dry edges and discolored fat.

Since the hams have a dry cure, soaking in water around 8 hours before cooking is often desirable. Use fresh water for cooking. Fill large roaster about $^{1}/_{2}$ full with water. Place ham on rack skin-side up. Start ham cooking at high heat, when water boils reduce heat to simmer and continue cooking until ham is tender. Cook approximately 30 minutes per pound or until meat thermometer registers 160 degrees. One tablespoon of brown sugar or molasses per quart of water may be added; $^{1}/_{4}$ cup vinegar or red wine may be added to the water if desired. Allow ham to cool in the juice 4 or 5 hours; this will bring the internal temperature to 170 degrees. Remove from broth and skin ham. Use your favorite glaze.

Baking Country Ham. Prepare as for boiling. Place ham, skin-side up, on a rack in an open pan. Start ham covered or in aluminum foil in a 375 degree oven for 1 hour. Reduce heat to 200 to 225 degrees and cook until the center of the ham registers 160 degrees on a meat thermometer. This will take about 45 to 50 minutes per pound for whole hams. Hams continue to cook after removal from oven. For well done meat, internal temperature should reach 170 degrees. Remove skin and allow ham to cool slightly. Either serve as is or glaze.

Note: Baked hams are much easier to slice when chilled. Cut slices thin and perpendicular to the bone.

To glaze baked or boiled ham: After ham is cooked remove skin with sharp knife, score, cover with glaze, stick cloves about every inch and bake at 350 to 400 degrees for about 30 minutes or until lightly browned. Glaze may be made of combinations of brown sugar and fruit juice, crushed pineapple or honey. Serve hot or cold.

Fried Country Ham. Skin should only be removed from the area where the slices will be taken. Cut ham slices ¼ to ⅜-inch thick. Do not trim any excess fat from the slices until after frying. Use heavy skillet that will distribute heat evenly. Fat edges should be scored to prevent curling. Place slices in skillet with fat edges toward the center. Do not cover; fry slowly at medium heat. Turn frequently. Do not over-fry or cook on high heat; grease should not splatter. Cook until both sides of ham are very lightly browned. Best served hot.

Sausage Crepes

1   pound hot bulk pork sausage
¼   cup chopped onion
½   cup grated Cheddar cheese
1   3-ounce package cream cheese
1   cup sour cream
1   tablespoon milk
16 crepes
4   tablespoons butter, softened

Cook sausage and onion until brown. Drain. Stir in both cheeses. Mix well. Add ¾ cup sour cream and 1 tablespoon milk. Place 2 tablespoons sausage mix down center of each crepe. Roll crepes up. Arrange in a shallow baking dish. Combine the butter and ¼ cup sour cream. Spread over center of crepes. Bake, covered, in a 375 degree oven for 20 minutes. Yield: 6 servings

Cabbage Rolls

1   pound lean ground beef
½   pound bulk pork sausage
½   cup cooked rice
⅓ to ½ cup milk
3   tablespoons diced green pepper
    Salt
    Garlic salt
    White pepper
½   teaspoon nutmeg
1   large head cabbage
1   16-ounce can tomato sauce
4 to 5 tablespoons brown sugar

Mix ground beef, sausage, cooked rice, milk, green pepper, salt, garlic salt, white pepper, and nutmeg. Set aside for 30 minutes. Core and boil the cabbage for 1 to 3 minutes until the leaves begin to separate. Gently lift from pot and drain. Cool until it can be handled. Use the large outside leaves and fill each with a small portion of the meat mixture. Roll the leaf around the meat, tucking in the ends. Place seam-side down, side-by-side in an ovenproof glass dish. Pour tomato sauce over the rolls. Sprinkle with more nutmeg and brown sugar. Cover tightly in foil and bake for 1½ hours in a 300 degree oven. May be made ahead and refrigerated. Freezes well. Yield: 4 to 6 servings

Beef Stroganoff

1   tablespoon all-purpose flour
½   teaspoon salt
1   pound beef sirloin, cut into ¼-inch strips
2   tablespoons butter
1   3-ounce can sliced mushrooms, drained
½   cup onion, chopped
1   clove garlic, minced
2   tablespoons butter
3   tablespoons all-purpose flour
1   tablespoon tomato paste
1¼ cups cold beef stock or 1 10½-ounce can condensed beef broth
1   cup sour cream
2   tablespoons dry white wine
    Hot buttered noodles

Combine 1 tablespoon flour and the salt; sprinkle over the meat. Melt 2 tablespoons butter in skillet; add meat and brown quickly on both sides. Add mushrooms, onion, and garlic; cook until crisp-tender for 3 or 4 minutes. Remove mixture from pan. Add 2 tablespoons butter to pan drippings. Blend in 3 tablespoons flour. Add tomato paste; stir in beef stock. Cook and stir until thickened and bubbly. Return meat mixture to skillet. Stir in sour cream and wine; cook slowly until hot. Do not boil. Serve over noodles. Yield: 4 to 5 servings

Stuffed Peppers

6 large green peppers
1 pound ground beef
1 16-ounce can tomato sauce
1 cup cooked rice
2 teaspoons salt
¼ teaspoon pepper
¾ cup onion, chopped

Cut a thin slice from the top of each pepper. Remove all seeds and membranes. Cook peppers in boiling water for five minutes. Mix rest of ingredients. Stuff peppers lightly with mixture. Place upright in a large covered baking dish. Bake for 45 minutes in a 350° oven. Uncover and bake for 15 minutes longer. Yield: 6 servings

Gourmet Meat Loaf

1 pound lean ground chuck
¼ pound lean ground pork
1 large onion, finely chopped
2 cloves garlic, crushed
1 tablespoon Italian seasoning
Salt to taste
Cayenne pepper to taste
2 loaves frozen bread dough
1½ cups grated Cheddar cheese

Mix chuck, pork, onion, garlic, and seasonings. Cook in skillet until done but not brown. Drain off any fat. Taste and adjust seasonings. Cool. Thaw frozen dough enough to roll loaves together to form rectangle. Spread cooled meat over dough; press gently with fork onto dough leaving edges clean. Spread cheese over meat mixture. Roll up jelly-roll style, using a folding over motion, rather than rolling. Fold ends over well. May be brushed with butter. Bake according to frozen bread dough directions. Yield: 8 servings

Spaghetti Meat Sauce

Olive oil
2 green peppers, chopped
1 large bunch celery
4 large onions, chopped
1 bunch green onions, chopped
6 cloves garlic, finely chopped
7 pounds ground beef
Salt and pepper to taste
1 14½-ounce can tomatoes
3 8-ounce cans tomato sauce
1 6-ounce can tomato paste
3 cans water
Worcestershire sauce
A-1 sauce
"57" sauce
Hot sauce
2 tablespoons wine vinegar
1 teaspoon sugar
1 11-ounce can mushroom pieces
1 6-ounce jar stuffed olives, sliced

Grease bottom of large cast aluminum roaster with olive oil. Sauté 1½ cups chopped pepper, chopped outside stalks of celery, two chopped onions, ½ the chopped green onion, and ½ the garlic in roaster. Add meat a little at a time; when meat is half cooked, add seasonings, tomatoes, tomato sauce, and tomato paste. Measure three cans of water in the whole tomatoes can and add to mixture. Add bottled sauces to taste, wine vinegar, sugar, and any other sauces desired. Stir well while adding sauces. In another bowl, chop and combine remaining pepper, chopped celery hearts, onion, green onion, and garlic. Add mushrooms and olives, and then pour into cooked sauce. Cook, covered, for about 1 hour. Remove cover and simmer about 1½ hours longer. Stir often. Sauce can be kept frozen for four months. Yield: 15 servings

If you must wait a few minutes before serving spaghetti, toss the cooked, drained spaghetti with a tablespoon of cooking oil to prevent sticking.

Baby Lamb Chops

6   lamb chops
1/4 teaspoon salt per chop
1/4 teaspoon pepper per chop
1/4 teaspoon garlic powder per chop
1/8 teaspoon marjoram per chop
1/8 teaspoon basil per chop
1/8 teaspoon rosemary per chop
1/3 cup vinegar

Liberally sprinkle lamb chops with salt, pepper, and garlic powder. Lightly sprinkle chops with marjoram and basil. Sprinkle rosemary on each chop. Set aside at room temperature for 1 or 2 hours. Place a large cast iron skillet, which can be fitted with a lid, on a burner and turn heat on high. When pan is very hot, sear lamb chops for 2 minutes on each side. Reduce heat to low and continue cooking 5 minutes. Pour vinegar into pan and cover immediately. Cook chops an additional 2 or 3 minutes on each side. Remove from pan and serve with pan juices. Yield: 6 servings

Veal Pot Roast

4   tablespoons butter
1   6-pound veal rump roast
2   medium onions, chopped
2   cups sour cream
1   to 3 cups chicken stock
2   teaspoons dill weed
1   teaspoon seasoned salt
1/4 teaspoon red pepper flakes

Melt the butter in a Dutch oven. Brown the roast in butter over medium-high heat. Remove the meat from the pot and set aside. Place the onion in the pot and sauté until light brown. Stir in the sour cream, 2 cups chicken stock, dill weed, seasoned salt and pepper flakes. Return the veal roast to the pot and baste well with the sauce. Cover the pot tightly and simmer over low heat for 2 to 3 hours, or until the meat is fork-tender,

adding more chicken stock as needed. Place the meat on a heated platter and serve immediately. Serve the sauce separately in a gravy boat. Yield: 6 servings

Grillades

4   pounds veal scallopini
1 1/2 tablespoons salt
1   teaspoon pepper
3/4 cup bacon drippings
1/2 cup all-purpose flour
2   cups chopped onions
3/4 cup chopped celery, including ribs and leaves
6   thinly sliced green peppers
3   cups chopped green onions
3   cloves garlic, minced
3   cups chopped tomatoes
1   teaspoon thyme
3   bay leaves
     Hot sauce to taste
     Worcestershire sauce to taste
1 1/2 cups warm water
3/4 cup parsley
     Hot cooked grits
     Gravy

Season veal with salt and pepper. In a heavy Dutch oven, brown meat in four tablespoons of the drippings. Remove veal; keep covered and warm. Add remaining drippings and flour to Dutch oven, stirring constantly over low heat to make a chocolate brown roux. Add onion, celery, peppers, green onion, and garlic. Sauté until limp. Add only enough of the tomatoes to add a pink tint to the roux which should retain its brown color. Add seasonings and stir in water. Place meat in roux, cover and cook slowly about one hour. Remove bay leaves and stir in parsley. Serve piping hot, spooned over grits with lots of gravy. Overnight refrigeration enhances the flavor of the sauce. To reheat, add a small amount of warm water or beef stock. If veal is unavailable, tender beef round is a good substitute. Yield: 8 to 10 servings

Veal with Mushrooms

2 pounds veal, thinly sliced
  Flour
4 tablespoons of butter
1 cup of water
1/4 pound mushrooms, thinly sliced
1 cup heavy cream
2 tablespoons cognac
  Salt
  Pepper

*R*oll veal in flour. Brown in butter. Remove to an ovenproof dish and add water and mushrooms to butter. Cook 5 minutes and pour over meat. Stir in cream. Bake in a 400 degree oven for 15 minutes. Just before serving, add cognac, salt and pepper. Yield: 6 servings

Liver in Wine

2 pounds calves liver
1/2 cup vegetable oil
2 tablespoons lemon juice
2 tablespoons vinegar
1 teaspoon salt
1/2 teaspoon oregano
6 slices bacon
2 cups sliced onions
2 tablespoons butter
1/2 cup all-purpose flour
1/2 cup white wine
1 4-ounce can sliced mushrooms, 1/4 cup liquid reserved
1 teaspoon salt
1/8 teaspoon pepper
2 tablespoons chopped fresh parsley

*M*arinate liver for 2 hours in oil, juice, vinegar, salt, and oregano. Fry bacon and crumble. Sauté onions in drippings until transparent. Add butter. Drain liver, coat with flour, and quickly brown on both sides. Place liver in 2-quart casserole. Stir wine, mushroom liquid, salt, and pepper into pan drippings. Heat to boiling. Place mushrooms on liver. Cover with sauce. Sprinkle with bacon and parsley. Bake, uncovered, in a 350 degree oven for 30 minutes. Yield: 4 servings

Savory Pork Pub Pie, page 138.

To test fish for doneness, no matter how it is prepared, pierce it with a fork. If it flakes easily, it is ready to be served.

Seafood au Gratin

1/4 cup butter
1/4 cup all-purpose flour
3 cups whole milk
4 egg yolks
1 cup oysters
2 cups shrimp, cooked and cleaned
1 cup crab meat
1/4 cup sherry
1 tablespoon lemon juice
1/2 teaspoon salt
   Pinch of red pepper
   Fine bread crumbs
   Grated cheese
   Extra butter

Combine butter and flour in a double boiler. Add milk and cook over boiling water until it begins to thicken. Beat egg yolks lightly, and slowly add some of hot milk mixture. Return all to double boiler. Cook for five minutes, stirring constantly. Combine all seafood. Pour sherry on top. Add seasonings to sauce. Mix lightly with seafood. Pour all into greased baking dish. Sprinkle bread crumbs and grated cheese over the top. Dot with butter. Bake in a 350 degree oven until top begins to brown and casserole is bubbly. Easy to prepare ahead. Yield: 6 servings

Shrimp Creole

1 cup diced onion
1 cup diced celery
1/2 cup diced green pepper
1/4 cup vegetable oil
3 1/2 cups canned tomatoes
1 8-ounce can tomato sauce
2 bay leaves
1 tablespoon sugar
1 teaspoon salt
1 tablespoon chili powder
1/8 teaspoon hot sauce
2 pounds cleaned, raw shrimp
1/4 cup all-purpose flour
1/4 cup water
   Hot cooked rice

Sauté onions, celery and pepper in oil until tender. Add tomatoes, tomato sauce, bay leaves, sugar, salt, chili powder, and hot sauce. Mix well. Simmer 30 minutes. Remove bay leaves. Add shrimp. Simmer 30 minutes longer. Mix flour and water to a paste; add a cup or two of tomato mixture and stir with wire whisk until blended. Add flour mixture to tomato mixture. Cook until creole is thickened, about 5 minutes. Serve over rice. Yield: 6 servings

Shrimp De Jonghe Soufflé

   Butter
   Grated Parmesan cheese
1/3 cup butter
1/3 cup all-purpose flour
1 1/4 cups milk
1/4 cup dry white wine
1/2 cup shredded Gruyère or Swiss cheese
1 tablespoon parsley flakes
1/2 teaspoon garlic powder
1/2 teaspoon paprika
1/4 teaspoon salt
6 eggs, separated
3/4 teaspoon cream of tartar
1 6-ounce package tiny frozen cooked shrimp, thawed and drained

Butter bottom and sides of a 2 to 2 1/2-quart soufflé dish or straight-sided casserole. Dust with Parmesan cheese. Prepare a collar by making a 4-inch wide band of triple-thickness aluminum foil long enough to go around dish and overlap 2 inches. Butter one side of band and dust with Parmesan cheese. Wrap band around dish, dusted side in, and fasten with straight pins, paper clips or string. Collar should stand at least 2 inches above rim of dish. Set aside. In medium saucepan over medium-high heat, melt butter. Blend in flour. Cook, stirring constantly, until mixture is smooth and bubbly. Stir in milk all at once. Cook and stir until mixture boils and is smooth and thickened. Stir in wine. Remove from heat. Stir in Gruyère cheese and seasonings until cheese is melted. Set aside. In large mixing bowl, beat egg whites with cream of tartar at high speed until stiff but not dry, just until whites no longer slip when bowl is tilted. Thoroughly blend egg yolks and shrimp into reserved sauce. Gently, but thoroughly, fold whites into yolk mixture. Carefully pour into prepared dish. For a "top hat," hold spoon upright and circle mixture to make a ring about 1 inch from side of dish and 1-inch deep. Bake in a 350 degree oven until puffy, delicately browned and souffle shakes slightly when oven rack is moved gently back and forth, about 35 to 45 minutes. Quickly, but gently, remove collar. Serve immediately. Yield: 4 to 6 servings

Tuna Au Gratin

  2 **7-ounce cans tuna, drained and flaked**
  ²/₃ **cup chopped onion**
  ¹/₄ **cup chopped green pepper**
  ¹/₄ **cup chopped pimiento**
  ²/₃ **cup mayonnaise**
  ¹/₄ **cup fine dry bread crumbs**
  ¹/₄ **cup grated fresh Parmesan cheese**

Combine first five ingredients. Spoon into small seafood shells. Sprinkle with bread crumbs and cheese. Bake in a 350 degree oven for 20 minutes, or until browned. Yield: 5 to 6 servings

Open Faced Shrimp Salad Sandwich

  1 **1-pound package cooked salad shrimp**
  1 **cup chopped celery**
  ¹/₂ **cup chopped green onion**
  ¹/₂ **to ³/₄ cup mayonnaise**
  1 **teaspoon seasoning salt**
  ¹/₂ **teaspoon dried dill weed**
    Swiss cheese, sliced
    Rye or whole wheat bread, sliced

Combine first 6 ingredients. Chill until ready to serve. To make sandwich, place 1 slice cheese on bread. Top with a scoop of shrimp salad. Place another slice of cheese on top of shrimp. Place in a 400 degree oven until cheese melts. Yield: 4 to 6 servings

Note: Shrimp salad may also be served chilled on a bed of lettuce.

Cheese, Avocado, and Bacon Croissants

  4 **frozen Sara Lee All-Butter Croissants**
  4 **slices Cheddar cheese**
  4 **slices Swiss cheese**
  8 **slices tomato**
    Alfalfa sprouts, optional
  8 **slices bacon, cooked until crisp, optional**
  ¹/₂ **avocado, peeled, sliced**

Cut frozen croissant in half horizontally; leave together. Heat frozen croissants on ungreased baking sheet in preheated 325 degree oven for 9 to 11 minutes. Layer 1 slice each of Cheddar and Swiss cheeses on croissant bottom half. Top with 2 tomato slices; some alfalfa sprouts, if desired; 2 bacon slices, if desired; and several avocado slices. Top with remaining croissant half. Yield: 4 servings

Cream Cheese, Marmalade and Bacon Croissants

4 frozen Sara Lee All-Butter Croissants
3 ounces cream cheese, softened
1/4 cup orange marmalade
8 slices bacon, cooked until crisp

Cut frozen croissants in half horizontally; leave together. Heat frozen croissants on ungreased baking sheet in preheated 325 degree oven for 9 to 11 minutes. Spread 1 1/2 tablespoons cream cheese on each croissant bottom half. Spoon on 1 tablespoon marmalade and top with 2 bacon slices. Top with remaining croissant half. Yield: 4 servings

Curried Shrimp Croissants

Delicious croissant sandwiches, pages 145-146.

4 frozen Sara Lee All-Butter Croissants
1/4 cup chopped onion
1/4 cup chopped celery
3 tablespoons butter
3/4 teaspoon curry powder
1/4 cup all-purpose flour
1 1/2 cups light cream
1/4 teaspoon ground ginger
1 teaspoon lemon juice
1/3 cup light or dark raisins
10 ounces medium shrimp, cooked or 1 6 1/2-ounce can tuna, drained and flaked
    Chopped peanuts or sliced green onion tops, optional

Cut frozen croissants in half horizontally; leave together. Heat frozen croissants on ungreased baking sheet in preheated 325 degree oven for 9 to 11 minutes. Sauté onion and celery in butter. Stir in curry powder; cook 1 minute. Stir in flour; heat until bubbly. Stir in cream, ginger and lemon juice. Cook over low heat, stirring until thickened. Stir in raisins and shrimp. Heat 2 to 3 minutes longer. Serve spooned over croissant bottom halves. Garnish with peanuts, if desired. Top with remaining croissant halves. Yield: 4 servings

Desserts

Apricot Brandy Cake

1/2 cup butter
1/2 cup margarine
3 cups sugar
6 large eggs
3 cups all-purpose flour
1/2 teaspoon salt
1/4 teaspoon baking soda
1 cup sour cream
1/2 teaspoon lemon extract
1 teaspoon orange extract
1/4 teaspoon almond extract
1/2 teaspoon rum extract
1 teaspoon vanilla
1 cup apricot brandy
4 cups confectioners' sugar
6 tablespoons melted butter
1 teaspoon vanilla
1/4 cup apricot brandy

Cream butter and margarine until light. Add sugar 1 cup at a time. Cream until light and fluffy. Add eggs one at a time, beating well after each addition. Beat three minutes after adding last egg. Combine flour, salt, and soda. Combine sour cream and extracts. Add flour mixture and sour cream alternately to the batter. Blend well. Fold in 1 cup apricot brandy. Bake in well-greased and floured 10-inch tube pan at 375 degrees for 70 minutes or until a skewer inserted in center comes out clean. Cool for 15 minutes in pan; remove from pan and cool on wire rack. Make frosting by combining remaining ingredients and blending until smooth. Apply to cooled cake with spatula. Yield 10 to 12 servings

Coconut Bavarian Custard Cake

1 large angel food cake, broken into bite-sized pieces
Sherry
1 cup sugar
2 tablespoons all-purpose flour
4 egg yolks
1 teaspoon vanilla
2 cups milk
1 package unflavored gelatin dissolved in 1/4 cup cold water
2 cups heavy cream, whipped
4 egg whites, stiffly beaten
1 6-ounce package fresh frozen coconut, thawed

Sprinkle cake pieces with sherry and set aside. Mix sugar, flour and egg yolks, add vanilla and blend well. Stir milk into mixture and blend thoroughly. Cook over low heat, stirring constantly until thickened (about 10 to 12 minutes). Stir in gelatin. Blend until gelatin is thoroughly dissolved; set mixture aside to cool. When cool fold in 1/2 the whipped cream and the stiffly beaten egg whites. In a large greased tube pan, alternate layers of broken cake pieces and sauce, ending with layer of sauce. Chill for at least 24 hours. When ready to serve, turn cake out onto serving platter. Frost with remaining whipped cream. Sprinkle generously with coconut. Yield: 12 to 14 servings

To store extra egg yolks, place them in a glass jar and cover with water. Cover and store in refrigerator. Drain off water before using.

Icebox Pineapple Angel Food Cake

1   8-ounce can crushed pineapple with juice
     Juice and grated rind of 1½ lemons
2   3-ounce packages lemon gelatin
1½ pints heavy cream, whipped or 3 packages Dream Whip, whipped
1   angel food cake
     Mandarin oranges
     Pineapple tidbits

*U*sing pineapple juice and lemon juice in the liquid, prepare gelatin. Chill until slightly thickened; mix in drained pineapple and grated rind. Fold in ⅔ of the whipped cream. Break up angel food cake into small pieces and fold into pineapple mixture. Pour all into a lightly oiled tube pan. Chill for 24 hours. Garnish with remaining whipped cream, mandarin oranges and pineapple pieces. Yield: 10 to 12 servings

For best results, egg whites should be at room temperature when whipped. Use a whisk and a glass bowl, both of which must be absolutely free of water, grease, or egg yolk. If a drop of yolk gets in the whites, a bit of shell is the best thing to use to remove it. Always separate eggs over a cup, then add to your mixing bowl. This will keep you from mixing in a bad egg.

Fresh Carrot Cake with Cream Cheese Frosting

4   eggs
1½ cups vegetable oil
2   cups all-purpose flour
2   cups sugar
2   teaspoons baking powder
2   teaspoons baking soda
3   teaspoons cinnamon
1   teaspoon salt
3   cups firmly packed grated raw carrots
1½ cups chopped black walnuts

*B*eat eggs and oil. Mix dry ingredients. Add to egg and oil mixture. Beat well. Add carrots and walnuts. Blend. Pour into 3 greased 9-inch layer pans. Bake in a 350 degree oven for 25 minutes. Yield: 8 to 10 servings

Frosting

1   1-pound box confectioners' sugar
1   stick butter, softened
1   8-ounce package cream cheese, softened
1½ cups chopped black walnuts, optional

*B*lend ingredients. Spread on cake. Refrigerate cake.

Fresh Coconut Cake

1   cup butter
2   cups sugar
4   eggs, separated
1½ teaspoons vanilla
2⅔ cups cake flour
1½ teaspoons baking powder
½ teaspoon salt
1   coconut
½ cup milk
     Frosting

*C*ream the butter (do not use margarine) and sugar together until light. Separate the eggs, setting whites aside. Beat egg yolks into butter and sugar mixture, one at a time. Add vanilla. Sift the cake flour before measuring. Resift measured flour with baking powder and salt. Pierce the coconut and strain ½ cup of the liquid into a measuring cup. Combine the coconut liquid and the milk in a small bowl. Add the sifted dry ingredients to the butter and sugar mixture in three parts, alternating with the coconut-milk mixture. Beat well after each addition. Beat the egg whites until stiff and fold into the batter. Pour into 3 greased 9-inch cake pans and bake in a 350 degree oven for 30 minutes. Remove from pans before completely cooled. Spread on Frosting. Yield: 8 to 10 servings

Frosting

1½ cups sugar
2 egg whites
5 tablespoons water
  Pinch of cream of tartar
6 large marshmallows
1 teaspoon vanilla
2 cups freshly grated coconut

*P*lace all ingredients except vanilla and coconut in the top of a double boiler over simmering water. Heat for about 7 minutes, beating constantly with an electric mixer on high speed. The frosting should be stiff and glossy. Remove from heat and stir in vanilla. When cool, spread on layers. Grate coconut meat and sprinkle between each layer and on top and sides of cake.

Chocolate Buffet Cake

2 eggs, separated
½ cup sugar
1¼ cups unsifted all-purpose flour
1 cup sugar
½ cup unsweetened Hershey's cocoa
¾ teaspoon baking soda
½ teaspoon salt
½ cup vegetable oil
1 teaspoon vanilla
1 cup buttermilk or sour milk
  Chocolate Rum Filling
  Chocolate Glaze
  Sweetened whipped cream
  Maraschino cherries, optional

*L*ine a 15½x10½x1-inch jelly roll pan with aluminum foil; generously grease and flour foil. Set aside. Beat egg whites in large mixer bowl until foamy; gradually add ½ cup sugar, beating until stiff peaks form. Combine flour, 1 cup sugar, cocoa, soda and salt in large mixer bowl. Add oil, vanilla, buttermilk, and egg yolks; beat until smooth. Gently fold egg whites into batter; spread evenly in prepared pan. Bake in a 350 degree oven for 25 to 30 minutes or until cake springs back when lightly touched in center. Cool 3 minutes; invert onto a large cooling rack. Carefully remove foil; cool. Prepare Chocolate Rum Filling. Cut cake in half crosswise to form 2 equal pieces. Place one layer on serving tray; spread with filling and top with remaining layer. Chill while preparing glaze. Glaze cake; refrigerate 2 to 3 hours or until set. To serve; top with dollops or rosettes of sweetened whipped cream arranged atop cake. Garnish with maraschino cherries, if desired. Yield: 12 servings

Note: To sour milk: Use 1 tablespoon vinegar plus milk to equal 1 cup.

Chocolate Rum Filling

½ cup unsalted butter
⅔ cup sugar
⅓ cup unsweetened Hershey's cocoa
1 large egg
2 tablespoons rum
½ cup heavy cream, beaten stiff

*C*ombine first 5 ingredients; blend until smooth. Fold in whipped cream just until blended.

Chocolate Glaze

2 tablespoons butter
3 tablespoons unsweetened Hershey's cocoa
3 tablespoons water
½ teaspoon vanilla
1¼ cups confectioners' sugar

*M*elt butter in small saucepan over low heat. Stir in cocoa and water. Cook, stirring constantly until mixture thickens; do not boil. Remove from heat; stir in vanilla and confectioners' sugar, beating or whisking until smooth.

If your heavy cream won't whip, try chilling the bowl and beaters. Place the bowl in a larger bowl of ice cubes and whip. As a last resort, try adding a drop or two of lemon juice to the cream.

Three Chocolate Cake

- 1   18½-ounce package devil's food cake mix
- 1   4⅛-ounce package instant chocolate pudding mix
- ½   cup brewed coffee
- 4   large eggs
- 1   cup sour cream
- ½   cup vegetable oil
- ½   cup dark rum
- 2   cups semi-sweet chocolate chips

Combine all ingredients except chocolate chips. With an electric mixer, blend on low speed. Beat at medium speed for one minute. Scrape bowl and beat one minute longer. Fold in chocolate chips. Pour into a greased and floured bundt pan. Bake in a 350 degree oven for 55 to 60 minutes or until skewer inserted in center comes out clean. Turn out of pan and cool. Yield: 10 to 12 servings

Williamsburg Orange Cake

- 2¾   cups cake flour
- 1½   cups sugar
- 1½   teaspoons baking soda
- ¾   teaspoon salt
- 1½   cups buttermilk
- ½   cup butter, softened
- ¼   cup shortening
- 3   eggs
- 2   teaspoons vanilla
- 1   cup chopped golden raisins
- ½   cup chopped nuts
- 1   tablespoon grated orange peel
- ½   cup soft butter
- 3   cups sifted confectioners' sugar
- 3   tablespoons orange liqueur (or fresh orange juice)
- 2   tablespoons grated orange peel

Blend first 12 ingredients in a large mixing bowl on low speed for 30 seconds, scraping bowl constantly. Beat three minutes on high speed, scraping bowl occasionally. Pour into greased and floured 13x9x2-inch pan. Bake in a 350 degree oven for 45 to 50 minutes or until a skewer inserted in center comes out clean. Set aside to cool. For frosting, combine butter and sugar. Stir in liqueur and orange peel. Beat until smooth. Spread on cake. Yield: 12 to 16 servings

Japanese Fruit Cake

- 1   cup butter
- 2½   cups sugar
- ½   cup milk
- 6   eggs, beaten
- 4   cups all-purpose flour
- ¼   teaspoon salt
- 1   teaspoon ground cloves
- 1   teaspoon ground allspice
- 1   teaspoon ground cinnamon
- 2   teaspoons baking powder
- 1   cup chopped nuts
- 1   cup seedless raisins
- 2   cups sugar
- 1   cup coconut milk
- 1¾   cups cake batter
      Juice and grated rind of 2 lemons
- 1   coconut, grated or 2 cans
- 1   cup chopped nuts
- 3   tablespoons melted butter
- ¼   cup chopped candied cherries
- ¼   cup chopped candied pineapple

Cream butter and sugar; add milk. Beat well. Add beaten eggs. Combine dry ingredients and mix into batter. Add nuts and raisins. Reserve 1¾ cups of batter for filling. Bake remaining batter in 3 greased 8-inch cake pans in a 375 degree oven for 25 minutes. Set out to cool. Prepare filling by combining sugar and coconut milk and boil until slightly syrupy. Add the reserved cake batter, lemon juice and rind. Cook until thickened, stirring constantly. Add coconut, nuts, butter, and candied fruits. Spread between layers and on top of cooled cake. Yield: 8 to 10 servings

Egg Nog Cake

2 cups pitted prunes, quartered
1/4 cup Jamaica rum or orange juice
1 cup butter or margarine, softened
1 1/4 cups sugar
2 1/4 cups all-purpose flour
1 teaspoon baking powder
1/2 teaspoon salt
2 1/2 teaspoons nutmeg
1/4 cup sour cream
5 eggs
1 cup chopped walnuts
Whole pitted prunes
Colored sugars
Candied cherries
Confectioners' sugar
Nutmeg Cream

*I*n small bowl toss prunes with rum. Set aside 15 minutes. In large bowl, combine butter, sugar, 2 cups of the flour, baking powder, salt, nutmeg, sour cream and rum drained from prunes. With electric mixer at medium speed, beat until smooth, about 3 minutes. (Mixture will be thick.) Add eggs 1 at a time, beating 1 minute after each addition. Toss prunes with remaining 1/4 cup flour. Fold prunes and walnuts into batter to blend thoroughly. Spoon into greased and floured 10-inch tube pan. Bake in 325 degree oven about 1 hour 10 minutes until top is browned and springy to the touch. Cool on rack 15 minutes before turning out of pan onto rack to cool completely. Garnish with prunes rolled in colored sugar and topped with cherries. Dust with confectioners' sugar. Slice to serve; top with Nutmeg Cream. (Ungarnished cake may be securely wrapped and frozen up to 1 month.) Yield: 14 to 16 servings

Nutmeg Cream

*B*eat 1 cup whipping cream to form soft peaks. Beat in 2 tablespoons confectioners' sugar and 1 teaspoon nutmeg. Fold in 1/2 cup sour cream. Chill.

Fudge Cake

3/4 cup butter
2 1/4 cups sugar
1 1/2 teaspoons vanilla
3 eggs
3 1-ounce squares unsweetened chocolate, melted
3 cups sifted cake flour
1 1/2 teaspoons baking soda
3/4 teaspoon salt
1 1/2 cups ice water
Date Cream filling
Fudge Frosting (Recipe is on page 152)

*C*ream butter, sugar and vanilla with mixer. Add eggs and melted chocolate. Beat well. Sift dry ingredients; add alternately with water to chocolate mixture. Pour batter into 3 greased and floured 8-inch layer pans. Bake in a 350 degree oven for 30 to 35 minutes. Cool. Prepare and put layers together with Date Cream Filling. Frost with Fudge Frosting. Yield: 8 to 10 servings

Date Cream Filling

1 cup milk
1/2 cup chopped dates
1 tablespoon all-purpose flour
1/4 cup sugar
1 egg, beaten
1/2 cup chopped nuts
1 teaspoon vanilla

*C*ombine milk and dates in top of double boiler over simmering water. Combine flour and sugar and add beaten egg, blending until smooth. Add to hot milk. Cook, stirring until thick. Cool. Stir in nuts and vanilla. Spread between cake layers.

Is your cake done? For layer cakes and cupcakes, touch the cake lightly in center with fingertip. It should spring back. The sides of the cake will also begin to pull away from the pan when it is done. For pound cakes, insert a skewer in the center of the cake. It will come out clean when the cake is done.

Cool layer cakes in their pans for 10 minutes, then turn out onto wire racks to cool thoroughly. Sheet cakes can be cooled in the pan. Pound cakes should be cooled in the pan for 5 minutes and then turned onto a wire rack to complete cooling.

Fudge Frosting

2 cups sugar
1 cup light cream
2 1-ounce squares unsweetened chocolate, grated

*C*ombine all ingredients in heavy saucepan. Boil over medium-high heat 3 minutes without stirring. Reduce heat and continue to cook until it reaches soft-ball stage (238 degrees). Cool. Beat until creamy and of spreading consistency. Add cream if too thick. Spread on sides of cake first then over top edge. Frost top layer last.

Cream Cheese Pound Cake

1 1/2 cups chopped pecans
1 1/2 cups butter or margarine, softened
1   8-ounce package cream cheese, softened
3   cups sugar
6   eggs
3   cups sifted cake flour
    Dash of salt
1 1/2 teaspoons vanilla

*S*prinkle 1/2 cup pecans in a greased and floured 10-inch tube pan; set aside. Cream butter and cream cheese; gradually add sugar, beating until light and fluffy. Add eggs, one at a time, beating well after each addition. Add flour and salt, stirring until combined. Stir in vanilla and remaining pecans. Pour batter into prepared pan. Bake in a 325 degree oven for 1 1/2 hours, or until a skewer inserted in center comes out clean. Cool in pan 10 minutes. Turn out and cool on wire rack. Yield: 10 to 12 servings

Five Flavor Pound Cake

1   cup butter or margarine
1/2 cup shortening
3   cups sugar
5   eggs, well beaten
3   cups all-purpose flour
1/2 teaspoon baking powder
1   cup milk
1   teaspoon coconut extract
1   teaspoon rum extract
1   teaspoon butter extract
1   teaspoon lemon extract
1   teaspoon vanilla

*C*ream butter, shortening and sugar until light and fluffy. Add eggs. Combine flour and baking powder. Add to creamed mixture alternately with milk. Stir in extracts. Spoon mixture into greased 10-inch tube pan and bake in a 325 degree oven for 1 1/2 hours, or until a skewer inserted in center comes out clean. Add glaze if desired or cool in pan about ten minutes before turning out. Yield: 10 to 12 servings

Strawberry Pie

1 cup sugar
1 cup hot water
3 tablespoons cornstarch
3 tablespoons wild strawberry gelatin
1 pint fresh strawberries, washed and drained
1 9-inch pie crust, baked and cooled
  Whipped cream

*M*ix sugar, hot water, cornstarch and gelatin. Cook until thickened. Cool. Place strawberries in pie crust. Pour sugar mixture over. Place in refrigerator until firm. When ready to serve top with whipped cream. Yield: 6 to 8 servings

Lemon Chess Pie

1/2 cup butter
2   cups sugar
1   tablespoon cornstarch
4   eggs
    Juice of 2 lemons
    Grated rind of 1 lemon
1   9-inch unbaked pie crust

Cream butter. Blend together sugar and cornstarch; add to butter. Add eggs one at a time, beating well after each addition. Blend in lemon juice and rind. Pour into unbaked pie crust. Bake in a 350° oven until firm, about 35 minutes. Yield: 6 to 8 servings

French Silk Chocolate Pie

- ¹/₂ cup butter
- ³/₄ cup sugar
- 2 squares unsweetened chocolate, melted
- 1 teaspoon vanilla
- 2 eggs, chilled
- 1 9-inch pie crust, baked and cooled
  Whipped cream
  Slivered almonds

Cream butter and sugar until light and fluffy. Blend in chocolate and vanilla. Add the chilled eggs, one at a time, beating two minutes after each addition. Pour into pie crust. Chill at least 3 hours before serving. Top with whipped cream and almonds. Yield: 6 to 8 servings

Japanese Fruit Pie

- ¹/₂ cup margarine
- 1 cup sugar
- 2 eggs, well-beaten
- ¹/₂ cup coconut
- ¹/₂ cup raisins
- ¹/₂ cup nuts, chopped
- 1 teaspoon vanilla
- 1 teaspoon vinegar
- 1 9-inch unbaked pie crust

Melt margarine and sugar over low heat, stirring constantly. Remove from heat; add eggs. Stir in coconut, raisins, and nuts. Stir in the vanilla and vinegar. Pour into pie crust; bake in a 300 degree oven for 30 minutes. Yield: 6 to 8 servings

French Coconut Pie

- 3 eggs, beaten
- ¹/₄ teaspoon salt
- 1 teaspoon vanilla
- ¹/₄ teaspoon almond extract
- ¹/₄ teaspoon coconut extract
- 1¹/₂ cups sugar
- 2 tablespoons all-purpose flour
- 1 tablespoon vinegar
- ¹/₂ cup butter, melted
- 1 cup coconut
- 1 9-inch unbaked pie crust

Blend eggs, salt, vanilla, almond, and coconut extracts. Combine sugar and flour and stir into egg mixture. Add vinegar. Stir in melted butter. Mix well. Fold in coconut. Pour into unbaked pie crust. Bake in a 300 degree oven for 1 hour. Yield: 6 to 8 servings

Coconut Cream Pie

- ²/₃ cup sugar
- ¹/₄ cup cornstarch
- ¹/₂ teaspoon salt
- 3 cups milk
- 4 egg yolks, beaten
- 2 tablespoons butter
- 4 teaspoons vanilla
- 1 10-ounce can flaked coconut
- 1 10-inch pie crust, baked and cooled
- ¹/₂ cup heavy cream, whipped

In saucepan, combine sugar, cornstarch and salt. Combine milk and egg yolks and gradually stir into sugar mixture. Cook over medium heat, stirring constantly until mixture thickens and comes to a boil. Boil and stir for one minute. Remove from heat and blend in butter and vanilla. Add ³/₄ can of coconut. Pour into pie crust. Refrigerate. Before serving, top with whipped cream (you may sweeten this to taste) and sprinkle with remaining coconut. Yield: 6 to 8 servings

Apple Ribbon Pie

6   to 8 tart apples
    Pastry for 2-crust pie
1   cup sugar
1   tablespoon all-purpose flour
1/4 teaspoon nutmeg
1/2 teaspoon cinnamon
2   tablespoons butter or margarine
1/4 cup grated sharp Cheddar cheese
1 1/2 teaspoons poppy seed

Pare and core apples; slice thin. Line 9-inch pie pan with pastry. Combine sugar, flour and spices; rub a little of this mixture into pastry in pie pan. Fill pie pan with sliced apples; add remaining sugar mixture. Dot with butter or margarine. Divide remaining pastry into two equal portions. Roll out 1 portion 1/8-inch thick; top with grated cheese; fold over in 3 layers; roll out again. Cut into 5 strips 10 inches long by 3/4-inch wide. Repeat with remaining portion of pastry, using poppy seed instead of cheese. Weave strips, lattice fashion, on pie, alternating cheese strips and poppy seed strips; trim and flute edge. Bake in a 425 degree oven for 40 to 45 minutes, or until apples are tender. Yield: 6 to 8 servings

Apple Cream Pie

3   cups chopped tart apples
1/2 cup sugar
1   tablespoon all-purpose flour
1/4 teaspoon mace
1   9 inch unbaked pie crust
2   tablespoons butter
    Cream Filling

Combine apples, sugar, flour and mace. Spread apple mixture in pie crust. Dot with butter and bake in a 450 degree oven for 10 minutes. Reduce temperature to 350 degrees and bake 35 minutes longer or until apples are tender. Cool; spread with Cream Filling.

Cream Filling

1 1/2 cups milk
1/4 cup sugar
1/4 teaspoon salt
3   tablespoons all-purpose flour
1   egg, beaten
1   tablespoon butter
1/2 teaspoon vanilla

Scald 1 cup milk over boiling water. Mix sugar, salt, flour and remaining milk together. Stir into hot milk. Cover and cook slowly for 4 minutes or until thickened, stirring constantly. Add egg slowly to mixture and cook 1 minute longer. Add butter and vanilla. Pour over apples in pie crust. Yield: 6 to 8 servings

Amelia Island Mud Pie

21 Oreo cookies, crushed
6   tablespoons butter, melted
1   quart chocolate ice cream, softened
4   tablespoons brewed coffee
2   tablespoons brandy
2   tablespoons coffee liqueur
1   cup heavy cream, whipped
1   12-ounce jar fudge sauce (or your favorite homemade)
    Toasted almonds and cherries to garnish

Mix cookie crumbs with butter. Press into nine or ten-inch pie pan. Freeze. Whip ice cream with coffee, brandy and liqueur. Add 4 tablespoons whipped cream to ice cream mixture and continue to whip. Spread in frozen pie shell. Freeze until very hard. Dip knife in hot water, working quickly spread fudge sauce on top of frozen pie. Cover with whipped cream. Garnish with toasted almonds and cherries. Freeze. Yield: 8 servings

Bourbon Chocolate Pecan Pie

1 cup sugar
³/₄ cup butter, melted
3 eggs, slightly beaten
³/₄ cup light corn syrup
¹/₄ teaspoon salt
2 tablespoons bourbon
1 teaspoon vanilla
¹/₂ cup pecans, chopped
¹/₂ cup chocolate chips
1 9-inch pie shell

Cream sugar and butter. Add eggs, syrup, salt, bourbon and vanilla. Mix well. Spread pecans and chocolate chips in bottom of pie shell. Pour filling into shell. Bake in a 375 degree oven for 40 to 50 minutes. Yield: 6 to 8 servings

Peach Cobbler

8 to 10 medium peaches
Lemon juice
¹/₂ cup solid shortening
2 cups all-purpose flour
¹/₄ teaspoon salt
¹/₃ cup ice water
Butter
³/₄ cup sugar
4 tablespoons butter, cut into small pieces
Sugar

Peel and slice the peaches; sprinkle with lemon juice and set aside. Place the shortening in the refrigerator to chill. Sift the flour and salt into a mixing bowl. Cut the chilled shortening into the flour with a knife or pastry blender until the mixture resembles coarse crumbs. Mix gently with fingers to remove any lumps. Sprinkle the ice water gradually into the mixture, mixing with the fingers until the dough sticks together. Form into a ball and set aside for 15 minutes. Divide the dough in half and roll out very thin. Store between sheets of wax paper in the refrigerator until ready to use. Preheat oven to 450 degrees. Butter a heavy casserole or baking dish and place half of the sliced peaches in the bottom. Sprinkle with half of the sugar and dot evenly with half of the butter. Place one sheet of pastry over the peaches. Top with the remaining peaches, sugar and butter, and cover with the second sheet of pastry. Pinch the pastry to the edges of the casserole and plunge a small sharp knife into the cobbler four or five times piercing through both sheets of pastry. Brush the top with melted butter and sprinkle with a little sugar. Place the cobbler in the oven, reduce heat to 425 degrees and bake for 45 minutes, or until the cobbler is bubbling and is lightly browned on top. Cool for 10 to 15 minutes before serving. Yield: 6 to 8 servings

Apple Ribbon Pie, page 154.

If you don't have a double boiler, set a smaller pan inside a larger one containing simmering water or place the smaller pan on a steamer rack in a larger pot.

Apple Cranberry Cobbler

    4   cups thinly sliced apples
    1   cup cranberries
    1   cup sugar
    1   teaspoon cinnamon
    1/2 teaspoon nutmeg
    1/4 teaspoon salt
    1/2 cup water
        Baking powder biscuit dough
    1   egg, slightly beaten
    1   tablespoon water

Cook apples until just tender in small amount of water; add cranberries; cook 5 minutes longer; drain; pour into shallow baking dish. Blend sugar, spices, salt and water; pour over apple mixture. Prepare your favorite recipe for baking powder biscuits, using 2 cups flour and adding 2 tablespoons sugar. Or use 2 cups biscuit mix according to package directions, adding 2 tablespoons sugar. Roll out 1/2-inch thick; cut with round cutter. Cut each round in half, crosswise, and arrange around rim of baking dish with rounded side in. Combine egg and water; brush over biscuits. Bake in a 425 degree oven for about 25 minutes or until cobbler is bubbly and biscuits golden brown. May be served with plain or with whipped cream or whipped topping. Yield: 8 servings

Peach Bavarian with Raspberry Sauce

    2   eggs, separated
    1   3-ounce package peach gelatin
    1/8 teaspoon salt
    1   cup boiling water
    1/4 teaspoon vanilla
    1/4 teaspoon almond extract
    2   tablespoons sugar
    1   cup diced peaches, drained
    1   cup heavy cream, whipped
        Raspberry Sauce

Beat egg yolks; add gelatin and salt. Pour in water and stir until dissolved. Add vanilla and almond extracts; set aside. Beat egg whites until stiff, gradually adding sugar. Fold gelatin into egg white mixture. Fold in peaches and whipped cream. Pour into a 6-cup mold and chill until firm. Serve with Raspberry Sauce. Yield: 6 to 8 servings

Raspberry Sauce

    1   6-ounce package frozen red raspberries
    1   teaspoon cornstarch
    1   tablespoon water
    1/4 cup sugar
    1/2 cup red currant jelly
    1   tablespoon all-purpose flour
    1/4 cup cherry Cointreau

Thaw berries, heat and strain through a sieve. Mix cornstarch and water; combine with strained berries in a saucepan. Cook and stir for 5 minutes. Add sugar and jelly and heat until fully dissolved. Add flour and Cointreau. Stir until well blended. Serve over fresh sliced peaches, canteloupe, ice cream or cake, or Peach Bavarian.

Blueberry Ice Cream

    1   envelope unflavored gelatin
    1/2 cup cold milk
    1/2 cup milk, heated to boiling
    2   cups fresh blueberries
    3/4 cup sugar
    2   cups whipping or heavy cream, whipped

In a 5-cup blender, sprinkle unflavored gelatin over cold milk; set aside 3 to 4 minutes. Add hot milk and process at low speed until gelatin is completely dissolved, about 2 minutes. Cool completely. Add blueberries and sugar; process at high speed until blended. Pour into large bowl and chill, stirring occasionally, until mixture mounds slightly when dropped from spoon. Fold whipped cream into gelatin mixture. Pour into two 4x10-inch freezer trays or one 8-inch baking pan; freeze until firm. Yield: 1½ quarts ice cream

Brandy Spiked Ice Cream

³/₄　cup chopped pitted prunes
3　tablespoons brandy
4　egg yolks
1½　cups sugar
2　cups scalded milk
1　pint coffee ice cream, optional
1　pint chocolate ice cream, optional
　　Chocolate curls, for garnish
8　whole pitted prunes

*M*arinate chopped prunes in brandy to soften several hours or overnight. In mixing bowl beat yolks until pale, 1 to 2 minutes; gradually beat in sugar. On medium speed gradually beat in milk until well blended; cool. Stir in marinated prune mixture; freeze until slushy, 2 to 3 hours. Beat smooth with electric mixer; return to freezer until firm (ice cream will not harden completely). Serve scoops of prune ice cream with coffee and chocolate ice creams. Garnish with chocolate curls and a prune. Yield: 1 quart

Chocolate Ice Box Dessert

4　ounces semi-sweet chocolate
1　cup butter
　　Salt
1　cup sugar or 2 cups confectioners' sugar
6　eggs, separated
18　lady fingers
18　macaroons
　　Whipped cream

*M*elt chocolate. Cream butter and beat into chocolate. Add pinch of salt. Beat sugar into egg yolks. Stir into chocolate mixture. Whip egg whites and fold into mixture. Pour into bowl lined with lady fingers. Crush macaroons and sprinkle on top. Store in refrigerator and serve with whipped cream. Yield: 8 servings

Peanutty Chocolate Cheesecakes

²/₃　cup graham cracker crumbs
2　tablespoons sugar
2　tablespoons butter, melted
1　8-ounce package cream cheese
1　3-ounce package cream cheese
½　cup sugar
1　teaspoon vanilla
½　cup milk
2　eggs
½　cup Hershey's semi-sweet chocolate chips
¼　cup creamy peanut butter
　　Sweetened whipped cream or topping
　　Chopped peanuts

*C*ombine graham cracker crumbs, 2 tablespoons sugar and butter in a small bowl. Press 1 level tablespoon of crumbs on bottom of 12 paper-lined muffin cups (2½-inch diameter). Combine both packages of cream cheese, ½ cup sugar and vanilla in small mixer bowl. Beat until smooth and creamy. Add milk and eggs, beating just until blended. Melt chocolate chips; gradually stir 1½ cups cheese mixture into melted chocolate. Add peanut butter to remaining cheese mixture, beating on low speed just until blended. Spoon 2 tablespoons of peanut butter mixture into each muffin cup. Spoon 2 tablespoons chocolate mixture evenly over the peanut butter mixture, filling cups almost full (mixture rises only slightly during baking). Bake in a 325 degree oven for 20 to 25 minutes or until set. Cool on wire rack. Chill. To serve, peel off papers and garnish with sweetened whipped cream or topping and chopped peanuts. Yield: 12 servings

Rum Cheesecake

2 cups graham crackers, crushed
$^1/_2$ cup butter, melted
4 8-ounce packages cream cheese, softened
$^1/_8$ teaspoon salt
2 teaspoons vanilla, divided
4 eggs
1 cup sugar
$^1/_2$ cup light rum
2 cups sour cream
$^1/_2$ cup sugar

Combine graham crackers and butter; press into 9-inch pie plate. Beat together cream cheese, salt, 1 teaspoon vanilla, eggs, 1 cup sugar and rum until smooth. Pour into crust. Bake in a 375 degree oven for 40 minutes. Cool 30 minutes. Combine sour cream, 1 teaspoon vanilla and $^1/_2$ cup sugar; pour over cake. Bake in a 450 degree oven for 5 minutes. Refrigerate several days before serving to enhance the flavor. Yield: 6 to 8 servings

Chocolate Mousse

4 ounces unsweetened chocolate
8 eggs, separated
1 cup sifted confectioners' sugar
$1^1/_2$ ounces bourbon
$^3/_4$ cup heavy cream, whipped with 1 tablespoon sugar and 1 teaspoon bourbon

Melt chocolate. Beat yolks, adding confectioners' sugar gradually, until yolks are pale yellow. Slowly mix yolks into chocolate over low heat until very smooth. Add bourbon. Beat whites until almost stiff. Gently fold whites into chocolate mixture until blended. Refrigerate, covered, overnight. When ready to serve top with whipped cream. Yield: 8 servings

Chocolate Mousse Party Puffs

$^1/_2$ cup water
$^1/_4$ cup butter or margarine
$^1/_8$ teaspoon salt
$^1/_2$ cup unsifted all-purpose flour
2 eggs
  Chocolate Cream Mousse
$^1/_4$ cup red and green candied cherries, quartered, optional

Heat water, butter and salt to rolling boil in saucepan. Add flour all at once; stir vigorously over low heat about 1 minute or until mixture leaves sides of pan and forms a ball. Remove from heat; cool slightly. Add eggs, one at a time, beating until smooth and velvety. Drop dough by heaping spoonsful onto ungreased baking sheet forming 10 mounds about 2 inches apart. Bake in a 400 degree oven for 30 to 35 minutes or until puffed and golden brown. Remove from oven and slice off small horizontal portion of top; reserve. Remove any soft filaments of dough; cool. Prepare Chocolate Mousse filling; spoon into puffs. Garnish with candied cherries, if desired. Replace tops; chill. Yield: 10 puffs

Chocolate Cream Mousse

1 teaspoon unflavored gelatin
1 tablespoon cold water
2 tablespoons boiling water
$^1/_2$ cup sugar
$^1/_4$ cup unsweetened Hershey's cocoa
1 cup heavy cream, very cold
1 teaspoon vanilla
$^1/_2$ cup chopped nuts

Sprinkle gelatin over cold water in small bowl; stir and set aside 1 minute to soften. Add boiling water; stir until gelatin is completely dissolved. Stir together sugar and cocoa in small cold mixer bowl; add heavy cream and vanilla. Beat at medium speed until stiff peaks form; pour in gelatin mixture and beat until well blended. Add nuts; chill about 10 minutes before filling puffs.

English Trifle

  1½ quarts milk
  1½ cups sugar
  2 tablespoons cornstarch
  6 eggs
  ½ cup sherry
  2 cups cream
  1½ pounds pound cake, sliced
     Raspberry or strawberry preserves

*P*our milk into top of a double boiler. Combine the sugar, cornstarch and eggs until smooth. Add to the milk; heat until mixture is thickened, stirring constantly. Set aside to cool. Add sherry to the cooled custard. Whip the cream and set aside. Arrange cake slices in a large 3-quart baking pan. Spread with preserves, then top with a layer of custard and a layer of whipped cream. Repeat until all ingredients are used. Chill. Yield: 6 to 8 servings

Lemon Tea Cookies

  2 teaspoons lemon juice
  ½ cup milk
  1¾ cups all-purpose flour
  1 teaspoon baking powder
  ¼ teaspoon baking soda
  ¼ teaspoon salt
  ½ cup butter or margarine
  ¾ cup sugar
  1 egg
  1 teaspoon finely grated lemon rind
     Lemon Icing

*C*ombine lemon juice and milk. Sift next 4 ingredients together. Cream butter; add sugar. Beat until light and fluffy. Add egg and lemon rind. Add

flour mixture and milk mixture alternately to the batter, beating well after each addition. Drop by rounded teaspoonsful 2 inches apart onto ungreased cookie sheets. Bake in a 350 degree oven for 12 to 14 minutes. Cool cookies on wire rack. Spread with Lemon Icing. Yield: 4 dozen

Lemon Icing

  1¾ cups sifted confectioners' sugar
  1 tablespoon butter, melted
  2 tablespoons lemon juice
  2 drops yellow food coloring

*C*ombine all ingredients until well blended. Spread on cookies.

Assorted chocolate Valentine treats, pages 162-164.

Double Chocolate Brownies

4   1-ounce squares unsweetened chocolate
1   cup butter
4   eggs
1   cup sugar
1   cup brown sugar
1½ cups all-purpose flour
1   teaspoon baking powder
2   teaspoons vanilla
1   cup chopped pecans or walnuts, or mixed
½   cup miniature marshmallows

Melt chocolate and butter in top of double boiler. Beat eggs, add sugars, then flour sifted with baking powder. Stir in vanilla and nuts, then chocolate mixture. Turn into a greased and lightly floured 15x10x1-inch pan. Bake in a 325 degree oven for 25 to 30 minutes. Prepare Frosting. Remove from oven; immediately spread marshmallows over top.

Frosting

½   cup butter
3   1-ounce squares unsweetened chocolate
1   cup sugar
1   small can evaporated milk
1   1-pound box confectioners' sugar
1   teaspoon vanilla

Do not wash the double boiler chocolate pot. Add to it ½ cup butter, chocolate, sugar and evaporated milk. Cook in double boiler until well blended. Beat in sugar and vanilla. Pour immediately over hot marshmallow-covered brownies. Cool for 4 hours. Yield: 6 dozen

Walnut Cookies

½   cup margarine, softened
½   cup sugar
1   egg, separated
1   teaspoon grated lemon rind
1   cup all-purpose flour
¼   teaspoon ground cinnamon
    Pinch of ground cloves
1¾ cups finely chopped walnuts
½   cup apricot preserves

Cream margarine; gradually add sugar, beating until light and fluffy. Add egg yolk and lemon rind; beat well. Combine dry ingredients and 1 cup walnuts; stir into creamed mixture. Cover dough, and chill at least 30 minutes. Beat egg white lightly. Shape dough into 1-inch balls. Dip each ball in egg white, roll in remaining walnuts, and place on greased cookie sheet. Make a thumbprint in center of each cookie, and fill with preserves. Bake in a 350 degree oven for 15 minutes. Cool on wire rack. Yield: 3 dozen cookies

Cinnamon Crackers

½   cup butter
½   cup margarine
½   cup sugar
2   packages of cinnamon graham crackers
1   to 1½ cups chopped pecans

Place butter, margarine and sugar in saucepan and heat for 3 minutes, stirring until sugar dissolves. Place foil on cookie sheet. Break cinnamon crackers into individual pieces and place on foil. Spoon butter mixture over crackers. Place pecans on top. Bake in a 350 degree oven for 10 minutes. Yield: 4 dozen

Cathedral Window Cookies

1   12-ounce package chocolate chips
½   cup butter
1   10-ounce package colored miniature marshmallows
1   cup chopped walnuts
1   7-ounce package coconut

Melt chocolate chips and butter; cool. Add marshmallows and nuts. Divide mixture in half and form 2 large rolls. Roll in coconut and wrap in wax paper. Chill for 24 hours. Slice to serve. Yield: 3 dozen cookies

Grandma's Sugar Cookies

    2 cups sugar
    1 cup shortening
    2 eggs
    1 teaspoon vanilla
    1 teaspoon lemon extract, optional
    1 teaspoon baking soda
    1 cup sour milk
    4 to 5 cups all-purpose flour
    2 teaspoons baking powder
    1 teaspoon grated nutmeg
      Sugar

Cream sugar and shortening, add eggs one at a time, beating well after each addition, add extracts. Dissolve baking soda in milk; sift 4 cups flour with nutmeg and baking powder. Add sour milk and flour alternately to creamed mixture. Add enough additional flour to make dough easy to handle. Chill dough for 2 hours. Flour hands and pastry board. Roll out dough about 1/4 to 1/2-inch thick; cut with a 2 to 3-inch cookie cutter. Place cookies on greased cookie sheets, sprinkle with sugar. Bake in a 400 to 425 degree oven for 8 minutes or until lightly browned. Watch carefully. Yield: 6 dozen cookies

Note: 1 tablespoon lemon juice or vinegar may be mixed with sweet milk to make 1 cup sour milk.

Old-Fashioned Molasses Cookies

    1/2 cup butter, softened
    1/3 cup brown sugar
    1 egg
    1/2 cup molasses
    1/4 cup milk
    2 cups all-purpose flour
    1/2 teaspoon salt
    1/2 teaspoon ginger or ground cloves
    1/2 teaspoon cinnamon
    1 teaspoon baking soda

Cream butter and sugar until fluffy. Add egg, molasses and milk. Sift remaining ingredients and add to creamed mixture. Blend well. Mixture should be stiff. Spoon onto well-greased cookie sheets leaving space for spreading during baking. If mixture is too thin add more flour. Bake in a 375 degree oven for 10 minutes. Yield: 3 to 4 dozen cookies

Peanut Butter Jumbos

    1 cup butter or margarine
    1 cup peanut butter
    1 cup sugar
    1 cup firmly-packed brown sugar
    2 eggs
    2 cups all-purpose flour
    1 teaspoon baking soda
    1 1/2 cups peanut "M & Ms"

Beat together butter, peanut butter, and sugars until light and fluffy; blend in eggs. Combine flour and soda. Blend into peanut butter mixture. Stir in "M & M's". Drop dough by level 1/4 cup measures onto greased cookie sheet, about three inches apart. Press three to four additional candies into each cookie, if desired. Bake in a 350 degree oven for 14 to 16 minutes, or until edges are golden brown. Cool cookies on sheet for 3 minutes; remove to wire rack and cool. Yield: 24 four-inch cookies

Cool cookies on a wire rack. Store in an airtight container when completely cooled.

Peanutty Chocolate Cheesecake, page 157; Chocolate Mousse Party Puffs, page 158; Chocolate Buffet Cake, page 149.

Chocolate Peanut Brittle

$^{1}/_{4}$ cup unsweetened Hershey's cocoa
1   teaspoon baking soda
1   tablespoon butter
1   cup sugar
$^{1}/_{2}$ cup light corn syrup
$^{1}/_{4}$ cup heavy cream
$1^{1}/_{4}$ cups salted peanuts

*L*ightly butter a cookie sheet; set aside. Combine cocoa and soda in small bowl; add butter. Set aside. Combine sugar, corn syrup and cream in a heavy 2-quart saucepan. Place over medium heat and stir constantly until sugar is dissolved. Stir in peanuts. Continue cooking and stirring frequently until mixture reaches 300 degrees on candy thermometer (hard-crack stage). Remove from heat; stir in cocoa mixture. Immediately pour onto cookie sheet; quickly spread and pull into $^{1}/_{4}$-inch thickness. Place on wire rack to cool completely. Snap into pieces; store in airtight container. Yield: About 1 pound candy

Oatmeal Cookies

1   cup sugar
1   cup firmly-packed brown sugar
1   cup all-purpose flour
$3^{1}/_{2}$ cups quick-cooking oats
1   scant teaspoon baking soda
1   can coconut
1   cup vegetable oil
1   teaspoon salt
1   teaspoon vanilla
2   eggs, beaten

*P*lace all ingredients in a large container and mix thoroughly. Form into small balls; place on cookie sheet and bake in a 350 degree oven for 8 to 10 minutes. Yield: About 8 dozen cookies

Peanutty Chocolate Pinwheels

1   12-ounce package Hershey's semi-sweet chocolate chips
$^{3}/_{4}$ cup sweetened condensed milk
$^{3}/_{4}$ cup creamy peanut butter
1   tablespoon butter or margarine, melted
1   cup confectioners' sugar
3   tablespoons milk
1   teaspoon vanilla

*C*ombine chocolate chips and sweetened condensed milk. Cook over low heat, stirring constantly, until melted and smooth. Remove from heat; cool slightly. Pat or spread evenly into 12x9-inch rectangle on wax paper; set aside. In a small mixer bowl, combine peanut butter and butter. Add confectioners' sugar, milk and vanilla, beating until well combined. Pat or roll into a 12x9-inch tangle on sheet of wax paper. Invert peanut butter onto chocolate; remove top sheet of wax paper. From long end, roll up jelly-roll style. Wrap tightly; chill until firm. Slice into 1/4-inch slices. Yield: About 40 slices

Peanut Butter Balls

1   cup peanut butter
1/3 cup instant nonfat dry milk
1/4 cup sesame seed
1/4 cup raisins
1/4 cup honey
1/2 cup unsweetened coconut

*C*ombine all ingredients. Form into balls. Chill and serve. Good lunchbox treat or breakfast addition. Yield: 4 1/2 dozen

Pecan Dreams

2   sticks butter
1/2   cup confectioners' sugar
2 1/4 cups all-purpose flour
2   teaspoons vanilla
1   teaspoon water
1   cup pecans, chopped
      Confectioners' sugar

*C*ream butter and sugar. Add flour, vanilla, and water; mix well. Add pecans. Place small balls of mixture on cookie sheet. Bake in a 325 degree oven for 30 minutes. Roll in confectioners' sugar. Yield: 3 to 4 dozen

Fantastic Fudge

2/3 cup evaporated milk
2/3 cup butter or margarine
3   cups sugar
1   12-ounce package Hershey's semi-sweet chocolate chips
1   7-ounce jar marshmallow creme
1   cup coarsely chopped nuts
1   teaspoon vanilla

*C*ombine evaporated milk, butter and sugar in a heavy 2 1/2 to 3-quart saucepan. Bring to full rolling boil, stirring constantly to prevent scorching. Boil 5 minutes over medium heat or until candy thermometer reaches 234 degrees, stirring constantly. Remove from heat; stir in chocolate chips until melted. Add marshmallow creme, nuts and vanilla; beat until well blended. Pour into greased 8 or 9-inch square pan. Cool; cut into squares. Yield: About 3 pounds fudge

Chocolate-Marshmallow Turtles

1 1/2 cups Hershey's semi-sweet chocolate chips
1   tablespoon vegetable shortening
12   large marshmallows
1 1/2 cups pecan halves

*M*elt chocolate chips and shortening in top of double boiler over hot, not boiling water; remove from heat. Cool mixture to 85 degrees stirring constantly. Meanwhile, cut marshmallows in half horizontally; flatten with rolling pin. Set aside. On wax paper-covered tray, form head and hind feet of turtle by arranging 3 pecan halves with ends touching in center; for front feet, place 1 pecan quarter on each side of head. Arrange 24 of these clusters as bases for turtles. Spoon 1/2 teaspoon melted chocolate mixture into center of each cluster of pecans. To make turtle shell, place flattened marshmallow half in center of pecans on top of chocolate; press lightly to adhere. Spoon a small amount of chocolate onto marshmallow and spread with spatula to cover top and edges of marshmallow. Chill. Store covered in refrigerator. Yield: About 2 dozen turtles

To flame a spectacular dessert, warm brandy before pouring over dessert and igniting. The alcohol will burn off, leaving only the essence of the brandy flavor.

Chocolate Fudge Candy and Icing

2   cups sugar
$^1/_4$ cup butter
$^1/_2$ cup margarine
$^2/_3$ cup milk
$2^1/_2$ squares semi-sweet chocolate
$^1/_2$ teaspoon vanilla

*B*ring all ingredients to a boil; reduce heat to medium. Cook 3 minutes for icing, 5 minutes for fudge. Beat until thick. Yield: 2 pounds of fudge or enough icing for 1 cake

Note: Use above recipe for vanilla fudge by leaving out the chocolate.

Chocolate Truffles

$^1/_2$ cup heavy cream
$^1/_3$ cup sugar
6   tablespoons sweet or regular butter
1   cup Hershey's semi-sweet chocolate Mini-Chips
1   teaspoon vanilla
1   12-ounce package Hershey's semi-sweet chocolate chips
2   tablespoons vegetable shortening

*C*ombine heavy cream, sugar and butter in saucepan; bring just to a boil. Remove from heat; immediately add 1 cup Mini Chips. Stir until chips are melted; add vanilla. Pour into bowl; cool, stirring occasionally. Cover; chill in refrigerator several hours, preferably overnight, to allow mixture to ripen and harden. Form mixture into $^1/_2$-inch balls working quickly to prevent melting. Place on wax paper-covered tray; cover loosely. Chill several hours. Prepare chocolate coating by melting remaining chocolate chips with shorten-

ing in top of double boiler over hot water (avoid getting water in chocolate). Cool to 85 degrees, stirring constantly. With fork, dip each truffle into chocolate; gently tap fork on side of bowl to remove excess coating. Invert truffle on wax paper-covered tray. Decorate top of coated center with small amount of chocolate. Repeat until all are coated. Chill completely. Yield: About 30 truffles

Minted Chocolate Drops

1   12-ounce package Hershey's semi-sweet chocolate chips
2   tablespoons shortening
1   cup finely chopped nuts
1   3-ounce package cream cheese, softened
2   tablespoons butter
2   cups confectioners' sugar
$1^1/_2$ teaspoons vanilla
$^1/_4$ teaspoon peppermint extract
5 to 6 drops red food coloring
5 to 6 drops green food coloring

*O*ver hot (not boiling) water, melt chocolate with shortening until mixture is smooth. Stir in chopped nuts. Drop by slightly rounded teaspoonful onto wax paper-lined cookie sheet. Flatten slightly with spatula forming $1^1/_2$-inch round drops about $^1/_4$-inch thick. Chill 5 to 10 minutes or until set. In a small bowl, combine cream cheese and butter until blended. Gradually add sugar, vanilla and peppermint extract; beat until creamy. Divide mixture in half. Add red food color to $^1/_2$; green to the other. Using a star tip pastry tube pipe a rosette or swirl a small amount of mint cream with a spatula onto top of each chocolate round. Chill to set. Yield: About 3 dozen candies

Note: Pipe any remaining mint cream onto wax paper; use later as a garnish on pies, cakes, mousses.

Accompaniments

Bread and Butter Pickles

2   gallons cucumbers
14 small onions
4   large green peppers
³/₄ cup pickling salt
10 cups sugar
1   teaspoon turmeric
1   teaspoon ground cloves
¹/₄ cup mustard seed
2¹/₂ quarts vinegar

*S*lice vegetables and sprinkle salt over all. Set aside for 3 hours. Drain. Heat sugar, turmeric, cloves, mustard seed, and vinegar. Do not boil. Add to vegetables. Pack in hot, sterilized jars and seal. These are best when stored three weeks before opening. Yield: 7 quarts

Vegetable Relish

12 medium onions
1   medium cabbage
10 green tomatoes
12 green peppers
6   sweet red peppers
¹/₂ cup pickling salt
6   cups sugar
2   tablespoons mustard seed
1   tablespoon celery seed

1¹/₂ teaspoons turmeric
4   cups cider vinegar
2   cups water

*G*rind all vegetables and sprinkle with salt; set aside overnight. Rinse and drain. Combine remaining ingredients and pour over vegetables. Heat to boiling. Simmer 3 minutes. Seal in hot, sterilized jars. Leave a small amount of space in top. Yield: 8 pints

Tomato-Pepper Relish

20 cups (50 to 60) ripe tomatoes
4   cups juice from tomatoes
5   cups jalapeño or chile peppers
5   cups chopped onion
1   cup tarragon vinegar
2   cups white vinegar
1   cup thinly sliced garlic
1   cup sugar
5   tablespoons pickling salt
¹/₂ teaspoon garlic powder
2   tablespoons seasoned salt

*P*lace tomatoes in boiling water until the skins split. Peel, chop, and drain, reserving juice. Seed and chop peppers. Place all ingredients in a large pot and simmer 2 to 2¹/₂ hours, stirring occasionally. Pack into hot, sterilized pint jars. Yield: 12 pints

Ground spices lose their savor after about six months, whole dried herbs and spices after about a year. When you get a new can or bottle, glue a label on the bottom and record the purchase date. Write a reminder on your engagement calendar twice a year to check the spice rack, discard, and restock. Keep herbs and spices away from sunlight and heat from appliances. Refrigerate cayenne, paprika, chili powder, and red pepper during the summer.
Go easy when adding spices—more is not better. Usually $1/2$ to $3/4$ teaspoon of coarsely ground or $1/4$ to $1/2$ teaspoon of finely ground spice seasons a four-serving dish. One teaspoon of dried ground herb equals 1 tablespoon of fresh. Add ground spices during the last 15 minutes of cooking, however, whole spices can simmer longer.

Cranberry Relish

1   pound cranberries
1   orange, peeled, seeded and sectioned
2   cups sugar
$1/2$ cup water
1   teaspoon grated orange rind

Combine all ingredients in saucepan and simmer about 10 minutes or until berries pop open. Skim foam and cool. Yield: 12 servings

Pickled Okra

Vinegar, heated
Uncut okra
1   clove of garlic
Wedge of onion
Several peppercorns
$1/2$ teaspoon mustard seed
1   teaspoon sugar
1   teaspoon pickling salt

Pour hot vinegar over all and seal. Yield: 1 pint

Corn Relish

6 ears yellow corn
1 pint ripe tomatoes
1 pint onions
6 green peppers
6 red peppers
6 hot peppers
2 tablespoons salt
2 cups sugar
1 pint vinegar

Cut corn from cob. Chop all vegetables. Add sugar, salt and vinegar. Bring to a boil. Cook for 20 minutes. Pour into hot, sterilized jars and seal. Yield: 2 pints

Hot Pepper Jelly

5   cups sugar
$1^1/2$ cups cider vinegar
$3/4$ cup finely chopped, seeded green pepper
$1/2$ cup finely chopped, seeded jalapeño pepper
1   6-ounce bottle liquid fruit pectin

In a large pot, combine sugar and vinegar: bring to a boil. Add peppers and return to a boil. Stir in pectin and boil 1 minute. Strain liquid through a colander into a large bowl. Pour into hot, sterilized jars and seal. Yield: 3 pints

Apple Butter

16 cups cored, chopped, unpeeled cooking apples
2   cups apple cider
2   cups sugar
2   teaspoons ground cinnamon
$1/4$ teaspoon ground cloves

Combine apples and cider in a slow-cooker. Cover and cook on low for 10 to 12 hours. Purée in food processor. Return puréed mixture to pot and add sugar, cinnamon and cloves. Cover and cook on low for 1 hour. Pour into hot, sterilized jars and seal. Yield: 4 pints

Berry Blueberry Jam

2   cups fresh blueberries
$1/3$ cup sugar
2   teaspoons grated orange peel
1   envelope unflavored gelatin
1   cup water

*I*n medium saucepan, combine blueberries with sugar. Cook 5 minutes, crushing berries slightly. Bring to a boil; then boil rapidly, stirring constantly, 3 minutes. Stir in orange rind. In small bowl, sprinkle unflavored gelatin over water. Set aside for 1 minute. Add to blueberries; stir over low heat until gelatin is completely dissolved, about 5 minutes. Ladle into jars; cover and cool slightly before refrigerating. Yield: 2 cups jam

Strawberry Preserves

1 quart strawberries
4 cups sugar, divided
2 tablespoons water
1 teaspoon lemon juice

*C*ap and wash berries. Cut berries in half; add 2 cups sugar and 2 tablespoons water. Bring to a boil and cook for 5 minutes, stirring constantly. Add remaining sugar and lemon juice. Return to a boil and cook for 5 minutes longer. Remove from heat and partially cool before pouring into hot, sterilized jars and sealing. Yield: 2 pints

Note: You may substitute other berries of your choice.

Beet Relish

1 pint chopped, boiled beets
1 pint chopped cabbage
2 ribs celery, diced
1/3 cup grated horseradish
1/4 teaspoon white pepper
   Dash cayenne pepper
1/2 teaspoon salt
3/4 cup sugar
1 cup vinegar

*C*ombine all ingredients in large saucepan. Cook until thoroughly heated. Pour into hot, sterilized jars and seal. Yield: 3 to 4 pints

Lemon Curd

1 cup butter
2 cups sugar
3 tablespoons finely grated lemon rind
2/3 cup lemon juice
1/8 teaspoon salt
4 eggs

*P*lace butter in the top of a double boiler over simmering water. Add next 4 ingredients, stirring until sugar is dissolved, 2 to 3 minutes. Beat eggs until foamy. Stir 1 cup lemon mixture into eggs. Add lemon-egg mixture to remaining mixture in double boiler. Cook for 6 to 10 minutes or until thickened. Pour into jars, cover and cool at room temperature. Store in refrigerator. This is excellent served with cakes, breads, rolls, and cookies. Yield: 2 pints

Winter Salad, page 90.

Equivalents Chart

Food	Amount	Equal to
Apple	1 medium	1 cup chopped
Bacon	1 lb.	24 slices
crisply fried, crumbled	1 lb.	3 cups
Butter or margarine	1 lb.	2 cups
Cheese		
Cheddar-type, shredded	1 lb.	4 cups
cottage cheese	1 lb.	2 cups
cream cheese	3 oz.	6 tablespoons
	8 oz.	1 cup
Chocolate		
pieces (chips)	6 oz.	approx. 1 cup
unsweetened baking	8 oz.	8 squares
Cocoa	8 oz.	2 cups
Coconut, shredded or flaked	4 oz.	$1^1/_3$ cups
Cream		
sour	1 lb.	2 cups
whipping cream	$^1/_2$ pint	1 cup
whipped	$^1/_2$ pint	2 cups
Egg whites	12 eggs	$1^1/_4$ cups
	1 egg	5 tablespoons
Egg yolks	12 eggs	$^3/_4$ cup
	1 egg	approx. 4 teaspoons
Flour		
all-purpose	1 lb.	$3^1/_2$ to 4 cups
whole-wheat	5 lbs.	about $18^1/_3$ cups
Graham crackers	1 lb.	about 4 cups crumbs
Lemon juice	1 lemon	3 to 4 tablespoons
Lemon peel, grated	1 lemon	approx. 2 teaspoons
Nuts, shelled		
almonds	1 lb.	3 cups
peanuts	1 lb.	3 cups
pecans		
halves	1 lb.	4 cups
chopped	1 lb.	$3^1/_2$ to 4 cups
walnuts		
halves	1 lb.	$3^1/_2$ cups
chopped	1 lb.	$3^1/_2$ cups
Onion	1 large	$^3/_4$ to 1 cup chopped
chopped fresh	$^1/_4$ cup	1 tablespoon dried
Orange juice	1 orange	6 to 8 tablespoons
Orange peel	1 orange	3 to 4 teaspoons
Solid shortening	1 lb.	2 cups
Sugar		
brown, packed	1 lb.	$2^1/_4$ cups
granulated	1 lb.	3 cups
powdered, unsifted	1 lb.	3 to 4 cups
Yeast		
active dry	$^1/_4$ oz.	1 scant tablespoon
cake	0.60 oz.	4 teaspoons

Blackberry Jam

5 cups mashed blackberries
5 cups sugar

*M*ash blackberries thoroughly. Bring to a boil and cook for 3 minutes. Add sugar and cook about 20 minutes or until mixture coats spoon. Skim and pour into hot, sterilized jars and seal. Yield: 2 pints

Carrot Relish

6   large carrots
6   green tomatoes
6   medium onions
2   small red sweet peppers
1   6-ounce jar prepared mustard
4   cups sugar
2   teaspoons pickling salt
$1^1/_2$ pints vinegar
$^1/_2$ cup all-purpose flour

*P*rocess carrots, tomatoes, and onions in food chopper or food processor. Combine vegetables, mustard, 3 cups sugar, salt and 1 pint vinegar. Bring to a boil. Simmer for 20 minutes. Add remaining ingredients, stirring to blend well. Heat 10 minutes longer. Pack into hot, sterilized jars and seal. Yield: 8 pints

Index

Order Additional Copies

Buy additional copies of *Gracious Entertaining, Southern Style* or Daisy King's other cookbooks for yourself and your friends from your local book store. If you are not near a store that carries her cookbooks, you may order copies from Rutledge Hill Press at the retail price plus $1.75 postage and handling for each shipment (even if more than one book is ordered). Tennessee residents must add 7.75% for sales tax. If you want to send copies as gifts, Rutledge Hill Press will enclose a gift card signed with your name at no additional charge.

Recipes from Miss Daisy's is the enormously popular cookbook created for the patrons of Miss Daisy's Tearoom in Franklin, Tennessee. Major sections of the book include luncheon menus and recipes, recipes ideal for use at home, "Sunday Down South" buffets, and recipes and menus for special occasions. $5.95, spiral bound.

Miss Daisy Entertains begins with a section of special occasion menus and recipes for breakfasts, brunches, lunches, dinners, a buffet supper, and a Fourth of July picnic. Following this section, the book is arranged by categories. The easy, clear directions will make even the most inexperienced cook an expert in Southern hospitality. Ideal as a gift for a beginning cook. $6.95, spiral bound.

The Original Tennessee Homecoming Cookbook contains original recipes and others handed down from generation to generation sent to Daisy King from all across Tennessee. The recipes were selected and kitchen tested. Contains 31 full-color photographs. $14.95, hardcover.

Gracious Entertaining, Southern Style is $19.95, hardcover.

- -

To: Rutledge Hill Press
   513 Third Avenue South
   Nashville, Tennessee 37210

Please send me the following books. I enclose the cost of the book, $1.75 for postage and handling per order, and sales tax if the books are to be mailed to Tennessee residents. The total enclosed is _____. (Make check payable to Rutledge Hill Press and send to the above address.)

Name _____

Address _____

City _____ State _____ Zip _____

For additional copies to be sent to your friends, please include their names and addresses, tell us whether you want us to send a card or not, and enclose $1.75 postage and handling for each shipment in addition to the cost of the book and tax if mailed to Tennessee residents.